RETURN MIGRATION IN LATER LIFE

International perspectives

Edited by John Percival

First published in Great Britain in 2013 by

Policy Press
University of Bristol
6th Floor
Howard House
Queen's Avenue
Clifton
Bristol BS8 1SD
UK
t: +44 (0)117 331 4054
f: +44 (0)117 331 4093
tpp-info@bristol.ac.uk
www.policypress.co.uk

North America office:
Policy Press
c/o The University of Chicago Press
1427 East 60th Street
Chicago, IL 60637, USA
t: +1 773 702 7700
f: +1 773 702 9756
sales@press.uchicago.edu
www.press.uchicago.edu

Cover design by Anne Percival
Front cover image: © Anne Percival 2013
Printed and bound in Great Britain by TJ International,
Padstow.
Policy Press uses environmentally responsible print partners.

Contents

List of tables and figures

Tables

Figure

Notes on contributors

Alison Blunt is professor of geography at Queen Mary, University of London, UK. Her research focuses on home, migration and diaspora, with ESRC- and AHRC-funded projects on the Anglo-Indian community in India, Britain and Australia and a project funded by The Leverhulme Trust on 'Diaspora Cities: imagining Calcutta in London, Toronto and Jerusalem.' Her books include *Anglo-Indian women and the spatial politics of home* (Blackwell, 2005) and, with Robyn Dowling, *Home* (Routledge, 2006). She edits *Transactions of the Institute of British Geographers* and is co-director of the new Centre for Studies of Home.

Claudio Bolzman is professor in the Department of Social Work at the University of Applied Sciences Western Switzerland (HES-SO) and senior lecturer at the Department of Sociology, University of Geneva. He received his PhD in sociology from the University of Geneva in 1991. Since 2004, he has been head of the Research Centre on Cultural Diversity and Citizenship at HES-SO. This is an interdisciplinary centre associating more than 30 researchers from different disciplines and interested mainly in social and health issues. Claudio Bolzman was also general secretary of the International Association for Intercultural Research (ARIC) between 2001 and 2007. His research interests include migration and the lifecourse, transnational practices and immigration policies. His recent publications include 'Democratization of ageing: also a reality for elderly immigrants?' in *European Journal of Social Work*, 2012; 15(1):97–113.

Jayani Bonnerjee completed her PhD from Queen Mary, University of London (QMUL), UK, as part of The Leverhulme Trust-funded 'Diaspora Cities' project in 2010 focusing on ideas of neighbourhood, identity and belonging for Calcutta's Anglo-Indian and Chinese communities. Her postdoctoral work has focused on shared religious spaces in Chinatowns of Calcutta and Singapore (at the Nalanda-Sriwijaya Centre, Singapore) and on the AHRC-funded scoping study Connected Communities: Diaspora and Transnationality (QMUL). She is currently a teaching assistant at QMUL.

Anastasia Christou is reader in sociology in the School of Law at Middlesex University, London, UK. Anastasia has expertise in social and cultural geography researching within critical perspectives and an interdisciplinary approach to social and cultural theory. She has widely published on issues of migration and return migration, the second generation and ethnicity, space and place, transnationalism and identity, culture and memory, gender and feminism, home and belonging, and emotion and narrativity.

Dennis Conway is professor emeritus of geography at Indiana University, USA. He has written over 140 articles and book chapters, and co-authored nine books on Caribbean urbanisation, internal and transnational migration, economic development, alternative tourism and their geographical consequences and globalisation's wider structural impacts. He has also studied Caribbean immigration to the US and migration-development relationships in the Caribbean. He is currently conducting qualitative research on the transnational lives of the 'next generations' and interpreting the migration-stories of youthful professionals who have returned to Trinidad and Tobago in mid-career and mid-life.

Johanne Eliacin is a clinical psychologist and psychological/medical anthropologist. She holds a PhD from the Department of Comparative Human Development at the University of Chicago, USA. Currently, she is a postdoctoral resident in psychology at Cornell University. Dr Eliacin's research has been funded by the National Science Foundation and the National Institute of Mental Health among other funding agencies. Her research interests include health disparities, the intersections of race, gender, culture and mental health, social neuroscience and psychosis. Her latest research project is an ethnography of the 'epidemic' of schizophrenia among individuals of African-Caribbean heritage in England.

Noah Hysler-Rubin is a lecturer in the department of Architecture at the Bezalel School of Art and Design, Israel. She holds a PhD in geography and is a trained town planner. Her main research interests include the multidisciplinary origins of town planning, planning across the British Empire, and colonial and post-colonial cities. Her book, *Patrick Geddes and town planning: A critical view*, has recently been published by Routledge.

Martin Klinthäll has a PhD in economic history and is associate professor at the Institute for Research on Migration, Ethnicity and Society, Linköping University, Sweden. His research interests are primarily in the domain of economic demography, in particular migration and labour market integration. He has published work on return migration, migration and health, and self-employment among immigrants, as well as on economic structural change and household income disparity. He is currently heading the research project Competence and Contacts on social networks and labour market integration among second-generation immigrants in Sweden.

Gerard Leavey is director of the Bamford Centre for Mental Health and Wellbeing at the University of Ulster, Northern Ireland. Professor Leavey holds honorary posts with the University of Ulster and University College London. He is a health services researcher with a long-standing interest in ethnicity, culture and religion.

K Bruce Newbold is professor in the School of Geography and Earth Sciences at McMaster University, Canada. He received his PhD in geography from McMaster University in 1994, and worked at the University of Illinois Urbana-Champaign between 1994 and 2000, before returning to McMaster University in 2000. His research interests focus on population issues as they relate to internal migration, immigration, ageing, and intersections with population health issues.

Erik Olsson is professor in international migration and ethnic relations at Stockholm University, Sweden, and former director for the Centre for Research in International Migration and Ethnic Relations. Currently Olsson is coordinator of the research programme Transnational Migration in the Department of Social Anthropology. His research is mainly in the field of transnational migration and diaspora, and he has conducted work on transnational educational careers and welfare practices in transnational spaces. His recent publications include, 'From exile to post-exile: historical contexts in the diasporisation of Chileans in Sweden', *Social Identities*, 15(5):659–76 and *Making the final decision: The representation of migration in Swedish repatriation practice*, Prague Occasional Papers in Ethnology No 8: Migration, Diversity and Their Management, Institute of Ethnology of the Academy of Sciences of the Czech Republic: Prague.

John Percival is research associate at University of Bristol, UK, and has a background in social work and social gerontology. He is also an independent research consultant, working predominantly in the fields of social care, health and housing. He has led ethnographic studies examining older people's housing needs and aspirations; the uses of assistive technology by people with disabilities; end of life care in nursing and residential care homes; and the impact of vision impairment on the social inclusion of people with sight loss. John is currently researching innovative end of life care community provision in south-west England.

Robert B Potter is professor of human geography at the University of Reading, UK. His research and teaching interests span development geography and development studies, urban geography, return migration, transnationality and issues of identity. He is the founding editor-in-chief of the interdisciplinary journal *Progress in Development Studies*, published by Sage. Rob Potter was elected to the Academy of Social Sciences in 2006, and in 2007 was awarded the degree of Doctor of Science by the University of Reading in recognition of his contributions to the fields of geographies of development and urban geography.

Godfrey St Bernard is senior research fellow at the Sir Arthur Lewis Institute of Social and Economic Studies (SALISES) at The University of the West Indies (UWI), Trinidad and Tobago. He has worked extensively on Trinidadian and Tobagonian demographic patterns, including work as a statistician with the Central Statistical Office of Trinidad and Tobago. Born in Trinidad, after undergraduate training at UWI, Jamaica, he completed his PhD in social demography in 1992 at the University of Western Ontario, Canada. In 1993 he became a research fellow at the Institute for Social and Economic Research (now SALISES), where he is today.

Brad Ruting conducted his research at the School of Geosciences in the University of Sydney, Australia. His past research has covered a range of topics, including cultural festivals in rural Australia, urban sustainability and the evolution of gay urban districts over time. He is also an economist with interests in labour markets and migration, and currently works for the Australian Government.

Acknowledgements

The editor would like to thank Professor Tony Warnes for his encouragement and advice when first presented with the germ of an idea for this book. He would also like to thank colleagues and research participants, past and present, who have been generous in providing time and thought to the subject of return migration and, in doing so, have helped bring about this book. Additionally, gratitude is extended to Emily Watt, Laura Greaves and all the team at Policy Press for their support. Finally, he would like to thank his family for their insights and patience during the lengthy process of the book's inception to its culmination, and in particular his wife, Anne, who designed the cover of this book.

ONE

Charting the waters: return migration in later life

John Percival

It may be that the satisfaction I need depends on my going away, so that when I've gone and come back, I'll find it at home.

Rumi (translated by Coleman Banks, 1995, Penguin Classics)

Introduction

The main objective of this book is to explore the motivations, decision-making processes and consequences, when older people consider or actualise return migration to their place of origin; and also to raise the public policy profile of this increasingly important subject. The collection will examine in detail a range of themes affecting return migrations, including: autonomy and personal imperatives; socioeconomic considerations; cultural assimilation and psychological adjustment; belonging and attachment to place; kinship and friendship needs; and health and resource planning.

Return Migration in Later Life is unusual in four important ways. First, the collection has a wide remit and does not exclusively focus on refugee, political, heritage, lifestyle, or family-oriented return, but encompasses all these constituent parts and, in so doing, highlights core themes as well as particular issues and comparative factors. Second, chapters reflect a variety of quantitative, qualitative and ethnographic methods of enquiry, by researchers from different disciplines, representing social gerontology, anthropology, migration and human geography perspectives. Third, there are varying emphases on permanent return, non-permanent returns, and visits to place of origin, which reflects variety in strategic approaches and also recognises that visits are important signifiers of a return home. Finally, *Return Migration in Later Life* is unique, as far as I know, in bringing this breadth and depth of exploration to bear on *older* people's return movements, providing a focused synthesis that allows a neglected subject to receive due attention in an era of ageing and more mobile societies. As such, it is hoped that the book will be of practical use and interest not only to those from academic disciplines mentioned above, but also to social welfare professionals, policy makers and practitioners involved in tourism, as well as older people considering return migration.

There are two important and related reasons for this consolidated focus: a need for more detailed research on return migration; and a general lack of attention to migration in later life.

The experience of 'going back' has generally been absent from migration literature (Baldassar, 2001:4), as it has within anthropology (Stefansson, 2004), and as a result we have limited knowledge of motivations, socioeconomic influences, or cultural impact on home or host country. While emigration has long been a topic of historical enquiry, generating teaching, media coverage, cultural tourism and academic research, there have been few such outcomes in respect of return migration (Harper, 2005). Stefansson (2004) suggests that it is time to explore the driving forces behind homecoming in an era of globalisation, an argument supported by an online resource, *Diasporic constructions of home and belonging* (CoHab, 2012), which states that changes in concepts of home and belonging present 'cultural, social and political changes and challenges'. We need to unpick the complex 'web' of competing factors that influence decision making, including personal and family priorities (Finch et al, 2009), and understand better the personal and social adjustments confronting migrants who do return (Phillips and Potter, 2009). In order to do this, we require greater insight into individuals' everyday lives, their family and community relationships and the influence of these on migration decisions (Conway and Potter, 2007) but, as Baldassar points out, few studies examine such processes at the 'micro' level of families and households (2007a:277).

If 'return migration is the great unwritten chapter in the history of migration' (King, 2000:7) return migrations of people in later life is even more of a footnote. There are relatively few international migration studies that focus on return movement by older people (Klinthäll, 2006) and we have limited understanding of the experiences and motivations of migrants in later life who return to their region or country of childhood (Longino and Warnes, 2005), despite the growing numbers of older people deciding to live permanently or part time abroad (Warnes, 2001) and the relatively new phenomenon of an ageing immigrant population (Bolzman et al, 2006). Furthermore, there is increasing evidence that retirement migrants are less healthy and wealthy than was historically the case; significant proportions have health problems or a disability; and a proportion have not always thought through the personal and social care implications of their decisions, which can lead to sudden return and prompt attention by home country services (Age Concern, 2007). Indeed, two recent studies of British emigrants exposed a woeful lack of pre-emigration planning in respect of welfare entitlements or health and welfare needs, in some cases with serious personal consequences, and with specific policy and financial implications for the home country government (Finch et al, 2010; Sriskandarajah and Drew, 2006).

Additionally, there has been virtually no detailed enquiry into the family or social reasons influencing older international migrants' motivation to return (Longino and Warnes, 2005), nor implications for aged care support across national boundaries (Baldassar, 2007a, 2007b), resulting in a very incomplete picture of the inter-relationship between factors such as health, income and social networks in respect of older people's migration decisions (Warnes and Williams, 2006). We do know from recent studies that a variety of issues may influence return, including family obligations, homesickness, poor health, financial concerns, relationship needs, and life-cycle factors including retirement (Huseby-Darvas, 2004; Harper, 2005; Thomson, 2005), all of which would benefit from further research in the context of later life. A useful strategy in this respect is to broaden our enquiries, to 'explore the intersection of three major fields of interest, those of migration, tourism and applied social gerontological studies' (Božić, 2006:1423) and to give more than peripheral attention to changes in social context and the passage of time in respect of migrants' 'negotiations of home and identity' (George and Fitzgerald, 2012).

In the remainder of this chapter I present a brief account of key themes, including migration patterns; identity and place attachment; lifecourse perspectives; family ties and obligations; and health and resource planning, in order to elucidate influences and priorities outlined above and provide useful context for the chapters that follow.

Migration patterns and accounting for numbers returning

Traditionally, returnees are classified according to three types: those who intended temporary migration; those who intended permanent migration but were forced to return; and those who intended permanent migration but chose to return (Gmelch, 1980:138; cited by Conway and Potter, 2007:28). Increasingly, transnational mobility has become more affordable and welcome, for migrants of all ages, albeit a 'marginal activity rather than mainstream element of migration' (Jeffery and Murison, 2011).

Transnationalism may be thought of as 'the processes by which immigrants forge and sustain multi-stranded social relations that link together their societies of origin and settlement'; transnational social fields are therefore those that span more than one nation-state and consist of familial, social, economic and cultural links between groups of people of common origin spread across the world (Basch et al, 1994:7; cited in Ruting, 2008). Put very simply, transnational mobility is therefore 'a process that encompasses regular flows between countries' (Sinatti, 2011:154). This most obviously occurs through holidays, family visits or seasonal migrations to warmer climates but, additionally, increasingly takes place through transnational care giving and attending to health and welfare needs, issues that are beginning to be examined in more detail and which are likely to be further illuminated by a focus on retirement migration (Baldassar, 2007b; Gustafson, 2008).

As with the recent phenomenon of international retirement migration (IRM) of older people who migrate in retirement to pursue lifestyle improvement and subsequently put down roots in the host country, people who emigrated as younger people and have aged in place abroad, share the experience of 'transnational identity formation'. This involves identification with both 'relinquishing and receiving countries', and a sense of home that is permeable and cognitive rather than physical and localised ... an increasingly complex and ambiguous entity' (George and Fitzgerald, 2012:241). Such an identity is marked by hybridity, which is 'caused by living between two worlds [and] is built into the narratives of exile' (Conway and Potter, 2007:29). The majority of George and Fitzgerald's post World War Two emigrants to New Zealand described 'feeling like they were some sort of hybrid identity' and the authors cite cultural theorist Stuart Hall's (1996) contention that identity formation is a continual process that includes negotiation of 'what is left outside' (2012:246).

The changing nature of migration and mobility between countries, and the fluid parameters and definitions, makes it difficult to undertake meaningful statistical analysis of the numbers of people return migrating (Harper, 2005), with the result that data on older migrants and immigration trends is limited (Rutter and Andrew, 2009). Additionally, return rates change over time and statistics struggle to deal with returnees who subsequently re-migrate to the host country, and do not, in any event, capture those who wished to return but were prevented from doing so because of financial or personal circumstances (Thomson, 2005:106). Also, statistical information in regard to migration may be based on subjective accounts. For example, analysis by the Australian Government's Department of Immigration and Citizenship (DIAC), of overseas arrivals and departures data, is 'based on people's travel intentions as recorded on their outgoing passenger card'. Reliance on intentions is a 'flawed approach', as suggested by independently commissioned research that revealed the majority of people intending to leave Australia permanently or long term do, in fact, return within 12 months (DIAC, 2012).

With this cautionary note in mind, it is interesting to note some possibly indicative figures: almost twice as many people aged over 65, compared to those aged between 60 and 64, permanently migrated from Australia between 1994 and 2007, and of those who returned from there to the UK in 2011 14 per cent were aged over 60 (DIAC, 2012); the numbers of long-term international migrants to the UK aged over 60 increased by 20 per cent for each five-year period between 1991 and 2012 (ONS, 2012); and 10 per cent of UK nationals who return migrate are over retirement age, a proportion that rises to 25 per cent if we include all those aged over 45 (Rutter and Andrew, 2009).

What we can say with some certainty is that the immigrant population is ageing. For example, according to White (2006), the number of immigrants aged over 60 living in Germany increased from 80,000 to over 700,000 in the period 1970 to 2002; the numbers of Turks and Moroccans aged over 60 living in the Netherlands more than doubled, in each case to around 10,000, in the period 1996 to 2003; and the number of immigrants aged over 60 living in Sweden grew from 12,631 in 1975 to 56,550 in 2002. In most cases, the rate of increase is exponentially faster in the 70–80 age range and, generally, the ageing of immigrant populations in Europe is likely to 'increase in intensity' in the near future (White, 2006). In the UK, the numbers of foreign-born residents aged over 60 rose from 920,000 in 2004 to 1,101,000 (personal correspondence, Office for National Statistics). Some of the demographic and socioeconomic factors affecting ageing immigrant populations and influencing return migration flows will be taken up in later chapters in this collection.

At this point it is useful to remind ourselves that the intention eventually to return home is common in many migration traditions (Conway and Potter, 2007) and is perhaps the basis of the great return migration narrative – Homer's *Odyssey*. As with Odysseus, today's returnees face various challenges, possibly including disparity between remembered home and its changes over time; family ties that have weakened; and reduced entitlements to sources of support (Longino and Warnes, 2005). Homecomings, then, may have unsettling consequences and bring in their wake a variety of practical problems; they can also be 'encouraging experiences', when returnees reflect on the skills they have brought with them; their deep sense of spiritual belonging in the home country; and their renewed attachments to home (Stefansson, 2004:4–11; Finch et al, 2010). The significance of belonging and attachment is the subject of our next key theme.

Identity, place and attachment

According to Relph (1976:147), 'A deep human need exists for associations with significant places.' Indeed, over millennia human behaviour has been interpreted according to its interaction with environment, a relationship whose integral features include 'symbolic and emotional meanings of places' (Rowles, 1978). In this time of increased international mobility and migration, there is a need to understand these meanings more clearly, not least in respect of those ageing abroad, perhaps in diasporas, yearning to return, or make extended visits, to their homeland. Relph also emphasises the significance of spiritual and psychological attachment as elements of an individual's roots in a place (Relph, 1976:38).

This rootedness was a core feature of the holistic framework Rowles (1983) was striving for when he proposed three dimensions of place attachment: physical, social and autobiographical, which he saw as integral to understanding how geographical experiences and associated meanings constitute links between environment and personal identity. Rubinstein also refers to identity being defined, in part, by 'an indivisible link between place and person' (Rubinstein, 2005:115, cited by George and Fitzgerald, 2012:252). This link between place and invocation of meaning underlines what Relph describes as 'authentic sense of place', that of 'belonging to *your* ... hometown ... region or ... nation [providing] an important source of identity' (Relph, 1976:65, original italics). Such insights support Gu's contention that 'Place plays a major role in the ongoing constitution of identity, especially for those who migrate across national borders' (2010:689).

'Home' itself has a core place in the human psyche according to those who see it as 'the foundation of our identity ... an irreplaceable centre of significance' (Relph, 1976:39), a 'state of mind centred on a sense of belonging and security' (McHugh and Mings, 1996:538) and a 'relation between material and imaginative realms and processes' (Blunt and Dowling, 2006:254). Furthermore, 'the call to home' can offer 'an antidote to partial belongings and unfulfilled dreams' elsewhere (Markowitz, 2004:22). Markowitz is really referring here to homeland,

6

a 'highly packed signifier that encapsulates a concept and a place ... memories and longings, spatialities and temporalities, immediate family and ancestors long gone' (2004:23). Basu is equally eloquent when he states how home, as a 'shrine of self' becomes 'material in homeland' (2007:228).

Homeland can also be appreciated as a psychological anchor, when trying to cope with settlement in a distant land (Baldassar, 2001; Stephenson, 2002), but it is love for one's homeland that Wyman sees as integral to the study of emigration, citing the experiences of post-World War Two displaced persons, who waited 50 years to again touch their native soil. 'All the wonders of the West ... could not stop them becoming return migrants' (Wyman, 2005:29). This sense of belonging to a land can be strong enough to override the terror that surrounded more recent departure, the case with elderly Bosnian refugee returners, interviewed by Stefansson, who insisted on returning because they belong 'under my own sky' (2004:2). Feelings of belonging in the host country may be ambivalent when there are strong cultural affinities with the home country or when the migrant has never felt truly settled or accepted in the host country (Leavey et al, 2004; Thomson, 2005).

Attachment to home(land) is also forged through nostalgia and memory. The word 'nostalgia' invokes home in its very meaning, derived as it is from the Greek words *nostos* (homecoming) and *algos* (pain) (Blunt and Dowling, 2006). Many of Basu's respondents alluded to nostalgia for a '"lost homeland" – a place of perceived stability, where traditions survive and where time seems to move more slowly' (2007:47), characteristics that clearly appealed to the majority, aged over 50, who were concerned about the hectic, chaotic or disparate nature of modern society, concerns likely to be shared by others living abroad, especially those in the oldest age groups. According to Cresswell (2004:85), 'Place and memory are, it seems, inevitably intertwined ... The very materiality of a place means that memory is not abandoned to the vagaries of mental processes and is instead inscribed in the landscape.' Place and memory are therefore interconnected in a way that may be particularly helpful to older people, inspiring them to exercise and thereby strengthen their grip on memory in a meaningful practice.

Furthermore, this interpretation of memory's relationship with place suggests that landscape, in addition to being a cradle of myth or object of beauty, fuels memory-making and continues to exert a real and dynamic influence in the present day. Indeed, as George and Fitzgerald point out, memory can be seen as a constituent that helps establish home as less random than other places we have encountered and more an 'emotional fulcrum from which a person sees life'. With increased time in the host country, however, and as lifecourse events unfold, memories will also be formed there, which in turn instils a sense of alternative home; an integrated sense of self requires attachment both to current and remembered place. Despite this, the power of a place where formative experiences helped shape identity lives on, a power more remarkable since it relies not on physical presence but only the act of remembering, which has deep resonance for migrants far from home (2012:249–252).

Affinity with homeland can also manifest itself through visits that connect to an individual's ancestral roots, and in this respect Baldassar has learned that going back to the home country often takes the form of a 'secular pilgrimage of enormous importance' for migrants, and can be 'a rite of passage' for their children born in the host country (2001:3). Indeed, a key reason for these visits is 'the desire or need to reconstruct elements of a displaced heritage within a place of cultural and historical significance' (Stephenson, 2002:393) and is important to those wishing to connect to their spiritual or ancestral 'home', whether or not they ever lived there (Murdoch, 2005). Such visits provide an important way to 'construct meaningful self-narratives ... and a more secure sense of home and self-identity' (Basu, 2007: Foreword). The construction of meaningful narratives is a key task in later life, according to life cycle and life review theories (Biggs, 2005; Coleman, 2005), and is also integral to lifecourse perspectives, our next theme for discussion.

Lifecourse perspectives on migration

In 1996 McHugh and Mings, looking ahead 15 years to when the first cohorts of baby boomers would be in their sixties, wondered how the migration and life histories of these large cohorts would shape the geography of ageing in the 21st century (1996). We are nearer, temporally at least, to providing some answers, and a lifecourse perspective can help.

The 'lifecourse' can be conceptualised as 'a sequence of age-linked transitions that are embedded in social institutions and history' (Bengtson et al, 2005:493). Bengtson puts forward five principles that define the lifecourse: 'linked lives' (importance of kinship bonds across the generations); 'time and place' (influence of social and historic context in shaping life); 'transitions and their timing' (adaptive variation according to stage in life); 'agency' (construction of life through planned effort); and 'life-long human development' (continuity and change according to earlier experience). Such a framework emphasises the 'interaction between the passage of individual time, family time, and historical time'

(Arber and Evandrou, 1993:10), and this interplay between time, life events and context has direct relevance to a consideration of migration motivations in later life.

Retirement is a time for acting on migration wishes, with studies showing an increase in the return rate as immigrants reach this age (Thomson, 2005). Indeed, the desire to retire at 'home' has been a 'pull' factor influencing return migration across the centuries (Grosjean, 2005:229). As work and financial responsibilities recede, nostalgia and emotional ties to country of origin may come to the fore more prominently (Klinthäll, 2006). Lifecourse events and transitions, such as divorce, relocation of children and changes in family relationships can all trigger geographical mobility (Litwak and Longino, 1987; McHugh and Mings, 1996; Baldassar, 2007a), as can bereavement, an increasingly frequent experience in later life and one that may be particularly poignant for ageing immigrants.

The death of close immigrant friends, or a spouse, reduces the opportunity to share common personal stories and experiences of homeland, which can be deeply regretted in old age (George and Fitzgerald, 2012). Such loss can stimulate thoughts of return 'home' where siblings still reside, as discussed by Percival (Chapter Six, this volume); widowhood certainly features across studies into the propensities to return in later life, as noted in studies by Klinthäll in Sweden and Newbold in Canada (both included in this volume).

Old age is also a time to consider end of life and the body's final resting place. George and Fitzgerald (2012) found that ageing immigrants commonly wished their remains to be close to children in the host country, a preference also noted by Percival (Chapter Six, this volume), although in Percival's study a number of respondents were very passionate about plans for the return of their ashes to a place or city in the homeland. Richards (2005:84–85) provides figures that illustrate the importance, to significant minorities of 19th-century emigrants to Australia, of their return to the British Isles at the end of life, and Stefansson has noted how Bosnian refugees made the heartfelt decision to return to their former war-torn land because of 'their wish to die at home' (2004:2).

A lifecourse perspective is also useful methodologically, as suggested by Warnes and Williams (2006) when they argue for more biographical and lifecourse perspectives in order to increase understanding of motives for migration in old age and the consequences of migration and ageing. In similar vein, Thomson (2005) indicates that only in-depth, life-story, explorations can highlight long-term influences on migration and return, not least in regard to the complex but often influential issue of family dynamics. This issue is the subject of the next contextual theme under consideration.

Family ties and obligations

Relationships with partners and children are a very close form of social capital, one relatively unexplored as regards return migration (Rodríguez and Egea, 2006) but likely to be weighed in the balance when reaching migration decisions (Stoller and Longino, 2001), along with issues of family proximity, intensity and responsibility. For example, the death of a spouse or desire to be nearer new grandchildren in the home country are significant reasons for return migration in later life (Rutter and Andrew, 2009); conversely, dwindling social contacts in the home country and the presence of grandchildren in the host country may produce a feeling of being more grounded in the host country (Leavey et al, 2004; Van der Geest et al, 2004).

Family connection is sometimes maintained despite leaving children behind in the former host country, when returnees form close ties with grandchildren who stay with them in vacations (Rodríguez and Egea, 2006), a valuable trade-off, perhaps, and one likely to appeal to returnees characterised by Longino and Warnes as more inclined to 'individualistic lifestyles' than close 'family-oriented' ones (2005:543). Migrants wishing to experience homeland living while minimising family disruption, and those with children in both places, may choose a back-and-forwards or 'va-et-vient' strategy, regularly spending periods of time between the host and home region or country (de Coulon and Wolff, 2005).

However, older people's caring responsibilities as regards young grandchildren can postpone the decision to return (Rodríguez and Egea, 2006) or eventually lead migrants to concede that their cherished wish to return is no longer viable, especially the case when the adult children whom they expected to accompany them on their return are loath to leave a reasonably strong economy for one less favourable (Wessendorf, 2011). Women are more likely than men to wish to remain in the host country if children are based there, despite missing their home country (Klinthäll, 2006), and this may cause marital conflict when husbands maintain an eagerness to return (Van der Geest et al, 2004).

For those who do return, family relationships in the home country can be equally important. Indeed, successful return is aided by maintenance of positive contact with relatives and friends in the homeland (Leavey et al, 2004). Moving to be nearer a sibling may rarely be a prime reason for return migration (Rodríguez and Egea, 2006), although it may influence those older people interested in the prospect of receiving informal care by extended family (Taylor, 2009), especially if widowed and in declining health (Warnes, 1992a, 1992b), and certainly arises as a significant attraction for those seeking increased social interactions or closer family bonding (Percival, Chapter Six, this volume). Cheaper telecommunication systems and new communication technologies also potentially play a part, as they enable more immediate contact with family at home and also appear to 'increase the desire for intermittent co-presence ... and the incidence of visits' (Baldassar, 2007b:171). Of course, older returnees not only relinquish close proximity to their adult children and grandchildren when they leave the host country, they also forfeit opportunities for care by the immediate family, should they need it. Despite the resourceful efforts of young family members to provide transnational care to ageing relatives abroad (Baldassar, 2007b), increasing care needs can be a challenge to ageing returnees. There are implications here for health and welfare service provision.

Health and welfare services

Interest in migration in later life inevitably directs us to issues such as health, welfare, tax, housing and sources of valued care, factors that influence older people's movements (Litwak and Longino, 1987; Thomson, 2005; Warnes and Williams, 2006), issues that may not receive sufficient attention in respect of older returnees (Rutter and Andrew, 2009).

In her pioneering work, Cribier (1975, 1999) carried out studies with retirees in Greater Paris in the 1970s and 1980s to examine how provincial citizens who had migrated to Paris during the 1940s–1960s now planned their return. Cribier unearthed a strong wish to return to local towns and regions of birth, particularly to well-serviced towns in the same region, where valued amenities and a lower cost of living could be found. In their study of Canadian seasonal migrants to Florida, Marshall et al (1989) learned of a preference for the home country health system, which results in preventative behaviour including stocking up on drugs before the trip and taking out health insurance for Canadians travelling abroad, strategies more important to those less able to afford US health care costs. Hunter's (2011) study of retired African immigrants living in France highlighted their interest in retaining a base in the host country, to safeguard adequate health care and to secure irreplaceable pensions, a priority that prevented permanent return home. Similar issues influence retired Bengali migrant labourers living in London (Jeffery and Murison, 2011).

Pension levels are certainly a major concern to prospective returnees, and those whose pensions are frozen on exit from the host country are seriously disadvantaged (Khant and Mawhinney, 2010); such resource allocation practices, as they apply in Europe, are considered by Ackers and Dwyer (2002), who report the development of mobility and welfare rights for older citizens who wish to exercise their right to move or return home on retirement. However, sources of information about returnees' benefit entitlements are often lacking (Rutter and Andrew, 2009).

Even *perceptions* of health and other public services in host and home settings can affect decision making. Wessendorf has shown that Italian migrants in Switzerland who judged local health and public services to be superior to those found in their home country saw this as a 'strong incentive' to stay in the host country as they age (2011:161). Leavey et al (2004) learned that Irish immigrants ageing in the UK were worried about returning to a country perceived to have a poorer-quality health service.

In some cases, perceptions of health services are being favourably manipulated by home countries intent on attracting immigrants back, through advertising medical and dental treatment at a much less expensive cost than comparable services in the host country, the experience of Hungarians who emigrated to North America after the 1956 revolution (Huseby-Darvas, 2004). Where Italian migrants' expectations of land inheritance on return to poor urban regions were not realised, blame could realistically be levelled at lack of help from regional government, bureaucratic obstacles, and competition for inadequate local resources, failings that might have been expected by those likely to unfavourably compare state institutions at home to those previously experienced abroad (King et al, 1985). Availability and cost of health and public services can, therefore, be a significant factor weighed in the balance by older migrants considering return.

Such resource issues are likely to have implications for country economies and policies. According to White (2006:1297) a 'strong case' can be made that ageing migrant populations constitute a 'significant structural shift ... in the general societal responses that are needed in terms of welfare and other support'; not to plan for their particular needs is a form of social exclusion. Indeed, retirement migration may in the future involve substantial relocations of social and health care costs (Gustafson, 2001; Sriskandarajah and Drew, 2006), and return migration may also present challenges for social workers and social policy planners

(Rodríguez and Egea, 2006); as yet, examples of public financing of health and care services for older migrants in the host country are limited (Gustafson, 2008). Furthermore, the circulation model, or 'va-et-vient' process, mentioned earlier, has important policy applications with respect to housing markets, economic growth, remittances or social assimilation (de Coulon and Wolff, 2005). Health services and resource planning, and family ties and obligations, are themes that receive concerted attention throughout this book.

Many questions arise from this brief account of the myriad issues involved in return migration in later life. For example, in what ways do lifecourse events in later life affect attachment to place? To what extent do different family ties in old age influence return strategies and successful adjustment? How do care and health issues affect ageing immigrants and decision making regarding return migration? To what extent are older people interested in circular or transnational movements and with what effect on personal, family and cultural life? What should public services be mindful of, and plan for, in respect of an ageing immigrant population and the return of migrants in later life? Between them the chapters in this book address these and other related issues.

The two chapters that follow this one consider *propensities and determinants* for returning to places of origin. Klinthäll considers patterns of old age return migration from Sweden, through examination of data on the complete immigrant population over 55, while Newbold explores Canadian census statistics to determine the incidence, composition, spatial patterning, and correlates of return by residents aged over 60, to regions within the country. The next three chapters explore *motivations and strategies* as regards return migration in later life. Bolzman blends the findings of quantitative and qualitative studies of older Italian and Spanish immigrants living in Switzerland to explore economic, social, health and cultural dimensions that affect motivation to return. Conway and colleagues consider patterns and processes of lifecourse planning that influence timing of return to the Caribbean from Europe and the United States of America, and develop a conceptual framework to help explain the behavioural dynamics involved. Percival also uses narrative data in Chapter Six in this volume, which is based on interviews with British immigrants in Australia who are considering return, and those who have returned to the UK, to highlight the interplay of lifecourse events and changes that affect belonging and identity in later life.

A trio of chapters then discuss *priorities and evaluations* in respect of homeland visits and variations in types of return. Blunt, Bonnerjee and

Hysler-Rubin discuss return visits to Calcutta by retired members of the Anglo-Indian and Jewish communities who have migrated to London, Toronto and Israel since 1947, and focus on how decisions to return are sometimes shaped by ideas about urban and community continuity and change. Ruting's account explores how return visits from Australia to Estonia, by those who left their homeland as children, during the turmoil of the Second World War, affects transnational mobility and sense of 'home'. In Chapter Nine, Christou explores first and second generation Greek-Danish migration and the spatial and temporal meanings associated with diasporic longing and cultural connection with the ancestral homeland.

The final two chapters adopt different methods of enquiry but each encompass a wide and yet detailed perspective on *personal and cultural consequences of return*. Leavey and Eliacin review relevant studies to probe the biological, environmental and cultural factors, as well as issues of race and class, that influence the psychological wellbeing of those who realise their wish to return to country of origin. Olsson focuses on political exile and transnational relationships between older returnees in Chile and the diaspora in Sweden, and contrasts post-dictatorship returnees in the 1990s, characterised by their politically motivated return to Chile, with later returnees, no less politically oriented but more motivated to return because of family and kin affiliations and a strong desire to reconnect with cultural roots. The book's final chapter summarises key messages, insights, and future strategies indicated by the editor's reflection on the volume as a whole.

Acknowledgement
I would like to thank Graeme Hugo, professor of geography and director of the Australian Population and Migration Research Centre at the University of Adelaide, for relevant migration statistical information.

References
Ackers, L. and Dwyer, P. (2002) *Senior citizenship? Retirement, migration and welfare in the European Union*, Bristol: The Policy Press.

Age Concern (2007) *When the sun sets on retirement abroad*, London: Age Concern.

Arber, S. and Evandrou, M. (1993) 'Mapping the territory. Ageing, independence and the lifecourse', in S. Arber and M. Evandrou (eds) *Ageing, Independence and the Lifecourse*, London: Jessica Kingsley Publishers.

Baldassar, L. (2001) *Visits Home: Migration experiences between Italy and Australia*, Melbourne: Melbourne University Press.

Baldassar, L. (2007a) 'Transnational families and aged care: the mobility of care and the migrancy of ageing', *Journal of Ethnic and Migration Studies*, 33(2): 275–297.

Baldassar, L. (2007b) *Families caring across borders. Migration, ageing and transnational caregiving*, New York: Palgrave Macmillan.

Basch, L., Glick Schiller, N. and Szanton Blanc, C. (1994) *Nations unbound: Transnational projects, postcolonial predicaments and deterritorialised nation-states*, Langhorne, PA: Gordon and Breach.

Basu, P. (2007) *Highland Homecomings: Genealogy and heritage tourism in the Scottish diaspora*, London: Routledge.

Bengtson, V.L., Elder, G.H. and Putney, N.M. (2005) 'The lifecourse perspective on ageing: linked lives, timing and history', in M. Johnson (ed) *The Cambridge Handbook of Age and Ageing*, Cambridge: Cambridge University Press.

Biggs, S. (2005) 'Psychodynamic approaches to the lifecourse and ageing', in M. Johnson (ed) *The Cambridge Handbook of Age and Ageing*, Cambridge: Cambridge University Press

Blunt, A. and Dowling, R. (2006) *Home*, London: Routledge.

Bolzman, C., Fibbi, R. and Vial, M. (2006) 'What to do after retirement? Elderly migrants and the question of return', *Journal of Ethnic and Migration Studies*, 32(8): 1359–1375.

Božić, S. (2006) 'The achievement and potential of international retirement migration research: the need for disciplinary exchange', *Journal of Ethnic and Migration Studies*, 32(8): 1415–1427.

CoHab (Diasporic Constructions of Home and Belonging) (2012) Online resource. Available at: www.itn-cohab.eu/

Coleman, P. (2005) 'Reminiscence: development, social and clinical perspectives', in M. Johnson (ed) *The Cambridge Handbook of Age and Ageing*, Cambridge: Cambridge University Press.

Conway, D. and Potter, R. (2007) 'Caribbean transnational return migrants as agents of change', *Geography Compass*, 1(1): 27–45.

Cresswell, T. (2004) *Place: A Short Introduction*, Chichester: Wiley-Blackwell.

Cribier, F. (1975) 'Retirement migration in France', in L.A. Kosinski and R.M. Prothero (eds) *People on the Move: studies on internal migration*, London: Methuen, pp 361–373.

Cribier, F. (1999) *Retirement Migration from the Paris Region*. Cahiers de la MRSH, Caen: University of Caen Basse-Normandie.

de Coulon, A. and Wolff, F-C. (2005) *Immigrants at Retirement: Stay/ Return or 'Va-et-Vient'?* Discussion Paper No 691. London: Centre for Economic Performance, London School of Economics and Political Science.

DIAC (Department of Immigration and Citizenship) (2012) *Trends in Migration: Australia 2010–11*. Available at: www.immi.gov.au/ media/publications/statistics/trends-in-migration/trends-in-migration-2010–11.pdf

Finch, T., Andrew, H. and Latorre, M. (2010) *Global Brit: Making the Most of the British Diaspora*, London: Institute for Public Policy Research.

Finch, T., Latorre, M., Pollard, N. and Rutter, J. (2009) *Shall We Stay or Shall We Go? Re-migration trends among Britain's immigrants*, London: Institute for Public Policy Research.

George, M. and Fitzgerald, R.P. (2012) 'Forty years in Aotearoa New Zealand: white identity, home and later life in an adopted country', *Ageing & Society*, 32:239–260.

Gmelch, G. (1980) 'Return migration', *Annals, Review of Anthropology*, 9:135–159.

Grosjean, A. (2005) 'Returning to Belhelvie, 1593–1875: the impact of return migration on an Aberdeenshire parish', in M. Harper (ed) *Emigrant Homecomings. The Return Movement of Emigrants, 1600–2000*, Manchester: Manchester University Press.

Gu, C-J. (2010) 'Culture, emotional transnationalism and mental distress: family relations and well-being among Taiwanese immigrant women', *Gender, Place and Culture*, 17:687–704.

Gustafson, P. (2001) 'Retirement migration and transnational lifestyles', *Ageing & Society*, 21:371–394.

Gustafson, P. (2008) 'Transnationalism in retirement migration: the case of North European retirees in Spain', *Ethnic and Racial Studies*, 31:451–475.

Hall, S. (1996) 'Introduction: who needs identity?', in S. Hall and P. du Gay (eds) *Questions of Cultural Identity*, London: Sage.

Harper, M. (2005) 'Introduction', in M. Harper (ed) *Emigrant Homecomings. The return movement of emigrants, 1600–2000*, Manchester: Manchester University Press.

Hunter, A. (2011) 'Theory and practice of return migration at retirement: the case of migrant worker hostel residents in France', *Population, Space and Place*, 17:179–192.

Huseby-Darvas, E.V. (2004) '*Extra Hungarian Non Est Vita*? The relationships between Hungarian immigrants and their homeland', in F. Markowitz and A.H. Stefansson (eds) *Homecomings. Unsettling Paths of Return*, Maryland: Lexington Books.

Jeffery, L. and Murison, J. (2011) 'The temporal, social, spatial, and legal dimensions of return and onward migration', *Population, Space and Place*, 17:131–139.

Khant, O. and Mawhinney, P. (2010) *The Costs of 'Returning Home': retirement migration and financial inclusion*, London: Runnymede Trust.

King, R. (2000) 'Generalizations from the history of return migration', in B. Ghosh (ed) *Return Migration: Journey of Hope or Despair*, Geneva: IOM (International Organization for Migration).

Klinthäll, M. (2006) 'Retirement return migration from Sweden', *International Migration*, 44(2): 153–180.

Leavey, G., Sembhi, S. and Livingston, G. (2004) 'Older Irish migrants living in London: identity, loss and return, *Journal of Ethnic and Migration Studies*, 30(4):763–779.

Litwak, E. And Longino, C.F. (1987) 'Migration patterns among the elderly: a developmental perspective', *The Gerontologist*, 27(3):266–272.

Longino, C.F. and Warnes, A.M. (2005) 'Migration and older people', in M. Johnson (ed) *The Cambridge Handbook of Age and Ageing*, Cambridge: Cambridge University Press.

Markowitz, F. (2004) 'The home(s) of homecomings', in F. Markowitz and A. Stefansson (eds) *Homecomings: unsettling paths of return*, Lanham: Lexington Books.

Marshall, V.W., Longino, C.F., Tucker, R. and Mullins, L. (1989) 'Health care utilization of Canadian snowbirds: an example of strategic planning', *Journal of Aging Health*, 1(2): 150–68.

McHugh, K.E. and Mings, R.C. (1996) 'The circle of migration: attachment to place in aging', *Annals of the Association of American Geographers*, 86(3): 530–550.

Murdoch, S. (2005) 'Children of the diaspora: the 'homecoming' of the second-generation Scot in the seventeenth century', in M. Harper (ed) *Emigrant homecomings. The return movement of emigrants, 1600–2000*, Manchester: Manchester University Press.

ONS (Office for National Statistics) (2012) *Long-Term International Migration 1991 to 2012 Age and Sex*, Newport South Wales: Office for National Statistics. Available at: www.ons.gov.uk/ons/publications/re-reference-tables.html?edition=tcm%3A77–235198

Phillips, J. and Potter, R. (2009) 'Questions of friendship and degrees of transnationality among second-generation return migrants to Barbados', *Journal of Ethnic and Migration Studies*, 35(4):669–688.

Relph, E. (1976) *Place and placelessness*, London: Pion Limited.

Richards, E. (2005) 'Running home from Australia: intercontinental mobility and migrant expectations in the nineteenth century', in M. Harper (ed) *Emigrant Homecomings. The return movement of emigrants, 1600–2000*, Manchester: Manchester University Press.

Rodríguez, V. and Egea, C. (2006) 'Return and the social environment of Andalusian emigrants in Europe', *Journal of Ethnic and Migration Studies*, 32(8):1377–1393.

Rowles, G. (1978) *Prisoners of Space? Exploring the geographical experience of older people*, Boulder, CO: Westview Press.

Rowles, G. (1983) 'Place and personal identity in old age: observations from Appalachia', *Journal of Environmental Psychology*, 3:299–313.

Rubinstein, N. (2005) 'Psychic homelands and the imagination of place: a literary perspective', in G. Rowles and H. Chaudhury (eds) *Place Attachment*, New York: Plenum Press.

Ruting, B. (2008) 'Touring the homeland: diasporic travel by Antipodean Estonians'. Paper presented to 'The Baltic Region: Antipodean Perspectives', Association for the Advancement of Baltic Studies, Australasian Chapter Conference, 6 September, The University of Melbourne.

Rutter, J. and Andrew, H. (2009) *Home sweet home? The nature and scale of the immigration of older UK nationals back to the UK*, London: Age Concern and Help the Aged.

Sinatti, G. (2011) '"Mobile transmigrants or unsettled returnees?" Myth of return and permanent resettlement among Senegalese migrants', *Population, Space and Place*, 17:153–166.

Sriskandarajah, D. and Drew, C. (2006) *Brits Abroad: Mapping the Scale and Nature of British Emigration*, London: Institute for Public Policy Research.

Stefansson, A.H. (2004) 'Homecomings to the future: from diasporic mythographies to social projects of return', in F. Markowitz and A.H. Stefansson (eds) *Homecomings. Unsettling Paths of Return*, Lanham, MD: Lexington Books.

Stephenson, M.L. (2002) 'Travelling to the ancestral homelands: the aspirations and experiences of a UK Caribbean community', *Current Issues in Tourism*, 5:378–425.

Stoller, E.P. and Longino, C.F. (2001) '"Going home" or "leaving home"? The impact of person and place ties on anticipated counterstream migration', *The Gerontologist,* 41(1):96–102.

Taylor, L. (2009) *Return migration in Ghana*, London: Institute for Public Policy Research.

Thomson, A. (2005) '"My wayward heart": homesickness, longing and the return of British post-war immigrants from Australia', in M. Harper (ed) *Emigrant Homecomings. The return movement of emigrants, 1600–2000*, Manchester: Manchester University Press.

Van der Geest, S., Mul, A. and Vermeulen, H. (2004) 'Linkages between migration and the care of frail older people: observations from Greece, Ghana and The Netherlands', *Ageing & Society*, 24:431–450.

Warnes, A.M. (1992a) 'Age-related variation and temporal change in elderly migration', in A. Rogers (ed) *Elderly Migration and Population Redistribution: A comparative study*, London: Belhaven, pp 35–55.

Warnes, A.M. (1992b) 'Migration and the lifecourse', in T. Champion and T. Fielding (eds) *Migration Processes and Patterns, Vol. 1, Research progress and prospects*, London: Belhaven, pp 175–87.

Warnes, A.M. (2001) 'The international dispersal of pensioners from affluent countries', *International Journal of Population Geography*, 7(6):373–388.

Warnes, A.M. and Williams, A. (2006) 'Older migrants in Europe: a new focus for migration studies', *Journal of Ethnic and Migration Studies*, 32(8):1257–1281.

Wessendorf, S. (2011) 'State-imposed translocalism and the dream of returning: Italian migrants in Switzerland', in L. Baldassar and D. Gabaccia (eds) *Intimacy and Italian Migration*, New York: Fordham University Press.

White, P. (2006) 'Migrant populations approaching old age: prospects in Europe', *Journal of Ethnic and Migration Studies*, 32:1283–1300.

Wyman, M. (2005) 'Emigrants returning: the evolution of a tradition', in M. Harper (ed) *Emigrant Homecomings. The return movement of emigrants, 1600–2000*, Manchester: Manchester University Press.

TWO

Older immigrants leaving Sweden

Martin Klinthäll

Introduction

Most research on temporary migration deals with labour migration by young people and large-scale quantitative studies of international return migration in old age are few. This study is the first to analyse patterns of old-age return migration in the complete immigrant population in a single country over a longer time period. The study analyses return migration from Sweden among immigrants 55 years or older during the period 1990–2007, a period of globalisation and increasing international mobility (United Nations, 2009). The study addresses the question of labour market attachment and return migration in later life.

Earlier studies have shown that return migration in working age often displays a positive selection in terms of education and income history in the host country, in that return migrants on average display higher levels of education and income compared with migrants who stay in the country of destination, leading to the conclusion that return migration is generally not the result of weak economic integration (Klinthäll, 2003; Nekby, 2006; Klinthäll, 2007). Regarding migrants of older age, the processes of migration and integration may however look different. Entry or re-entry into the labour market, as well as social integration and adaptation in the host country, may be more complicated for older migrants, depending on time since immigration and age at immigration. Hence, we may expect different types of return migration processes among older immigrants; older return migrants may be positively selected due to strategies of temporary migration that involve target-saving behaviour, resulting in relatively higher incomes among return migrants. 'Return of retirement' (Cerase, 1970) would thus be the result of an accomplished career in the host country.

However, retirement-return migration could also be the consequence of losing contact with working life in the host country. Older immigrants who have a weak position in the labour market and who exit employment before retirement may not consider a continued career as realistic. With few years left to retirement, re-entry into the labour market may not seem feasible and return migration appears as an option. Hence, we may also expect an increasing propensity for return migration in connection with exits from the labour market other than age retirement, such as unemployment or early retirement due to sickness or lay-offs. Regarding return migration in old age, we may therefore expect polarised patterns of return migration; positive selection due to target-saving behaviour and negative selection due to weak labour market integration.

Increased mobility can be expected at retirement, when the link between income and place of residence becomes weaker. Instead of wages and employment opportunities, considerations of costs of living and the value of pensions and savings become important (Dustmann, 2001; Dustmann and Weiss 2007; Dustmann and Mestres 2011). Research has shown that migration in old age is often directed from regions with high costs of living into regions with low costs of living (for example, Serow et al, 1986; Serow, 1987; Fournier et al, 1988a, 1988b; Walters, 2002, Sunil et al, 2007). There are also other important quality of life considerations, such as access to health care and other services, or a healthy and pleasant climate. Old age migrants moving from the North to the South in Europe and North America report the climate to be one of the most important determinants in the migration decision (for example, Meyer, 1987; Bohland and Rowles, 1988; López de Lera, 1995; King et al, 1998; King and Patterson, 1998; Rodríguez et al, 1998; Warnes and Patterson, 1998; Williams and Patterson, 1998; Walters, 2002; Gustafson, 2008; Warnes, 2009).

Among immigrants, an increased propensity for return migration would consequently be expected at the time of retirement, in particular when costs of living are lower in the country of origin, and when the migrant has a preference for the country of origin (Hill, 1987; Djajic and Milbourne, 1988; Dustmann, 1997; Klinthäll, 2006; Dustmann and Weiss, 2007). Labour migrants with a preference for the home country are assumed to be target savers and, thus, positively selected in terms of income compared with the rest of the immigrant population. They display high labour supply and high rates of saving while abroad, in order to be able to have a high level of consumption after returning to the country of origin.

However, the propensity for return migration declines with time in the host country (for example, Dustmann, 1996; Edin et al, 2000; Klinthäll, 2003; de Colon and Wolff, 2006). The accomplishment of a savings target requires a certain degree of socioeconomic integration in the country of immigration, which in turn may lead to a decline in the preference for the home country (see Bovenkerk, 1974). Such an 'acclimatisation effect' counteracts positive selectivity in retirement return migration. Empirical evidence is inconclusive; Klinthäll (2006) analyses return migration from Sweden 1979–96 among immigrants aged 51–80 and finds a tendency towards positive selection, whereas Yahirun (2009) finds negative selection patterns in return migration from Germany 1984–2007 among male immigrants aged 50 and over.

Regarding refugee immigrants, rates of return migration are expected to be low due to insecure and unstable circumstances in the countries of origin. Joly (2002) categorises refugee immigrants according to their attitudes towards return migration. 'Rubicon' refugees are oriented towards the host society and permanent settlement, while 'Odyssean' refugees are oriented towards their country of origin and view migration as temporary. Hence, the process of socioeconomic integration in the host country will differ between these refugee categories (Klinthäll, 2007). 'Rubicon' refugees have incentives for long-term investments in the host country, whereas 'Odyssean' refugees make their plans under great uncertainty, since the point in time when return migration can take place is unknown. The preconditions for integration are worse for 'Odyssean' refugees than for 'Rubicon' refugees and therefore, return migration among refugee immigrants is expected to be negatively selected.

One of the most important determinants of place of residence for older immigrants is contact with friends and family, in particular children. Studies on attitudes towards return migration from France find that many immigrants prefer a strategy of moving back and forth between home and host country after retirement (Attias-Donfut and Wolff, 2005a; de Coulon and Wolff, 2006), in particular immigrants who have children in both countries. Ahmadi and Tornstam (1996) and Emami and Ekman (1998) find similar considerations among elderly immigrants in Sweden. Bolzman et al (2004) find that among elderly immigrants in Switzerland, women have a stronger preference for settlement in the host country than men, mainly because they want to keep contact with their children, but also because they feel more independent in the host country. De Coulon and Wolff (2006) find similar gender differences regarding attitudes towards return migration among immigrants in France. Attias-Donfut and Wolff (2005b) also find that immigrant women have a higher preference for burial in France than immigrant men.

In the following analysis, we address the question of selectivity in return migration among older immigrants in Sweden. We expect determinants of return migration to differ among older immigrants compared with those at younger ages. When pensions replace income from work, the propensity for return migration should increase, in particular return migration to politically stable countries with lower costs of living and a warm climate. Successful socioeconomic integration in Sweden should decrease the propensity for return migration, leading to lower rates of return migration at higher income levels. However, certain immigrants may have had long-term plans for return migration and, therefore, there may also be positive selection in terms of income, due to savings target behaviour. Returning refugee immigrants, however, are expected to be negatively selected, due to lower levels of socioeconomic integration in Sweden. In addition, according to evidence from previous research, we also expect gender differences in the patterns of old-age return migration.

The literature on temporary migration has become increasingly concerned with double residence strategies. De Coulon and Wolff (2006) interview old-age migrants in France and find that 65 per cent of the respondents want to stay, 27 per cent prefer a double residence strategy and only 8 per cent report that they prefer permanent return migration. Bolzman et al (2006) find that 30 per cent of 55- to 64-year-old Spanish and Italian respondents in Switzerland wanted to stay permanently, 34 per cent preferred a double residence strategy and only 26 per cent return migration. Migration intentions are, however, a useful but not exact predictor of actual migration outcomes (see Bradley et al, 2008). When asked about their migration intentions in the 1984 wave of the German Socioeconomic Panel, 66 per cent of the immigrants stated that they intended to return, but 10 years later, only 11 per cent had realised their intentions (Dustmann 1996). There are a range of reasons why intentions are not actuated. One reason can be that preferred migration strategies stated by migrants do not always correspond to their resources (Cassarino, 2004).

Furthermore, recorded migration outcomes may not exactly reflect real migration outcomes. Migration outcomes in official registers tend to be biased towards permanent settlement, for two reasons: first, if the actual date of return migration is not reported by the migrant, the return will not be registered until the authorities conclude that the individual has left the country. Second, the occurrence of double residence strategies is hard to estimate, since residents often count as permanent although they may spend a large part of the year abroad. If the migrant adopts a strategy of moving back and forth between home and host country, the migration periods may be too short for a change of registered place of residence, or there may exist certain incentives to remain registered as a resident of the host country.

Data and definitions

This study uses data on actuated migration, that is, changes of place of residence reported to the tax authorities. The database consists of information compiled from a number of registers administered by Statistics Sweden containing a large range of socioeconomic and demographic information on the individual level. The database covers the period 1990–2008 and contains information on all individuals aged 16 or over who were registered as Swedish residents by December 31 in any year during the period.

In the dataset used in the following analysis, we have included all foreign-born individuals aged 55 or older for the period 1990–2007. The year 2008 was excluded due to lack of information on payments of early retirement compensation. Individuals may have immigrated before the age of 55, but in the analysis they are observed only from the year when they turn 55. Return migration is defined as emigration from Sweden to the country of birth. In the analysis, birth countries have been categorised according to history of migration to Sweden, such as North-western Europe, North America and Oceania, primarily sources of labour migration; Eastern Europe, which has been a source of both labour and refugee migration, and Asia, Africa and South America, primarily sources of refugee immigration.

Income is measured on the individual level and covers all kinds of officially registered income: income from work, capital income, sickness benefits, unemployment benefits, pensions, income support payments, housing subsidies and so on. In the regression models, incomes are categorised into income quintiles. Note that these are quintiles for the whole *immigrant* population aged 16 years and older, and not for the total population of Sweden. Assuming under-registration of emigration, observations where all types of income are equal to zero or missing are omitted.

The longitudinal character of the database provides a range of alternative methods. Because of the discrete character of the data (recorded on an annual basis) and that the concern is the probability of return migration in a given year, a standard binary logit approach was preferred for the empirical analysis. In the regression models, the probability of return migration in a given year is assumed to be dependent on the circumstances in the previous year: we estimate the impact of the situation in a certain year on the probability of return migration in the following year.

As Haas et al (2006) discuss, there is a lack of consensus on the concept 'retirement migration'. Although formal age retirement in Sweden may take place between ages 60 and 67, age 65 is still the standard age of retirement and therefore, we use age 65 as the point of age retirement in our models. There are three 'retirement variables' in the regression models; the variable *Age65* indicates whether an individual turns 65 in the observed year and measures the immediate retirement effect. *Retired* indicates whether the person is 65 years or older, and *Early retired* indicates whether the individual has received payments of early retirement compensation during the year, when the capacity for work is lost or reduced due to illness or injury. Figure 2.1 shows crude return migration rates by age. There is a peak in return migration at retirement age, which is in line with the findings by Poulain and Perrin (2002), who show that return migration from Belgium 1991–1997 decreases with age from around age 30 until retirement age, where there is a second peak in return migration rates.

The variables *Years since immigration* and *Age at immigration* are calculated from the last observed year of immigration to Sweden. Regarding *Civil status*, 'Unmarried' means never married, and 'Married'

Figure 2.1: Crude return migration rates 1990-2007, all immigrants resident in Sweden aged 55+. Average annual rates by age (%)

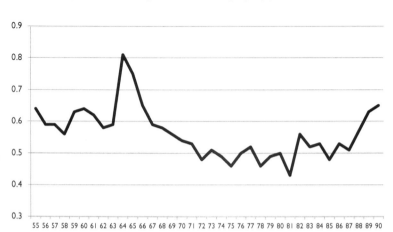

Source: REMESO database, Statistics Sweden

includes co-resident as well as separated married individuals. A remarried widowed or divorced person counts as married. Regarding *Education* 'Primary' denotes nine years of schooling or less, 'Secondary' up to three-year long completed post-primary education, and 'Tertiary' means that the individual has completed post-secondary education or higher.

Analysis

Tables 2.1–2.6 show binary logit regressions of the odds ratio of return migration from Sweden in the period 1990–2007. All regressions are estimated separately for males and females, since we expect gender differences regarding the mechanisms behind return migration decisions. A model which includes both sexes (not reported here) shows that return migration is about 30 per cent lower among women than among men aged 55+, controlling for demographic and socioeconomic factors.

The first model includes all foreign-born individuals who were registered as Swedish residents by December 31 in any year during the 18-year period between 1990 and 2007 and the results, displayed in Table 2.1, show that there is a clear retirement effect on the propensity for return migration. Whereas studies on the working population show that there is a negative effect of age on return migration propensity, the results in Table 2.1 show that the propensity for return migration is higher in ages 65+ than in ages 55–64, when controlling for demographic and socioeconomic characteristics. The indicator variable *Retired* shows that return migration is about 40 per cent higher among those who have reached retirement age, compared with those who are younger. This effect remains even when controlling for the peak at age 65, when return migration is significantly higher compared with the average of other ages. This peak, somewhat higher for men than for women, shows that there is an immediate retirement effect. The odds ratios for the indicator variable *Early retired* shows that there is an even stronger effect of early retirement on the propensity to return. The odds ratio for those who have received early retirement compensation is 1.73 for men and 1.88 for women, and the results are highly significant, with standard errors at 0.06 and 0.07 respectively.

The demographic variables show that civil status and the timing of immigration are important determinants for the propensity to return. One additional year since immigration is associated with a 4–5 per cent lower risk of return migration. This effect is however not completely linear; the inclusion of a quadratic term in the model (not presented

Table 2.1: Logistic estimation of return migration from Sweden 1990-2007.

All immigrants aged 55+. Separate estimations for males and females.

	Males	Females
Covariate	Odds ratio	Odds ratio
Calendar year	1.03***	1.04***
Years since immigration	0.95***	0.96***
Age at immigration	1.01*	1.02***
Age 65	1.28***	1.19***
Retired	1.41***	1.39***
Early retired	1.73***	1.88***
Civil status		
Married	*1.00*	*1.00*
Unmarried	1.67***	1.68***
Divorced	1.56***	1.25***
Widowed	1.34***	1.09**
Income		
First quintile	2.04***	2.09***
Second quintile	1.24***	1.31***
Third quintile	*1.00*	*1.00*
Fourth quintile	0.87***	1.12**
Fifth quintile	1.33***	1.39***
Education		
Primary	*1.00*	*1.00*
Secondary	0.66***	0.74***
Tertiary	0.75***	0.84***
Unknown	0.82***	0.63***
Observations	1,520,339	1,903,625
Individuals	198,263	236,717
Events	7,737	7,176

Asterisks denote significance level: ***) $p<0.01$, **) $p<0.05$, *) $p<0.10$

here) shows that the effect of time since immigration declines with each additional year since immigration, especially for women.

As expected, *Age at immigration* is associated with increased propensity for return migration; those who moved to Sweden at higher ages are more likely to return than those who came when they were younger. The results show that the effect is not highly significant for men, but this is primarily due to non-linearity; controlling for non-linearity yields a significant positive effect of *Age at immigration*. There are also large differences according to civil status. Being married is associated with significantly lower propensity for return migration for both men and women, compared with those who are unmarried, divorced or widowed. Unmarried people are generally more mobile and, as expected, they are more likely to return migrate than people in the other civil status groups. Divorced individuals in their turn display more return migration than widowed individuals. Although the ranking between civil status groups is the same for men and women regarding the propensity for return migration, there is an interesting gender difference regarding the size of the odds ratios for those who have left marriage. Divorced or widowed women seem to have lower return migration rates than divorced or widowed men. Models with interactions (not presented here) show that the risk of return migration for divorced or widowed men is about 30 per cent higher than for divorced or married women aged 55+, on top of the main effect of being male. Leaving marriage is apparently a more powerful trigger of return migration for older immigrant men than for older immigrant women in Sweden.

Regarding socioeconomic situation in terms of income and education, there seems to be a U-shaped relationship between return migration and the socioeconomic situation in the previous year. The lowest and the highest income quintiles display the highest odds ratios for both men and women, whereas the middle quintile is associated with lowest return migration for women and the fourth quintile is associated with lowest return migration for men. The odds ratios are particularly high for the first quintile, which can be interpreted as a partly negative self-selection: those with the lowest socioeconomic status are the ones most likely to return. However, the values for the lowest quintile may partly be exaggerated because income is measured in the year before return migration. Income may be lower than normal also in the year prior to the move if return migration has been a drawn-out process, due to lower presence in Sweden that year. Using a measure of accumulated income in Sweden over time, divided by the number of observed years, yields less high odds ratios for the first quintile.

There is also a tendency towards a U-shaped association between return migration and educational level, since the odds ratios for primary and tertiary education are higher than for secondary education. Return migration is highest among those who have the lowest status, that is those who only have primary education, which is similar to the pattern in terms of income. Thus, looking at the whole population of immigrants aged 55+ in Sweden, there seems to be a polarised pattern of return migration. In terms of income and education, those with the lowest socioeconomic status display the highest propensity for return migration, but also those at the other end, with high incomes and high education, show higher return migration than the groups in the middle.

One possible explanation for the U-shaped selectivity in terms of income and education may be that there are different patterns according to age, that self-selection patterns differ between those who are still of working age as compared with those who are retired. Table 2.2 shows the regression results of a model where only those who are below the age of 65 are included.

The results in Table 2.2 are similar to those in Table 2.1, although the negative effect of *Years since immigration* are weaker for the age group 55–64, whereas the positive effect of *Age at immigration* is stronger for

Table 2.2: Logistic estimation of return migration from Sweden 1990-2007.

Separate estimations for males and females. Odds ratios.

	Model A		Model B	
	Ages 55-64.		Ages 65+	
Covariates	Males	Females	Males	Females
Calendar year	1.02***	1.03***	1.03***	1.05***
Years since immigration	0.99	0.99*	0.94***	0.96***
Age at immigration	1.06***	1.06***	0.99***	1.01***
Early retired	1.99***	2.23***		
Age 65	1.20***	1.21***		
Unemployed	1.10	1.44***		
Civil status				
Married	*1.00*	*1.00*	*1.00*	*1.00*
Unmarried	1.72***	1.56***	1.73***	1.84***
Divorced	1.58***	1.16***	1.53***	1.34***
Widowed	1.24**	0.94	1.48***	1.15***
Income				
First quintile	1.98***	1.92***	2.33***	2.26***
Second quintile	1.22***	1.21***	1.35***	1.38***
Third quintile	*1.00*	*1.00*	*1.00*	*1.00*
Fourth quintile	0.87***	1.07	1.03	1.57***
Fifth quintile	1.58***	1.48***	1.24*	1.76***
Education				
Primary	*1.00*	*1.00*	*1.00*	*1.00*
Secondary	0.72***	0.77***	0.62***	0.74***
Tertiary	0.86***	0.90*	0.57***	0.72***
Unknown	1.20***	0.70***	0.73***	0.66***
Observations	884,625	937,563	635,714	966,062
Individuals	159,929	173,273	110,682	150,099
Events	4,215	3,166	3,522	4,010

Asterisks denote significance level: ***) p<0.01, **) p<0.05, *) p<0.10

the age group 65+. Men and women aged 55–64 who receive early retirement compensation display a much higher propensity for return migration and there is also a significant positive effect of unemployment for women. Women who received unemployment benefits in a given year have a 40–50 per cent higher risk of return migration in the following year. Unmarried men and women show higher propensity for return migration compared with the other civil status categories, and those who are divorced show higher than married and widowed persons. As in Table 2.1, the effect of being divorced is stronger for men than for women. The effect of being widowed is stronger in the age group 65+.

Regarding self-selection in terms of income and education, we find a similar U-shaped pattern in Table 2.2 as in Table 2.1. For both men and women, return migration is higher in the lowest and highest income quintiles and, in the age group 55–64, those who have secondary education as their highest level of education display lower propensity for return migration than those who have primary only or tertiary education. However, the odds ratios are highest in the first income quintile, for those who have only primary education, and for unemployed and early retired persons. Hence, we find a tendency towards a polarised pattern of return migration, although return migration is highest among those with weak attachment to the labour market, low income and low level of education.

Model B, which only includes those who are aged 65 years or older, shows that there is a significant retirement effect; those who turn 65 in a given year have a significantly higher propensity for return migration, compared with those who are older. Married retirees display lower return migration than those who are unmarried, divorced or widowed. As in the earlier models, we find a stronger effect of leaving marriage for men; the odds ratios for divorced and widowed men are higher than for women. This result indicates that preferences for the home country relative to a life in Sweden are stronger among men than among women. Unmarried persons display the highest propensity for return migration. Selectivity in terms of income and education seems to be stronger among those who are 65 years or older, and there are gender differences. Whereas the U-shaped income selection among male immigrants is weaker and somewhat more negative, female immigrants display a more pronounced U-shape, although the lowest income quintile still displays highest return migration. Regarding educational level, there seems to be negative selection, in the sense that those who have primary education only display higher return migration than higher education categories. In the age group 65+, primary education only is the most common level of education among immigrants as well as among native Swedes, but the results are significant for both men and women. Hence, when we do separate estimations for those above and those below retirement age, we still find polarised return migration patterns in terms of income selectivity, but for men and women aged 65+, we find negative self-selection in terms of educational level, although high education is not very common in these age groups.

Table 2.3 shows a model where we have introduced indicator variables for birth countries, grouped together into three large categories. The first category is labelled *North/West & Oceania*, and covers western and northern Europe, North America and Oceania. This category is a proxy for source countries of labour migration and other types of 'economic' or 'voluntary' migration. The second category, *Eastern Europe*, covers the Eastern European countries, Turkey and the states of the former Soviet Union. Before the 1990s, most of these countries were primarily sources of refugee immigration, and after 1990 immigration from these countries has been a mix of refugees, labour migrants, family migrants, students and so on. Turkey and the former Yugoslavia were first sources of labour immigration and later became sources of refugee immigration. In addition, the income levels in these countries are generally lower than in the countries of *North/West & Oceania,* and therefore these countries are expected to be less attractive to return to.

The third category is labelled *Asia, Africa, Latin America*. Although this category is very heterogeneous, it may be considered a proxy for source countries of refugee and family immigration. In recent years, Sweden has seen substantial labour immigration from countries such as India, Thailand and China, but compared with the numbers of refugees and tied movers from Asia, Africa and Latin America, they were few before 2008, especially in the age group 55+. There is considerable difference in return migration propensity between origin categories; men from *North/West & Oceania* display an odds ratio of 4.23 for men and 5.55 for women. Country of birth is apparently one of the most important characteristics to account for when analysing aggregate return migration. When introducing country/region of birth, we still find significant retirement effects, in particular regarding early retirement. There is an effect of turning 65 and the propensity for return migration is higher among those who have reached retirement age compared with those who are between 55 and 64 years old.

Introducing region of birth however affects the odds ratios of income category. The U-shaped selection pattern rather turns into a negative selection pattern, where the first and second income quintiles display

Table 2.3. Logistic estimation of return migration from Sweden 1990-2007.

All immigrants aged 55+. Separate estimations for males and females.
Model controlling for region of birth country/region. Odds ratios.

Covariate	Males	Females
Calendar year	1.04***	1.05***
Years since immigration	0.94***	0.93***
Age at immigration	1.01**	1.01***
Age 65	1.29***	1.17***
Retired	1.33***	1.52***
Early retired	1.70***	1.84***
Civil status		
Married	1.00	1.00
Unmarried	1.26***	1.42***
Divorced	1.27***	1.00
Widowed	1.25***	1.05
Income		
First quintile	1.53***	1.58***
Second quintile	1.29***	1.32***
Third quintile	1.00	1.00
Fourth quintile	0.77***	0.96
Fifth quintile	1.00	1.09
Education		
Primary	1.00	1.00
Secondary	0.72***	0.71***
Tertiary	0.92**	0.84***
Unknown	0.88***	0.75***
Birth country		
North/West & Oceania	4.23***	5.55***
Eastern Europe	1.17***	1.22***
Asia, Africa, Latin America	1.00	1.00
Observations	1,520,339	1,903,625
Individuals	198,263	236,717
Events	7,737	7,176

Asterisks denote significance level: ***) $p<0.01$, **) $p<0.05$, *) $p<0.10$

significantly higher return migration compared with the third, fourth and fifth quintiles. Apparently, 'Western' immigrants have both higher propensity for return migration *and* higher incomes than 'non-Western' immigrants and, therefore, the U-shaped income selectivity disappears when controlling for country/region of birth.

The next step is to run separate regressions according to region of birth, since the determinants seem to be different depending on immigrant category. Each model uses controls for calendar year, years since immigration, age at immigration, retirement effects, civil status, income and education. In order to keep tabulation to a limit, only the *Birth Country/Region* covariates are displayed in the following.

Table 2.4 shows the results of a model where only immigrants from *North/West & Oceania* were included. In this model we use indicator variables for region of birth within *North/West & Oceania*, categorised into western, northern or southern Europe, or outside Europe. Our results show that immigrants from southern Europe, that is Portugal, Spain, Italy and Greece, display much higher propensity for return migration, compared with other immigrants from 'Western' countries, even higher than the neighbouring Nordic countries.

Table 2.4. Logistic estimation of return migration from Sweden 1990-2007.

Immigrants aged 55+, born in 'Western' countries. Separate estimations for males and females. Odds ratios.

Covariate	Males	Females
Birth country/region		
Western Europe	*1.00*	*1.00*
Northern Europe	1.81***	1.74***
Southern Europe	4.34***	5.22***
North America, Oceania	1.87***	1.44***
Observations	943,506	1,267,017
Individuals	119,108	150,742
Events	5,761	5,196

Asterisks denote significance level: ***) p<0.01, **) p<0.05, *) p<0.10

This result indicates that the determinants of return migration in old age differ from return migration among younger immigrants. Earlier studies on return migration show that the attraction of a warm sunny climate and healthy environment has a strong influence on migration decisions in old age (for example, King et al 1998). While labour market circumstances are important reasons for return migration in younger ages, resulting in relatively high return migration rates to the United States, Western Europe and the Scandinavian countries (Klinthäll 2003), quality-of-life considerations dominate among older migrants, giving rise to relatively high return migration to Southern Europe. In addition, costs of living in these countries are relatively low, something which most likely has had a positive effect on retirement return migration.

Regarding selectivity in terms of income (not shown in the table), we find that the U-shaped selectivity pattern is weakened for men and disappears for women. Low incomes, that is first and second quintile are associated with higher propensity for return migration compared with higher incomes. On the other hand there is a U-shaped pattern according to educational level, where those with primary and tertiary education display higher return migration than those who have secondary education. There are evident retirement effects for both men and women; in particular the effect of early retirement is an increased propensity for return migration.

Table 2.5 shows results for a similar model as in Table 2.4, but run for immigrants from East European countries. Return migration is lower to these countries compared with 'Western' countries, partly because the immigrant population from these countries is a mix of labour migrants and refugees. In addition to the difference in the rate of return migration there are some interesting differences between 'Western' and East European immigrants. Firstly, there are considerable gender differences in return migration propensity by country/region of origin. Compared with the category 'Other Eastern Europe', men from former Yugoslavian countries display significantly lower return migration, whereas the opposite is true for women. A similar pattern is found for Polish immigrants. The lowest propensity for return migration is found for men and women who were born in Turkey. The results for the other covariates (not reported in the table) shows that, like return migration to 'Western' countries, there is a 'hook-shaped' selectivity in terms of income, although much steeper; low incomes are associated with high rates of return migration, in particular for women. Furthermore, the retirement effect is stronger for men than for women, and whereas unmarried 'Western' women display relatively

Table 2.5: Logistic estimation of return migration from Sweden 1990–2007.

Immigrants aged 55+, born in East European countries. Separate estimations for males and females. Odds ratios.

Covariate	Males	Females
Birth country/region		
Poland	0.63***	1.17
Former Yugoslavia	0.81***	1.49***
Turkey	0.58***	0.72**
Other Eastern Europe	1.00	1.00
Observations	394,027	447,356
Individuals	51,155	59,577
Events	1,175	1,231

Asterisks denote significance level: ***) p<0.01, **) p<0.05, *) p<0.10

high propensity for return migration, the corresponding figure for unmarried East European women is relatively low.

The final table shows a model where the regression is run separately for immigrants from Asia, Africa and Latin America. Return migration to these regions is lower compared with Western and Eastern European countries, primarily due to unstable political and socioeconomic situations in many countries. 'East Asia', 'Other Asia' and 'Other Latin America and Africa' are of course large and heterogeneous categories, but the groupings were constructed due to the relatively small number of immigrants in Sweden born in these countries. Table 2.6 shows that Middle Eastern countries display very low rates of return migration, especially for men. East Asian immigrants display higher return migration than those from 'Other Asia', but lower than those from Latin America and Africa. Chileans have high rates of return migration, which is consistent with earlier research that shows how a wave of return migration from Sweden to Chile started in 1990 after the fall of the Pinochet regime (Klinthäll, 2007).

Table 2.6: Logistic estimation of return migration from Sweden 1990-2007

Immigrants aged 55+, born in Asia, Latin America and Africa. Separate estimations for males and females. Odds ratios.

Covariate	Males	Females
Birth country		
Iran	0.34***	0.66***
Iraq	0.21***	0.25***
Lebanon	0.31***	0.47***
Syria	0.11***	0.23***
East Asia	0.69***	0.76*
Other Asia	0.55***	0.54***
Chile	1.89***	2.18***
Other Latin America, Africa	1.00	1.00
Observations	182,806	189,252
Individuals	27,736	26,177
Events	690	677

Asterisks denote significance level: ***) $p<0.01$, **) $p<0.05$, *) $p<0.10$

Return migration to Asia, Africa and Latin America is strongly associated with low incomes, in particular for women. On the other hand, women display a positive selection pattern in terms of education, whereas the pattern for men is U-shaped. As for the other categories, there are also retirement effects on the propensity for return migration to these regions, although the levels of statistical significance are weak due to a relatively low number of individuals in high ages.

Conclusions

There are gender differences regarding the propensity for return migration from Sweden. Women display 30 per cent lower rates of return migration, when demographic and socioeconomic factors are accounted for. This result is in line with earlier research, which has found that elderly women are more inclined to settle than men, often because they have children in the country of immigration, but also due to a feeling of more independence in the country of immigration compared with the country of origin. Since men are over-represented as immigrants to Sweden, this lower propensity for return migration among women tends to have a balancing demographic effect.

The analysis results show that, when looking at all immigrants aged 55+ in Sweden, married individuals display the lowest propensity for return migration. Unmarried men and women display the same high propensity to return compared with those who are married, while widowed or divorced men are more likely to return than widowed or divorced women. This result indicates that women who have become single after marriage and possibly have children in the country are less ready to return compared with men in the same situation, which is in line with the conclusions of previous studies. Gender differences in return migration propensity among divorced and widowed persons may, however, also to some extent be due to differences in rates of inter-marriage with native Swedes. A detailed investigation of the impact of family relations, time and space on return migration among old-age migrants requires new data on marriage patterns and the whereabouts of grown-up children.

For both men and women, there are clear retirement effects on the propensity for return migration. In the year of the 65th birthday, the standard age of retirement in Sweden, there is a 20–30 per cent increase in the propensity for return migration. Men and women who are 65 years or older display rates of return migration which are about 40 per cent higher compared with those who are 55–64 years old. Furthermore, those who are below 65, but have been early retired due to sickness or disability, display much higher propensity for return migration compared with those who have not received early retirement compensation. Apparently, there are immigrants who have a strong preference for living in the country of origin and return when the connection between income and place of residence weakens or disappears, many of them immediately in response to early retirement or in the year when they turn 65. In addition, unemployment in ages 55–64 increases the propensity for return migration, in particular for women.

An important question in this study regards the association between return migration and socioeconomic situation in the country of immigration. Looking at the whole immigrant population, there seems to be a polarised return migration pattern, where the lowest and the highest income and education categories are associated with higher return migration rates than the categories in the middle. This pattern is found for both men and women, and for those below and above retirement age alike. The U-shaped pattern among retirees indicates that return migration is most common among those who are less integrated in socioeconomic terms, and among those with high incomes, possibly because they are target savers with a plan to retire in the home country.

Separate estimations according to country/region of origin shows that this polarised pattern is explained partly by income differences by origin. Immigrants born in countries in Western Europe, North America and Oceania display both higher incomes and much higher rates of return migration compared with immigrants of other origins in Sweden. Separate regressions by region of origin yields 'hook-shaped' or L-shaped selectivity pattern in terms of income, where the first income quintile is associated with considerably higher and the second quintile with somewhat higher return migration than the upper quintiles. The third and fourth income quintiles are mostly associated with the lowest propensity for return migration. Selectivity in terms of educational level is generally U-shaped. Hence, those who are well-integrated in socioeconomic terms, but not with the highest education or incomes, are the ones most likely to stay permanently in the immigration country.

Older immigrants from 'Western' countries are the ones most likely to return migrate in old age, in particular those from Southern Europe, and retirement, not least early retirement, is associated with an elevated propensity for return migration. Many of today's old age immigrants arrived in Sweden as labour migrants in the 1960s and early 1970s, for work in the manufacturing industry. Many of these migrants, primarily from Finland and southern Europe, had heavy and monotonous work in the factories, which often led to early retirement due to occupational injury. Today, many of the early retired return to their countries of origin, bringing their pension rights with them from Sweden, but also putting some new and possibly unexpected pressure on the health care sector in their home countries.

While previous research has shown that the propensity for return migration decreases with age and time spent in the immigration country, this study shows that return migration among older immigrants increases after reaching retirement age, and in connection with other exits from the labour market, such as unemployment and early retirement due to sickness or disability. Apparently, many immigrants nurture a dream of returning home, and the day when working life is over is a day to make it come true.

References

Ahmadi, F. and Tornstam, L. (1996) 'The old flying dutchmen: shuttling immigrants with double assets', *Journal of Aging and Identity*, 1(3):191–210.

Attias-Donfut, C. and Wolff, F-C. (2005a) '*Transmigration et choix de vie à la retraite*' [Transmigration and choice of living at retirement], *Retraite et Société*, 44(1):79–105.

Attias-Donfut, C. and Wolff, F-C. (2005b) 'The preferred burial location of persons born outside France', *Population*, 60(5–6):699–720.

Bohland, J.R. and Rowles, G.D. (1988) 'The significance of elderly migration to changes in elderly population concentration in the United States 1960–1980', *Journal of Gerontology: Social Sciences*, 43(5):145–52.

Bolzman, C., Poncioni-Derigo, R., Vial, M. and Fibbi, R. (2004) '"Older labour migrants" well being in Europe: the case of Switzerland', *Ageing and Society*, 24:411–429.

Bolzman, C., Fibbi, R. and Vial, M. (2007) 'What to do after retirement? Elderly migrants and the question of return', *Journal of Ethnic and Migration Studies*, 32(8):1359–1375.

Bovenkerk, F. (1974) *The Sociology of Return Migration: A Bibliographical Essay.* Publications of the research group for European migration problems. The Hague, Netherlands: Martinus Nijhoff.

Bradley, D.E., Longino, C.F., Stoller, E.P. and Haas, W.H. (2008) 'Actuation of mobility intentions among the young-old: an event-history analysis', *The Gerontologist*, 48(2):190–202.

Cassarino, J-P. (2004) 'Theorising Return Migration: a revisited conceptual approach to return migrants', *EUI Working Papers: RSCAS No. 2004/02.* Florence, Italy.

Cerase, F.P. (1970) 'Nostalgia or disenchantment: considerations on return migration', in S.M. Tomasi and M.H. Engel (eds) *The Italian Experience in the United States*, New York: Center for Migration Studies, pp 217–239.

de Coulon, A. and Wolff, F-C. (2006) 'The location of immigrants at retirement: stay/return or "va-et-vient"?', *IZA Discussion Paper No. 2224*, 2006, Bonn: IZA.

Djajic, S. and Milbourne, R. (1988) 'A general equilibrium model of guest-worker migration', *Journal of International Economics*, 25:335–351.

Dustmann, C. (1996) 'Return migration. The European experience', *Economic Policy*, 22:215–250.

Dustmann, C. (1997) *Return Migration and the Optimal migration Duration*, London: University College London, and CEPR, London: Mimeo.

Dustmann, C. (2001) 'Return migration, wage differentials and the optimal migration duration', *IZA Discussion Paper No. 264*, 2001, Bonn: IZA.

Dustmann, C. and Mestres, J. (2011) 'Savings, asset holdings, and temporary migration', *IZA Discussion Paper No. 5498*, 2011, Bonn: IZA.

Dustmann, C. and Weiss, Y. (2007) 'Return migration: theory and empirical evidence from the UK', *British Journal of Industrial Relations*, 45(2):236–256.

Edin, P-A., LaLonde, R.J. and Åslund, O. (2000) 'Emigration of immigrants and measures of immigrant assimilation: evidence from Sweden', *Swedish Economic Policy Review*, 7:163–204.

Emami, A. and Ekman, S-L. (1998) 'Living in a foreign country in old age: life in Sweden as experienced by elderly Iranian immigrants', *Health Care in Later Life*, 3(3):183–198.

Fournier, G.M., Rasmussen, D.W. and Serow, W.J. (1988a) 'Elderly migration as a response to economic incentives', *Social Science Quarterly*, 69(2):245–260.

Fournier, G.M., Rasmussen, D.W. and Serow, W.J. (1988b) 'Elderly migration: for sun and money', *Population Research and Policy Review*, 7(2):189–199.

Gustafson, P. (2008) 'Transnationalism in retirement migration: the case of North European retirees in Spain', *Ethnic and Racial Studies*, 31(3):451–475.

Haas, W.H., Bradley, D.E., Longino, C.F., Stoller, E.P. and Serow, W.J.(2006) 'In retirement migration, who counts? A methodological question with economic policy implications', *The Gerontologist*, 46(6):815–820.

Hill, J.K. (1987) 'Immigrant decisions concerning duration of stay and migratory frequency', *Journal of Development Economics*, 25:221–234.

Joly, D. (2002) 'Odyssean and Rubicon refugees: toward a typology of refugees in the land of exile', *International Migration*, 40(6):3–23.

King, R., Warnes, A.M. and Williams, A.M. (1998) 'International retirement migration in Europe', *International Journal of Population Geography*, 4(2):91–111.

King, R. and Patterson, G. (1998) 'Diverse paths: the elderly in Tuscany', *International Journal of Population Geography*, 4(2):157–182.

Klinthäll, M. (2003) *Return Migration from Sweden 1968–1996. A Longitudinal Analysis*, Stockholm: Almqvist & Wiksell International.

Klinthäll, M. (2006) 'Retirement return migration from Sweden', *International Migration*, 44(2):153–80.

Klinthäll, M. (2007) 'Refugee return migration: return migration from Sweden to Chile, Iran and Poland 1973–1996', *Journal of Refugee Studies*, 20(4):579–598.

López de Lera, D. (1995) 'Immigration in Spain at the end of the twentieth century. Those who come to work and those who come to relax', *Revista Española de Investigaciones Sociológicas*, 71–72:225–245.

Meyer, J.W. (1987) 'A regional scale temporal analysis of the net migration patterns of elderly persons over time', *Journal of Gerontology*, 42(4):366–375.

Nekby, L. (2006) 'The emigration of immigrants, return vs onward migration: evidence from Sweden', *Journal of Population Economics*, 19(2):197–226.

Poulain, M. and Perrin, N. (2002) 'The demographic characteristics of immigrant populations in Belgium', in W. Haug, P. Compton and Y. Courbage, (eds) *The Demographic Characteristics of Immigrant Populations*, Strasbourg: Council of Europe Publishing, pp 57–129.

Rodríguez, V., Fernandez-Mayoralas, G. and Rojo, F. (1998) 'European retirees on the Costa del Sol: a cross-national comparison', *International Journal of Population Geography*, 4(2):183-200.

Serow, W.J. (1987) 'Why the elderly move: cross-national comparisons', *Research on Aging*, 9(4):582–597.

Serow, W.J., Charity, D.A., Fournier, G.M. and Rasmussen, D.W. (1986) 'Cost of living differentials and elderly interstate migration', *Research on Aging*, 8(2):317–327.

Sunil, T.S., Rojas, V. and Bradley, D.E. (2007) 'United States' international retirement migration: the reasons for retiring to the environs of Lake Chapala, Mexico', *Ageing and Society*, 27(4):489–510.

United Nations (2009) *International Migration Report 2006. A Global Assessment*, New York: United Nations, Department of Economic and Social Affairs, Population Division.

Walters, W.H. (2002) 'Place characteristics and later-life migration', *Research on Aging*, 24(2):243–277.

Warnes, A.M. and Patterson, G. (1998) 'British retirees in Malta: components of the cross-national relationship', *International Journal of Population Geography*, 4(2):113-133.

Williams, A.M. and Patterson, G. (1998) '"An empire lost but a province gained": a cohort analysis of British international retirement in the Algarve', *International Journal of Population Geography*, 4(2):135-155.

Warnes, A.M. (2009) 'International retirement migration', in P. Uhlenberg (ed) *International Handbook of Population Aging*, New York: Springer.

Yahirun, J. (2009) *Take me 'home': Determinants of return migration among Germany's elderly immigrants*, On-Line Working Paper Series, CCPPR-2009–019, Los Angeles: California Center for Population Research, UCLA, http://papers.ccpr.ucla.edu/papers/PWP-CCPR-2009-019/PWP-CCPR-2009-019.pdf

THREE

Place and residence attachments in Canada's older population

K Bruce Newbold

Introduction

Over the past two decades, the literature associated with migration in the context of older people has provided increasing detail regarding motivations for migrations, spatial patterns and migration propensities within this age group. Among older people, motivations often include amenity-oriented migration among the 'young old' at the time of retirement or shortly afterward (Longino, 1979; Litwack and Longino, 1987), kin-oriented migrations, such as the return of African Americans from the north to the south (Stack, 1996), and migrations associated with dependency or health needs as individuals age (Longino and Serow, 1992; Hayward, 2000; Hayward and Lazarowich, 2001). Amenity or 'lifestyle' migrations tend to be more prevalent among the healthy, the 'young old', and those with greater disposable income. These migrations are often concurrent with retirement, motivated by amenities, cost of living, or housing considerations (Kupiszewski et al, 2001a, 2001b).

Retirement destinations typically dominate the spatial patterns of return migration, particularly in the United States, where older migration flows tend to be more 'channelised', focusing on a few key retirement states in the American West or Southeast, including the ever-popular Florida and Arizona (Longino, 1995). In Europe, popular destinations include the south of France and Spain. Although such spatial focusing is less visible in Canada, the western-most province of British Columbia is an important retirement destination, and smaller sub-provincial units across the country have become retirement destinations, in large part because of their amenities and scenic locations (see, for example, Shearmur and Polèse, 2005).

Embedded within these broader discussions of older migrations are return migrations (those migrations returning an individual to an earlier place of residence) and onward migrations (subsequent migrations that do not return an individual to their previous place of residence). Previous literature has established the importance of these types of migration as components of migration streams (Long, 1988; Newbold, 1996). While research has illuminated general age-related patterns, including variations in the age profiles of return and onward migrations, the literature has not typically focused on the older population specifically. Clearly, it is unreasonable to assume that return and onward migration of older people mirror those of labour-forced aged migrants. Moreover, much of this literature is based on returns to an individual's place of birth (see, for example, Long, 1988; Newbold and Liaw, 1994). While revealing spatial preferences and mobility, reliance on the place of birth to define return migration can be problematic (Newbold and Bell, 2001) and this is potentially magnified among the older population, given the likelihood that they have made multiple moves associated with education and employment opportunities over their lifespan. Consequently, consideration of return migrations based on a previous place of residence, as opposed to place of birth, may reveal certain other migration preferences and patterns among older people.

This chapter explores the understanding of repeated or multiple intra-nation migrations occurring within a defined period, in respect of Canada's older population. The tendency to move home several times over a relatively short time interval is often referred to as 'repeat' migration, a notion recognising that migration is more than a one-time event (Goldstein, 1954; Eldridge, 1965; Morrison, 1971; Newbold and Bell, 2001). In part, data limitations often meant that the population was classified as either 'migrants' or 'non-migrants' in early migration research. Over time, conceptual advances and improved data, including longitudinal files and increased detail on residential history in census-based files has allowed recognition of the fact that almost no one is a lifetime 'non-migrant'. Instead, the literature now recognises links between life cycle events and migration, the timing of migrations, and the fact that migrating once increases the likelihood of migrating again.

Specifically, the chapter examines return and onwards migration among Canada's older population (aged 60 and over) based on the 2001 Canadian census and using information on place of residence at three points in time – Census day, five years prior, and one year prior to the Census. In doing so, the chapter (i) makes comparisons to the overall (aged 20 and over) population, answering the question of 'who moves?' and the importance of repeat migrations among the older population relative to aggregate population movements; (ii) distinguishes between returns to the 1996 dwelling and more general returns to the 1996 province of origin; and (iii) distinguishes between the 'young old' and 'old old' by disaggregating the older population by age, reflecting the potential for age-variations in motivations and propensities to engage in return and onwards migration among the older population.

Background: return and onward migration among the older population

While migration rates among older people are comparatively low relative to those of younger segments of the population, the migration of older people still has significant implications from a public policy perspective, something which is likely to increase with general population ageing over the coming decades. The sheer increase in the numerical size of older populations will translate into more migrants in coming years, implying an increased potential for greater global mobility among the older population and changes to the age profile of sending and receiving regions by their relative shares of the older population. From a public policy perspective, the migration of older individuals raises significant issues and questions, including those around the transfer of non-earned income (such as pensions and investments) across regions and countries, as well as needs for service provision, including health care and related social services, along with long-term care, and their impact on the health profile of sending and receiving regions.

Much of the existing return migration literature ascribes motivations for return migrations to either failed initial migrations (Grant and Vanderkamp, 1986) or planned returns following short-term relocations for employment, retirement, or educational reasons (Bell, 1996). Relatively less discussion is given to the motivations and spatial patterns of return and onwards migration among the older population. Moreover, the research that is available is often based on returns to the place of birth, or so-called lifetime return migrations. 'Fixed interval' return migrations, which reference return migrations to a previous residence as opposed to the place of birth, may provide further insight into propensity to return, particularly since location-specific capital, including property and/or family and friends, is more likely to be embedded in a recent place of residence.

Since 1991, Statistics Canada has collected data on usual place of residence both one and five years prior to the Census enumeration date, enabling return migration to be referenced to a previous place of residence and offering several advantages over return migrations based on place-of-birth data. These advantages include shorter intervals over which migration can be measured, the reduction of the effects of multiple moves in the overall data and capturing 'rapid' return migrations, or those which occur relatively quickly after the initial, primary migration (Linn et al, 1999). Furthermore, this definition of return migration potentially offers a more accurate measure of migration events and migrant characteristics, given that temporal change to personal effects such as education and employment status are more limited since such variables are less likely to change over the short time interval (Newbold and Bell, 2001). The literature has also observed a strong attraction among repeat older migrants toward the location of their adult children, an attraction that was stronger for the widowed (Liaw and Frey, 2003).

Typically, repeat migrations among older people are both numerically and proportionately small relative to the overall population (Newbold and Bell, 2001). At the same time, however, there is considerable diversity in the motivations for migration among the older population, with the literature constructing a typology of moves based on their underlying determinants (Litwack and Longino, 1987).

Although not necessarily sequential, the first migration is typically 'lifestyle' or amenity oriented, and more prevalent among the healthy, the 'young old', and those with greater disposable income. Lifestyle migrations are often concurrent with retirement, motivated by amenity, cost of living, or housing considerations (Liaw and Ledent, 1988; Serow et al, 1986). If this migration returns an individual to the place of birth, it may be defined as a *provincial* return migration. As a subset of amenity migrations, provincial return migrations are most probably undertaken because of existing knowledge of the destination. At the same time, onward migrations motivated by amenity issues are likely, with destinations including places where migrants had previously resided or vacationed (Cuba, 1991).

The second type of migration is typically motivated by the need for assistance or the desire to be closer to family as personal health declines. These migrations tend to occur more frequently among the older old, and may involve widowed individuals or those with poorer levels of health (Longino and Serow, 1992; Hayward, 2000). Finally, the third type of migration is often to institutions providing long-term care.

Data and methods

Data is derived from Statistics Canada's 2001 Public Use Microdata File (PUMF), a 3 per cent sample of the Canadian population offering information on the place of usual residence at the time of the Census, one year prior to the Census (2000), and five years prior (1996). Migrants and migrations are therefore defined by reference to changes in their usual residence over the 1996–2000 and 2000–01 intervals. The sample population is defined as those aged 60 and over on Census day in 2001 (aged 55 in 1996), although some comparisons are made to the population aged 20 and over. The sample further excludes the institutionalised population along with those who resided outside the country or did not report a place of residence in Canada on any one of the three dates. In addition, residents of Canada's three northern territories are excluded.

Based on the comparison of place of residence, five distinct groups of migrants could be identified:

- People who do not migrate between 1996–2001 (stayers);
- People who made an inter-provincial migration between 1996 and 2000 but did not migrate between 2000 and 2001;
- People whose province of residence was unchanged between 1996 and 2000 but who migrated between 2000 and 2001;
- People who migrated between 1996 and 2000 and who returned to their province of origin between 2000 and 2001;
- People who made an inter-provincial migration between 1996 and 2000 and who migrated again to a different region between 2000 and 2001.

The fourth group can be identified as return migrants, while the fifth group can be defined as onward migrants. Return migrants can be further subdivided to distinguish between those who returned to their 1996 place of residence ('home') and those who made a more general return migration to their 1996 province of origin.

The analysis proceeds through two sections, with the first focusing on the return and onward migration components of inter-regional migration of older citizens (aged 60+) through descriptive measures, including the count and proportion of migrants and migration events. In particular, the analysis focuses on the volume of migration, the personal characteristics of migrants, and spatial patterns. Mobility is measured with reference to the population 'at-risk' of making a return or onwards migration (the population who moved over the 1996–00 migration interval). In some cases and for purposes of presentation, provincial flows were aggregated to regional flows (Atlantic Canada, Quebec, Ontario, Prairies, and British Columbia) due to sparse place-to-place flows among older people.

The second section explores the determinants of older repeat migrations using binomial logistic models. Theoretically, the choices available to a potential migrant can be structured and modelled within multiple levels, including the departure, destination, and return and onward choice. For analytical convenience, the out-migration decision is focused upon in this chapter. In addition, given relatively sparse return and onward flows among the older population, their migration is set within the context of movements made by the population aged 20 and over, with interaction terms between age and personal factors (education, marital status) and age and provincial effects (climate, economic indicators) capturing age-dependent effects. The analytical model is defined by the following generic model:

$$\log\left(\frac{P_m}{1 - P_m}\right) = \alpha + \beta X_i$$

where P_m represents the probability of a migration, α and β are estimated coefficients, and X_i is a vector of personal and provincial attributes that defines the utility associated with migration. Two models are estimated, including (i) the decision to make a repeat (return or onward) migration in 2000–01 versus staying; and (ii) the decision to make a return to the dwelling versus a general return migration (a return to the region of origin). In both models, the direct effects (personal and provincial attributes) are forced into the model specification, while the age-dependent interaction terms are entered through stepwise regression. Variables significant at the p 0.05 level were entered and retained within the models, with both the set of included and excluded variables checked for endogenity and appropriateness relative to the literature.

The likelihood of migration is based on individual assessments of utility, expressed as a function of personal factors and a series of explanatory variables, selected based on previous results and migration theory. Personal attributes include *level of education* (less than high school, some post-secondary education, and bachelor's degree or higher); *tenure status* (own or rent residence); *marital status* (divorced-single-widowed, married, single (never married)); *age* (20–59[1], 60–69, 70–79, 80+); *immigrant status* (immigrant or native-born); *language* (English, French, other), and *sex*.

Provincial effects include *per capita income, unemployment rate*, and *employment growth rate* for the 2000–01 period to represent the economic opportunities in each province. Per capita income, unemployment, and employment growth rates represent the 2000–01 average value for each province. *Total population share*, defined by the province's 2001 proportional population share of the national population, was included to represent the availability of high-level service and general economic opportunities in each province. To represent the quality of the physical environment, an average index of *coldness* is used to represent the annual number of degree-days below 18°C, and *sun* captures the average number of sunny days.

The preference for living in a familiar cultural milieu is represented by *cultural similarity*, which reflects the cultural and language heterogeneity of Canada, with migration patterns strongly influenced by French and English language differences. Cultural similarity is defined as the proportional share of the 1996 provincial population by ethnic group that matched the mother tongue of the individual. Finally, all values are weighted according to population weights provided by Statistics Canada. In order to avoid artificially inflating the *t*-values associated with the multivariate analyses, the original weight variable (equal to Canada's total population excluding institutional residents) was scaled so that the sum of the scaled weight variable was equal to the sample size.

Propensities and patterns

Counting older migrants and migrations

Table 3.1 sets out the breakdown of inter-regional migration between 1996–2000–2001, divided according to the type of move and the timing of the move for individuals aged 60 and over. In order to effectively examine repeat migration, a distinction must be made between migrants and migration. The former refers to the number of individuals that make one or more moves during the observed period, while the latter refers to the aggregate number of moves recorded (Newbold, 2001). Since some people move more than once, the number of movers is typically smaller than the number of moves. Therefore, by combining data from 1996–2000 and 2000–01, Table 3.1 indicates a total of 69,923 inter-provincial migrations by older people. However, since some of these moves represent people who migrated in both the 1996–2000 and 2000–01 intervals, the total number of migrants is determined by subtracting all return and onward moves, leaving a total of 66,969 older migrants. If data were limited solely to the transitions between 1996 and 2000, with no information on place of residence in 2000, the number of older migrants would be further reduced to 64,311, since no return migrations would be identified.

Table 3.1: Return and onward migration: 1996–2001, aged 60+

Type of migration	Number	2000–01	1996-2001	All	Total
Did not migrate	4,766,845				
Return migration					
To 1996 home	1,144	7.9	2.1	1.6	0.0
To province	1,514	10.4	2.7	2.2	0.0
Total return migrations	2,658	18.3	4.8	3.8	0.1
Onward migration	296	2.0	0.5	0.4	0.0
Total repeat (onward + return migrations)	2,954	20.3	5.3	4.2	0.1
Migrated 2000–01 only	11,600	79.7	21.0	16.6	0.2
All 2000–01 migrations	14,554	100.0	26.3	20.8	0.3
Migrated 1996–2000 only	52,415		94.7	75.0	1.1
All 1996–2000 migrations	55,369		100.0	79.2	1.1
Total migrations	69,923			100	1.4
Total migrants	66,969				1.4
Recorded migrations 1996–2001	64,311				1.3
Total population	4,833,813				100.0

Table 3.1 also indicates the intensity of repeat migration during the period. Of the more than two million older migrants in the 1996–00–01 interval, 2,954 made inter-provincial moves in both periods. Of these, 2,658, or nearly 90 per cent of all chronic migrants returned to their 1996 place of origin. While large, the percentage engaging in a return migration is not all that different from what is observed elsewhere, although returns typically represent approximately 80 per cent of repeat migration flows (Newbold, 2001). Return migration can be further divided, revealing that approximately 39 per cent of all return migrants (1,144) returned to their original (1996) home, while the remainder returned to their province of residence in 1996. Only a small number (296) of older migrants participated in an onward migration, perhaps reflecting limited options or reasons for engaging in this sort of migration, and/or the relatively short time-frame over which these migrations would have occurred.

The significance of return and onward migration can be noted by examining the 2000–01 flow values. Of those who moved outside their place of origin over the one-year period, 20.3 per cent had made a previous inter-provincial move between 1996 and 2000. Therefore, 18.3

per cent of all 2000–01 migrants were returning to the region where they originally resided in 1996. Contrary to earlier work, only a small proportion (2 per cent) engaged in onward migration. Comparing to the broader (aged 20+) population (results not shown), a smaller proportion (approximately 7 per cent) of repeat migrants returned to their 1996 place of residence. Of these, 29 per cent returned to their 1996 home. Conversely, onward migrations accounted for 8.8 per cent of repeat migrations in 2000–01, while 27.2 per cent were returning to their 1996 province of residence. As such, while returns to the 1996 home are equally important and likely in both the older and overall (aged 20+) population (as measured relative to the 2000–01 flows), both onward and return migrations would appear to be somewhat more important among the total population, despite the expectation of the importance of return migrations among older people.

Personal characteristics

Table 3.2 references rates of return and onward migration for a set of personal characteristics among older people. Overall, the results are largely consistent with expectations and while rates of migration are relatively low, they are not unexpected for the age group. For example, individuals aged 60–69 tended to represent the near majority of both return and onward migrations, accounting for between 45 per cent and 50 per cent of all moves and potentially reflecting both the ability to migrate and a wider range of destination options incorporating amenity destinations as well as locations of previous residence or where family and friends are found. However, the propensity to return to the 1996 home tended to peak among those aged 80 and over, while both other returns and onward migrations peaked among those aged 70–79. No onward migrations were recorded for those 80 and over. While this may simply be a limitation of the data, it also reflects declining propensities, resources, and options to migrate among the very old.

Gender variations in return and onward migration are also apparent, with women tending to predominate in all three groups, but especially for 'other returns' (that is, back to their place of birth but not to their original 1996 home) and onward migrations, where they represent greater than 60 per cent of all migrations. Returns among the older population may be triggered by the need for health care, death of a spouse, or other circumstances, although relatively few of these are likely to occur within five years of the initial migration, with such migrations missed by the short, fixed interval used here (Newbold and Bell, 2001). Indeed, poor health and the need for health care are observed to be

Table 3.2: Return and onward migration by personal attributes among Canada's older citizens: 1996–2001

| | Percentage of total | | | | Percentage of 1996–2000 moves | | | |
| | Return to | | Total | | Return to | | Total | |
	1996 home	Other return	Return migration	Onward migration	1996 home	Other return	Return migration	Onward migration
Age:								
60–69	45.2	46.3	45.8	50.2	1.8	2.5	4.3	0.5
70–79	25.8	39.0	33.3	49.8	2.0	3.9	5.9	1.0
80+	29.0	14.7	20.8	0.0	5.0	3.3	8.3	0.0
Total	100.0	100.0	100.0	100.0	2.3	3.0	5.3	0.6
Sex:								
Female	51.7	68.3	61.2	62.7	2.2	3.8	6.0	0.7
Male	48.3	31.6	38.8	37.6	2.4	2.1	4.5	0.5
Total	100.1	99.9	100.0	100.3	2.3	3.0	5.3	0.6
Tenure status:								
Owned	72.5	42.5	55.1	37.5	2.4	2.0	4.4	0.3
Rented	27.5	57.5	44.9	62.5	1.7	4.9	6.7	1.1
Total	100.0	100.0	100.0	100.0	2.2	3.0	5.2	0.6

	Percentage of total				Percentage of 1996–2000 moves			
	Return to		Total		Return to		Total	
	1996 home	Other return	Return migration	Onward migration	1996 home	Other return	Return migration	Onward migration
Education status:								
< HS	48.4	58.6	54.2	25.1	2.6	4.1	6.6	0.3
Some uni	32.3	29.3	30.5	50.2	1.8	2.1	3.9	0.7
BA+	19.4	12.2	15.3	25.1	3.1	2.5	5.6	1.0
Total	100.0	100.0	100.0	100.3	2.3	3.0	5.3	0.6
Immigrant status:								
Native-born	67.8	70.7	69.5	50.0	2.2	3.0	5.1	0.4
Immigrant	32.2	29.2	30.5	50.0	2.7	3.2	5.9	1.1
Total	100.0	99.9	100.0	100.0	2.7	3.2	5.9	1.1
Language:								
English	71.0	65.9	68.1	50.0	2.4	2.9	5.3	0.4
French	3.2	12.2	8.3	25.0	0.8	3.8	4.6	1.5
Other	25.9	21.9	23.6	25.0	2.8	3.1	5.9	0.7
Total	100.0	99.9	100.0	100.0	2.3	3.0	5.3	0.6
Marital status:								
DSW	25.9	56.1	43.1	49.8	1.5	4.3	5.8	0.7
Married	58.1	39.0	47.3	50.2	2.4	2.2	4.6	0.5
Single	16.1	4.8	9.7	0.0	6.5	2.6	9.0	0.0
Total	100.0	99.9	100.0	100.0	2.3	3.0	5.3	0.6

prime motivators of migration in later life (Patrick 1980; Litwack and Longino, 1987; Hayward 2000; Kupiszewski et a,l 2000; Kawase and Nakazawa, 2009), as individuals relocate to seek care via family or in institutional settings. These migrations tend to occur more frequently among the older old as well as the widowed and those with poorer health (Speare et al, 1991; Burr and Mutchler, 1992; Longino and Serow, 1992; Hayward, 2000). For example, the onset of moderate to serious levels of disability has been shown to be a strong predictor of later-life migrations (Speare et al, 1991).

With respect to educational attainment, both return and onward migrations are dominated by individuals with less than a high school education, although there is little evidence of an age-educational profile. That is, for example, returns to the 1996 home and onward migrations were greatest among the better educated (those with a bachelors degree or higher), while the poorly educated (those with less than a high school education) were more likely to return to their province of origin, with the difference in return destination by education suggesting that the better educated had planned to return home following a temporary change in location, while the less educated were less likely to have planned on returning. Again, failing health or death of a spouse may have prompted a return to their original province given its familiarity.

Marital status poses an interesting contrast. While a small majority of return migrants were married, return migration propensities were highest among the divorced-separated-widowed, supporting arguments that return migration is facilitated by the death of a partner. Not surprisingly, the native-born represent the majority of repeat migrants, although the foreign-born generally had somewhat higher return migration propensities. Finally, French speakers had a somewhat lower propensity to return than either English or other (non-official) language speakers.

Somewhat different profiles are evident between individuals returning to their 1996 home, and those making 'other' return migrations, with returns to the previous home peaking later (aged 80+) than other returns, which peaked among the 70 to 79 year olds. Rates of 'other return' migrations tended to be highest for individuals who were less educated, French speakers, women, renters, and those who were divorced, separated or widowed. Moreover, nearly 45 per cent lived in rental accommodations following their return moves ('all returns'), in comparison to the nearly 73 per cent of individuals returning to their previous home who were also owners, reinforcing the idea of a planned return. For others, return migration may simply be one move in a series of migrations, potentially leading to residency within a long-term care environment.

Spatial patterns of older repeat migration

Table 3.3 sets out the rates of older return migration with respect to origin and destination regions, with the former representing the ability of each region to retain in-migrants, and the latter the ability to regain former out-migrants. On average, 4.8 per cent of the 1996–2000 inflow was lost through return migration, although there was considerable variation about the mean value. British Columbia, a long-time retirement and high-amenity destination, attracted some 13,743 older migrants between 1996 and 2000, and demonstrated a concomitantly strong ability to retain its in-migrants, with just 3.8 per cent making a return out-migration between 2000 and 2001. Quebec, while attracting a relatively modest number of in-migrants (3,725), also exhibited a strong retention rate (3.0 per cent return out-migration), most likely reflecting language differences and the retention of Francophone speakers. The Atlantic and Prairie provinces had relatively high out-migration rates among their 1996–2000 in-migrants.

Table 3.3: Interprovincial return migration among Canada's older citizens: 1996–2001

	2000–01 loss of 1996–2000 in-migrants			2000–01 gain of 1996–2000 out-migrants		
	Inflows	Returns		Outflows	Returns	
	1996–00	2000–01	%	1996–00	2000–01	%
Atlantic	7,077	480	6.8	6,049	222	3.7
Quebec	3,725	111	3.0	8,643	369	4.3
Ontario	14,071	517	3.7	12,663	629	5.0
Prairies	16,753	1,035	6.2	16,819	738	4.4
BC	13,743	517	3.8	11,195	702	6.3
Total	55,369	2,660	4.8	55,369	2,660	4.8

Prairies included the provinces of Alberta, Manitoba and Saskatchewan. Atlantic Canada included the provinces of Newfoundland and Labrador, Prince Edward Island, New Brunswick and Nova Scotia.

In terms of regional variations to regain previous out-migrants, Quebec's attraction was similar to the overall rate (4.3 per cent). British Columbia again demonstrated its ongoing role within the Canadian inter-provincial migration system, with an attraction rate of 6.3 per cent. The Atlantic region had the lowest attraction rate (3.7 per cent). While return migration has been noted as an important source of in-migrants to these provinces, it does not appear to function over the relatively short term. In other words, return migrants to this region had most likely left at a much earlier time in search of employment, returning upon retirement, and are therefore missed within the current analysis.

Population redistribution due to repeat migration

Table 3.4 represents population redistribution within the Canadian system, measured by net migration among old people. As observed within the broader literature, return migration generally worked counter to both primary and onward migration, reducing gains or losses associated with both. Concurrently, while onward migration has typically been noted to reinforce the effect of primary migration in the broader literature, its effect here was less consistent, although quantitatively limited. For example, onward migration reinforced the effects of return migration in the case of Ontario and the Prairies.
Prairies included the provinces of Alberta, Manitoba and Saskatchewan. Atlantic Canada included the provinces of Newfoundland and Labrador, Prince Edward Island, New Brunswick and Nova Scotia.
In relation to migrations during the 2000–01 interval, the bulk of

Table 3.4: Net gains and losses from return and onward migration among Canada's older citizens: 1996–2001

	Net migration 1996-2000	Net migration 2000-01			
		From return migration	From onward migration	From single migration	Total
Atlantic	1,249	−258	37	555	334
Quebec	−5,176	258	0	−664	−406
Ontario	1,185	112	111	−260	−37
Prairies	342	−297	−111	327	−81
BC	2,400	185	−37	42	190
Total	0	0	0	0	0

the demographic impact associated with migration was due to single, one-year migrations over the 2000–01 period. In other words, the demographic effect of single-year migrations often exceeded that of the net impact of repeat migrations. For instance, Atlantic Canada's net gain in the 2000–01 period was largely due to single migrations

(555), while it was reduced somewhat by return migration (−258) as noted above. Similarly, Quebec's net loss was due to single migrations out of the province between 2000 and 2001, although it had a modest net gain of return migrants during the same period. Only in British Columbia is the effect different. In this case, its net gain over the 2000–01 interval was due primarily to return migration, with a modest gain also associated with one-year migration. Once again, the character and spatial patterns of migration are visible, with Quebec experiencing a net loss in both 1996–2000 and 2000–01, and again probably reflecting the out-migration of English-speakers. British Columbia, on the other hand, had a net in-migration in both periods, reflecting its role as a retirement destination. The net gain observed in Atlantic Canada is probably due to the return of retirement-age individuals who had left the region at a much earlier date in search of employment opportunities, and therefore are not counted as return migrants in this analysis.

Determinants of older repeat migration

Tables 3.5 and 3.6 present the results of two logistic regressions, including (i) the decision to make a return to the 1996 home versus other returns (that is, returns to the province of origin in 2000–01 (Table 3.5); and (ii) the decision to make a repeat (return or onward) migration in 2000–01 versus staying (Table 3.6). Both models are estimated using measures of personal attributes and provincial variables (or regional dummies) to define the utility function. Recalling that the models incorporated migration decisions for the population aged 20 and over, interaction effects between age and individual factors were introduced to examine age specific effects. Model estimation required that the 80 and over age group be merged with the 70 to 79 age group.

With a rho-square of 0.235, Model 1 (Table 3.5) explores the decision to engage in a return migration to the 1996 home or a more general return migration to the 1996 province of residence. In this case, rather than a set of provincial attributes that would be common in both choice sets (to return to their previous 1996 home or to return to the province), a set of regional dummy variables was included that captures the 2000 place of residence. In effect, these ask the question whether or not individuals were more likely to return from particular regions. Overall, the 'young old' (aged 60–69) were more likely to return to their previous home, a phenomenon noted in the case of Australia by Newbold and Bell (2001). In addition, home owners and residents of Atlantic Canada in 2000 were more likely to return to their 1996 home.

Table 3.5: Logistic regression of return to the 1996 home versus other returns, 2000–01

		Coefficient	t-score
Constant		–2.184	–6.75
Personal attributes:			
Sex	Male	0.210	1.56
Age	60–69	2.342	3.99
	70+	0.080	0.13
Education	< High school	0.084	0.39
	Some post-secondary	0.241	1.52
Tenure status	Own	2.504	15.64
Immigrant status	Immigrant	0.168	0.68
Marital status	Married	–1.090	–6.87
Language ability	English	–0.458	–1.84
	French	–0.436	–2.64
2000 Region of residence	Atlantic	0.784	3.70
	Quebec	0.260	0.90
	Ontario	–0.277	–1.34
	Prairies	0.033	0.16
Interaction effects	Aged 60–69 own	–2.249	–2.93
	Aged 70+ married	2.331	2.73
Rho-squared		0.235	
Likelihood ratio		426.687	
N		1,501	
% Concordant		81.4	

Note: Other return migrations refer to return migration to the province of origin.

Conversely, individuals who were married or were French speakers were less likely to return to their earlier residence. Interactions between the various personal effects and age provide additional insight into repeat mobility among older people, with two interaction effects included in Model 1. First, reinforcing the age and home ownership effects already noted, home owners aged 60 to 69 were more likely to return, perhaps reflecting post-retirement migrations and a relocation. Second, married individuals aged 70 and over were more likely to return to their original home, again suggestive of a planned return. Such results also imply that older, non-married migrants were more likely to make

Table 3.6: Logistic results of repeat (onward or return) migration versus staying, 2000–01

		Coefficient	t-score
Constant		–4.901	–1.00
Personal attributes:			
Sex	Male	0.138	306
Age	60–69	–1.740	–8.60
	70+	–1.730	–9.31
Education	< High School	–1.117	–15.89
	Some post secondary	–0.659	–12.50
Tenure status	Own	–1.026	–21.2
Immigrant status	Immigrant	–0.313	–3.44
Marital status	Married	–0.708	–13.54
Language ability	English	0.407	4.50
	French	0.360	5.75
Provincial effects:			
Sun		–0.955	–0.53
Cold		0.237	0.95
Population		–0.071	–2.68
Unemployment rate		–0.087	–0.79
Employment growth		–0.122	–2.17
Personal income		0.142	1.25
British		–0.018	–3.03
French		0.002	0.36
Interaction effects:	Age 60–69 immigrant	0.878	2.44
	Aged 70+ immigrant	0.750	2.20
Rho-squared		0.111	
Likelihood ratio		2,938.673	
N		566,594	
% Concordant		74.1	

a more general return to their province of origin, perhaps seeking family and care options.

Model 2 (Table 3.6) represents the decision to engage in a repeat migration (either return or onward) versus staying in the 2000 place of residence. With a rho-square of 0.111, the model fit is not as good as that noted for the first model, although the estimated relationships are as expected. In terms of personal attributes, males and individuals who speak either French or English were more likely to engage in a repeat migration between 2000 and 2001, as opposed to staying. At the same time, people aged 60 and older are less likely to engage in a repeat migration as compared to their younger (aged 20–64) counterparts. Additionally, individuals with lower levels of education (less than non-graduates), immigrants, home owners and married people were less likely to make a repeat migration. In terms of provincial attributes, individuals were less likely to make a repeat migration out of provinces with a large population, higher employment growth, and that shared a similar cultural makeup. Interestingly, there is no indication that potential migrants were affected by amenity effects as represented by sunshine and coldness, even when interacted with age to capture potential migrations among older people. Finally, interactions with age suggested that immigrants aged 60 and over were more likely to make a repeat migration than their younger counterparts.

Conclusions

Defining return migration as movements which return an individual to their place of residence five years prior to the census, this chapter has examined return and onward migration in the context of Canada's older population, aged 60 and over, as of 2001. Underlying this inquiry is the need to understand repeat migration, and more specifically return migration among Canada's older population, along with age variations in repeat migration. A mix of multivariate and descriptive techniques helped to identify the attributes of these older repeat migrants. Overall, the rates of return and onward migration observed among the older population are comparatively low relative to individuals in the labour force. The propensity to engage in an onward migration is particularly low among older people and may reflect the importance of knowledge of the destination – knowledge that is gained by previous residency – in shaping the migration decision. In fact, it may be that many of the single-year migrations reflect movements associated with health or dependency needs (Liaw and Frey, 2003).

In general, older people were less likely to engage in any form of repeat migration, although there was some evidence of increased migration propensities between 2000 and 2001. In terms of personal attributes, older return migrants are similar in many ways to the general characteristics of return migrants, with a tendency to be better educated and home owners. With respect to age, returns to the 1996 home were somewhat more important among the oldest old (aged 80 and over), most likely corresponding to returns home for care and/or returns to their own home following a short-term stay in a continuing care or group home.

It is also the case that primary, return and onward migrations among older people have similar spatial effects to those observed more broadly within the literature. For instance, despite including interaction effects between age and provincial attributes, these effects were not statistically significant. In other words, while older return or onward migrants appear to move toward provinces with higher employment growth or personal incomes, they are probably not moving for these reasons per se. However, their movement reflects broader spatial patterns of migration in Canada. That is, provinces that are attractive to labour-force-aged people are also attractive to older people. In part, this could reflect older people following their adult children across the country (Liaw and Frey 2003). This is also reflected in the sense that return migrations tended to work counter to the net migration effects of primary and onward migration. Moreover, British Columbia displayed strong attraction and retention powers for older migrants, with the province known as an important retirement destination. Concurrently, Quebec lost migrants, most likely representing the ongoing exodus of English speakers from the province.

Still, some differences were observed. For example, although married people dominated repeat migration flows, the divorced-separated-widowed were more likely to make a repeat migration. In addition, onward migration is relatively rare among older people. This suggests that return migrations, when they do occur, dominate the decision process and reflect existing knowledge of a destination and/or the location of capital, family or friends. Spatial scale is, however, key to this distinction, with smaller spatial scales offering greater opportunities for onward migration (Newbold, 2001), and therefore represents an avenue of further research. Another avenue for exploration would include a larger sample of return and onward migrants, such that multivariate analyses could be conducted without the need to include the broader population to ensure consistent results. In this way, key attributes and determinants of return and onwards migration among older people could be teased out.

The implications of the work can also be considered within a broader agenda. Similar to the demographic shifts occurring in many countries, Canada's older population will grow significantly and the median age of its population will increase over the coming years (Ramlo et al, 2009). While older people are generally less likely to migrate, increasing numbers of older people will mean an increasing number of migrations. If Canada echoes trends in the US, migration will probably redistribute older people down the urban–rural hierarchy, out of the largest urban areas and into small- or medium-sized urban areas, with retirement communities being important destinations (Moore and Pacey, 2003; Plane et al, 2005). However, this movement will have demographic and other impacts for both sending and receiving regions. Rural areas, for instance, will be unlikely to benefit from in-migration, and will continue to lose population through out-migration. Moore et al (2000), for instance, noted that the geography of ageing is linked to economic disadvantage. That is, areas with high and growing proportions of elderly people are most likely to be those with slow growth and below-average incomes.

Whether migrants are returning from the south of Europe or western Canada, receiving areas, and more than likely families, will need to provide services and care for these elderly returnees. The interregional migration of seniors can further these economic and demographic differences, shifting people and their non-earned income away from slow-growth regions. Indeed, migration has been observed to redistribute non-earned income out of Quebec, Manitoba and Saskatchewan and into Alberta and British Columbia. However, this pattern is somewhat blurred in the Atlantic provinces where retirement savings and pension inflows make a significant contribution to their economies despite the relatively small numbers of in-migrants (Newbold, 2008). Similar patterns of income transfer are probably occurring at smaller spatial scales, whereby selected communities, such as retirement communities, benefit from the influx of older people and their retirement incomes (see, for example, Nelson, 2005).

This chapter has explored longer-term migrations and has not considered short-term movements and other types of return migrations, such as seasonal 'snowbirding', as older retirees seek out warm winter destinations in places such as Arizona and Florida. Such return migrations could fruitfully be explored, as could longer-term migrations to the US or elsewhere, followed by a return to Canada in old age. Unfortunately, statistical data that tracks such movements is limited.

However, the data and discussion of the migration of older Canadians put forward in this chapter does raise important policy and programme questions for both sending and receiving communities alike, but particularly for those communities that are faced with continued population loss. Can small and rural communities staunch the flow of their older population? Can they provide services and care for their older residents? Moore and Rosenberg (1997), for example, caution that the growth of the elderly population will pose service-delivery challenges to communities, potentially creating both service-rich and service-poor individuals and communities. Alternatively, limited health care resources may encourage out-migration of older people, and particularly those with health needs who are attracted to larger metropolitan areas precisely because of the availability of health care services. Who pays for services, including health care? (See, for example, Davenport et al, 2005; Carrière et al, 2008; Busby et al, 2009; Robson, 2009). Conversely, if communities can attract older migrants (for example, to retirement communities), is there an economic/fiscal benefit to them?

References

Bell, M. (1996) 'Repeat and return migration', in P.W. Newton and M. Bell (eds) *Population shift: Mobility and Change in Australia*, Canberra: Australian Government Publishing Service, pp 1–17.

Burr, J.A. and Mutchler, J.E. (1992) 'The living arrangements of unmarried elderly Hispanic females', *Demography*, 29(1):93–112.

Busby, C., Robson, W.P.B. and Desjardins, P.M. (2009) *'Stress Test: Demographic Pressures and Policy Options in Atlantic Canada', Backgrounder 120*, Toronto: C.D. Howe Institute.

Carrière, Y., Keefe, J., Légaré, J., Lin, X., Rowe, R., Martel, L. and Rajbhandary, S. (2008) *Projecting the Future Availability of the Informal Support Network of the Elderly Population and Assessing its Impact on Home Care Services*, Cat. 91F0015M – No. 009, Ottawa: Statistics Canada.

Cuba, L. (1991) 'Models of migration decision making re-examined: The destination search of older migrants to Cape Cod', *The Gerontologist*, 31:204–209.

Davenport, J., Rathwell, T.A. and Rosenberg, M.W. (2005) 'Service provision for seniors: challenges for communities in Atlantic Canada', *Longview Review*, 3(3):9–16.

Eldridge, H.T. (1965) 'Primary, secondary and return migration in the United States, 1955–60', *Demography*, 2:444–455.

Grant, E.K. and Vanderkamp, J. (1986) 'Repeat migration and disappointment', *Canadian Journal of Regional Science*, 9:299–322.

Goldstein, S. (1954) 'Repeated migration as a factor in high mobility rates', *American Sociological Review*, 19:536–541.

Hayward, L. (2000) 'Health and Residential Mobility in Later Life', *SEDAP Research paper No. 34*, Hamilton, ON: McMaster University.

Hayward, L. and Lazarowich, N.M. (2001) 'Cohort survival is not enough: Why local planners need to know more about the residential mobility of the elderly', *SEDAP Research paper No. 53*, Hamilton, ON: McMaster University.

Kawase, A. and Nakazawa, K. (2009) 'Long term care insurance facilities and interregional migration of the elderly in Japan', *Economics Bulletin*, 29(4).

Kupiszewski, M., Heikkilä, E., Nieminen, M., Durham, H., Rees, P. and Kupiszewska, D. (2000) 'Internal migration and regional population dynamics in Europe: Finland case study', *Working Paper 00/07*, School of Geography, University of Leeds, www.geog.leeds.ac.uk/wpapers/00–7.pdf

Kupiszewski, M., Illeris, S., Durham, H. and Rees, P. (2001a) 'Internal migration and regional population dynamics in Europe: Denmark Case Study', *Working Paper*, School of Geography, University of Leeds, http://eprints.whiterose.ac.uk/5018/1/01–2.pdf

Kupiszewski, M., Borgegard, L., Fransson, U., Hakansson, J., Durham, H. and Rees, P. (2001b) 'Internal migration and regional population dynamics in Europe: Sweden Case Study', *Working Paper*, School of Geography, University of Leeds, http://eprints.whiterose.ac.uk/5019/1/01–1.pdf

Liaw, K.L. and Frey, W. (2003) 'Location of adult children as an attraction for black and white elderly return and onward migrants in the United States: Application of a three-level nested logit model with census data', *Mathematical Population Studies*, 10:75–98.

Liaw, K.L. and Ledent, J. (1988) 'Joint effects of ecological and personal factors on elderly interprovincial migration in Canada', *Canadian Journal of Regional Science*, 11(1):77–100.

Linn, J.P., Liaw, K.L. and Tsay, C.L. (1999) 'Determinants of fast return migration of the labour force: evidence from the National Survey of Taiwan', *Environment and Planning A*, 31:925–945.

Litwack, E. and Longino, C.F. (1987) 'Migration patterns among the elderly: a developmental perspective', *The Gerontologist*, 27:266–272.

Long, L. (1988) *Migration and Residential Mobility in the United States*, New York: Russell Sage Foundation.

Longino, C.F. and Serow, W.J. (1992) 'Regional differences in the characteristics of elderly return migrants', *Journal of Gerontology: Social Sciences*, 47(1):S38–S43.

Longino, C.F. (1979) 'Going home: aged return migration in the United States, 1965–1970', *Journal of Gerontology*, 34:736–745.

Longino, C.F. (1995) *Retirement Migration in America*, Houston, TX: Vacation Publications.

Moore, E.G., McGuinness, D., Pacey, M.A. and Rosenberg, M.W. (2000) 'Geographic dimensions of aging: the Canadian experience 1991–1996', *SEDAP Research Paper 23*, Hamilton, ON: McMaster University.

Moore, E.G., and Pacey, M.A. (2003) 'Geographical Dimensions of Aging in Canada 1991–2001', *SEDAP Research Paper 97*, Hamilton, ON: McMaster University.

Moore, E.G. and Rosenberg, M.W. (1997) *Growing Old in Canada: Demographic and Geographic Perspectives*, Toronto: ITP Nelson Press.

Morrison, P.A. (1971) 'Chronic movers and the future redistribution of population', *Demography*, 8(2):171–184.

Nelson, P.B. (2005) 'Migration and the regional redistribution of nonearnings income in the United States: metropolitan and nonmetropolitan perspectives from 1975 to 2000', *Environment and Planning A*, 37(12):1613–1636.

Newbold, K.B. (1996) 'Income, self-selection and return and onward interprovincial migration in Canada', *Environment and Planning A*, 28: 1019–1034.

Newbold, K.B. (2001) 'Counting migrants and migrations: comparing lifetime and fixed-interval return and onward migration', *Economic Geography*, 77(1):23–40.

Newbold, K.B. (2008) 'Interprovincial migration and retirement income transfers among Canada's older population: 1996–2001', *Environment and Planning A*, 40(6):1501–1516.

Newbold, K.B. and Liaw, K.L. (1994) 'Return and onward interprovincial migration through economic boom and bust in Canada from 1976–81 to 1981–86', *Geographical Analysis*, 26: 228–245.

Newbold, K.B. and Bell, M. (2001) 'Return and onward migration in Canada and Australia: evidence from fixed interval data', *International Migration Review*, 35(4):1157–1184.

Patrick, C.H. (1980) 'Health and migration of the elderly', *Research on Aging*, 2(2):233–241.

Plane, D.A., Henrie, C.J. and Perry, M.J. (2005) 'Migration up and down the urban hierarchy and across the lifecourse', *Proceedings of the National Academy of Sciences*, 102(43):15313–15318.

Ramlo, A., Berlin, R. and Baxter, D. (2009) 'Canada to 2058: projections of demographic growth and change for Canada and its regions', *Urban Futures Institute report 74*. Available at: www.urbanfutures.com/reports/Report%2074.pdf

Robson, W.B.P. (2009) 'Boomer bulge: dealing with the stress of demographic change on government budgets in Canada', *E-brief 71*, Toronto: C.D. Howe Institute.

Serow, W.J., Charity, D.A., Fournier, G.M. and Rasmussen, D.W. (1986) 'Cost of living differentials and elderly interstate migration', *Research on Aging*, 8:317–327.

Shearmur, R. and Polèse, M. (2005) *'La géographie du niveau de vie au Canada, 1971–2001'* ['The geography of living in Canada, 1971–2001'], Montreal, Canada: *Institut national de la recherche scientifique, urbanisation, culture et société* [Institute for Scientific Research, urbanization, culture and society].

Speare, A.J.R., Avery, R. and Lawton, L. (1991) 'Disability, residential mobility, and changes in living arrangements', *Journal of Gerontology*, 46(3):S133–S142.

Stack, C. (1996) *Call to Home: African Americans Reclaim the Rural South*, New York, NY: Basic Books.

FOUR

Ageing immigrants and the question of return: new answers to an old dilemma?

Claudio Bolzman

Introduction

This chapter explores dilemmas that immigrants from Italy and Spain may face, when nearing retirement in Switzerland and considering their future country of residence. In particular, the chapter examines these dilemmas from two complementary theoretical perspectives: institutional and transnational. I will briefly discuss these perspectives before accounting for the methods employed in two particular studies, the themes and criteria arising from them, and implications for different models of return.

Institutional perspective and the question of return

The works of Sayad (1991, 1999) in France and of Dietzel-Papakyriakou (1993, 2001) in Germany are representative of the institutional perspective. According to this perspective, structure, and especially States' modes of organisation and immigration policies, is more important than agency in immigrants' lives. Sayad argues, following Hanna Arendt (1981), that in a world politically organised in nation-states international migration is an exception, an anomaly that should be justified. In a world governed by the logic of economics, the main justification for migration is work, but not all kinds of work. Migrants must prove that their presence in the host society is useful for the economy of the host country. They must also attest that they are not in competition with nationals for the same kinds of jobs.

From the moment that immigrants find themselves in a situation of 'vacancy' (unemployment, disability, illness, accident, welfare dependency and also retirement), that is, when they cease to be workers and to have a positive economic role, the legitimacy of their presence in the host society can be questioned and their lack of utility seen as problematic. According to Dietzel-Papakyriakou:'For the society of residence, with retirement the structural legitimation of extension of stay of older migrants who left the labour market is a problem: they become mere cost factors. Social acceptance is crumbling. The extension of their stay violates the agreement that led to their recruitment, which was based exclusively on employment' (1993:145, author's translation). Even when they are integrated in the labour market, their presence is considered as provisory. The designation of older immigrants as *Gastrentners* (guest pensioners) is also an indicator that they are not completely considered as a settled and accepted element of the national population.

Most immigrants share this perception. They see themselves as 'guest workers', because their initial project was not to settle permanently in the host society, but also because institutional settings both in the home country and in the host country expect immigrants to perceive permanent settlement in another country as unrealistic. Immigrants may reside in the host country with nostalgia for a place where they are considered to be more than guest workers, where they are perceived in a multidimensional perspective, as citizens and not just as denizens. Since immigrants are not fully recognised as part of the host society, they dream about return; not necessarily a real return, but a mythical return, regularly postponed, because structural and institutional conditions are limited for the majority and only a minority can accomplish that dream. Immigrants are then condemned to a 'double absence' (Sayad, 1999): not really integrated in the host society, neither really present in the home society; and this situation will last as long as immigrants cannot return home.

Therefore, according to the institutional perspective[1], in ageing immigrants more so than in other categories of older people, retirement marks a new stage in life by introducing changes in their social situation. It is an event that people look forward to but also dread. At the outset, most immigrants accepted that their presence in the host society was provisional. To them, and to the local population, the justification for their presence was in the work that they performed. Their status was one of 'foreign worker' or 'guest worker' (Piore, 1979; Sayad, 2001). As things turned out, the provisional stay became longer and longer. When they retire however, they cease to be 'workers' and the question of their status arises, together with that of the rationale for staying in or leaving the society of residence. At the same time, and for the first time, they have more favourable conditions to put into effect their plans. Thus, it can be argued, retirement may represent for immigrants not only a social transition, from work to retirement, but also a possible spatial transition, from living in one country to settlement in another country (Bolzman et al, 2001a). In that sense, it can be considered as a double change in lifecourse that can generate new dilemmas in couples and families.

Transnational perspectives and the question of return

On the other hand, the transnational perspective shows that migration does not disrupt social relations between migrants and their close network of significant persons that stayed in the home country (Vatz Laaroussi and Bolzman, 2010) and that migrants maintain and develop multiple social relations linking their home country and their host country. They build social spaces across geographical, cultural or political borders (Basch et al, 1994: 6). In fact, despite the distance and duration of separation, various forms of relationships, including intergenerational, take place between migrants and their network in the home country. These relations include reciprocal visits, but especially contacts at distance through various means (letters, telephones, internet and so on) that involve exchanging advice, emotional and moral support, money, goods and gifts (Baldassar, 2007; Le Gall, 2009). Thus, despite emigration, continuity of relationships and exchanges between those who left the country and those who stayed to some extent continues.

Furthermore, according to the transnational perspective, immigrants' agency is more significant than official structures: immigrants do not completely leave their home country; they never really cut off their relationship with that reality, creating their own social space that bridges here and there simultaneously. This process can also be defined as the construction of a duality of resources and references (Bolzman, 1994). Hence, according to the transnational perspective, the migrant's situation can be considered as a 'double presence'.

The main issue here is not the question of return but the one of circulation: to what extent are migrants still able to be mobile and keep in contact with both societies? Retirement can be seen as an opportunity to consolidate and develop a transnational way of life: immigrants have more freedom to move from one country to another, they can live part of the year in one place and part of the year in another place.

I shall endeavour in this chapter to determine under what conditions the 'duality of resources and references', observed in many studies on first-generation immigrants, represents a potential asset for a transnational life after retirement. In using the term 'duality of resources', I refer to the fact that the resource system of first-generation immigrants usually draws on the society of origin as well as on the society of residence, both as far as economic assets are concerned and with regard to family networks or broader social relationships (Bolzman, 1994). The term 'duality of references' refers to the fact that cultural and symbolic attachments are also shared between the two countries (Catani, 1983; Oriol, 1984). The immigrants' participation in the host country's labour market combined with regular contacts, both direct and indirect, with the native country, helps to propagate this duality. The immigrants' socio-cultural identity is thus shaped by those dual links and, in turn, helps strengthen them through symbolic activities Leser and Seeberger, 1992; Bolzman, 1996).

Empirical testing of both perspectives

In my view, both theoretical perspectives, institutional and transnational, are not necessarily contradictory and can be seen as complementary. The remainder of this chapter examines the relevance of both theoretical perspectives by considering data from a survey of the circumstances of Italian and Spanish immigrants nearing retirement in Switzerland, carried out as part of the Swiss *National Research Programme on Ageing*, together with data from qualitative interviews with these populations. Of all the immigrant populations from Southern Europe, Italians and Spaniards are the longest established in Switzerland. According to the Swiss Federal Office for Statistics, over the last four years (2007–10) migration between Switzerland and each of these countries has been relatively stable:[2] there is little variation in the number of arrivals and departures during this period (8,000–10,000 arrivals and 5,000–6,000 departures, as regards Italians; 2,000–3,000 arrivals and 2,000–4,000 departures in respect of Spaniards). Nowadays, Italians make up the largest foreign group in Switzerland (287,000 residents in 2010), while Spaniards come seventh in number with 64,000, after Germans, Portuguese, Serbs, Turks and the French.

Italian and Spanish immigrants arrived mainly as guest workers in Switzerland between the 1950s and the 1970s. They belong to a generation that experienced severe restrictions in their citizenships rights through state regulations, including limitations to family reunification and restrictions in access to housing and employment. Now retired or approaching retirement, in an era of globalisation, low cost flights and more freedom of circulation between EU countries and Switzerland, transnational possibilities are more likely. Therefore, immigrants who spent 30 to 40 years of their adult lives as guest workers in Switzerland, harbouring the idea that one day they will probably return to their home country, have progressively discovered that it may be possible to live a transnational life that allows them to be regularly in contact with their home country without completely leaving Switzerland.

In my view[3], intentions concerning the country (or the countries) of residence after retirement are related to issues of resources and their spatial location. Economic resources, family and social networks, health condition and cultural resources are four dimensions that play an important role in migrant decisions about whether to return permanently to their home country, to stay in the host country, or to go back and forth between these countries. I shall discuss how these different types of resources and their location influence intentions concerning the future country of residence. I shall also analyse to what extent preferences to stay or return are mutually exclusive or if these options include living arrangements that allow some transnational mobility. Before doing so, I need to explain the qualitative and quantitative nature of the data drawn upon in this chapter.

Qualitative interviews were carried out in three different periods: 1995–96, 2000 and 2008, among Italians and Spanish elderly populations. In 1995–96 colleagues and I interviewed 30 individuals who had completed a survey (discussed below); in 2000, we conducted 10 focus groups with a total of 26 Italian and 19 Spanish older migrants, focusing on their everyday lives and future plans (Bolzman et al, 2000); and in 2008 we interviewed 24 immigrants of different nationalities about transnational family reunification and their relationships to their home country (Bolzman et al, 2008).

The Pre-Retired Immigrants (PRI) quantitative survey, which also informs this chapter, was originally conducted in 1994 by drawing a random sample of 274 Italians and 168 Spaniards aged 55 to 64, that is just before the legal age for receiving old age insurance in Switzerland (PRI survey, Bolzman et al, 1998). I draw on this survey data for two main reasons: first, it is the only quantitative study existing in Switzerland on the question of return among these populations[4], and we were keen to explore such data to help understand the main factors that could have an impact on decisions about the place to live after retirement; second, revisiting this data offers a useful opportunity to examine it from my two alternative theoretical perspectives. The quantitative sample was chosen through accessing official lists of residents of Italian and Spanish nationalities in Basel City and Geneva. We selected this age period (55–64) because many empirical researches observed a significant proportion of respondents taking early retirement and/or of returning to the home country before the age or retirement

(Peil et al, 1988; Guillemard, 1992). The composition of the survey sample was made up of: 155 Italians in Geneva (78 women and 77 men); 119 Italians in Basel (60 women and 59 men); 108 Spanish in Geneva (56 women and 52 men); and 60 Spanish in Basel (30 women and 30 men).

Three possible options

Colleagues and I have previously observed that ageing immigrants in Switzerland have different intentions with respect to their future place of residence: one third planning to stay in Switzerland, another third preparing the return to the home country and the last third expecting to live part of the year in the host country and the rest of the year in the home country (Bolzman et al, 2006). The latter, halfway, alternative, between the extremes of return to the country of origin or settlement in the host country, is becoming a real option for many immigrants near retirement. They intend to 'come and go' between the two countries, living thus a mobile life across borders. This option is not really surprising given the transnational perspective, as previously discussed.

Many research studies about migrants show how important coming and going can be, especially when migrants form transnational communities (Guarnizo, 1994; Portes, 1996). However, these forms of transnational mobility have been chiefly observed among economically active workers. Among older migrants, transnational mobility has been discussed mainly in respect of migrations within the same country (Bond, 1990), or the migration of elderly EU citizens from northern Europe to southern EU countries (Casado-Diaz et al, 2004).

That this option appears to be so popular among foreign residents in Switzerland seems astonishing, since the regulations governing foreigners' residence in Switzerland legally exclude such mobility: according to the actual rules, a foreigner holding a long-term residence permit is not allowed to leave Switzerland during more than six months – or in some cases two years – if he wants to maintain his or her status as resident. Moreover, some payments related to national insurance schemes or welfare entitlements require the permanent presence in the host country of those who receive those benefits. Thus, this option requires living arrangements that take into account these kinds of legal constraints. Regarding future place of residence intention (see Table 4.1), we observe a distinction between the two age groups in our studies: the younger group (aged 55–59) showing a preference for 'coming and

Table 4.1: Intentions concerning future place of residence by age and gender * (% in column)

	Men 55–59	Women 55–59	Men 60–64	Women 60–64
Switzerland	21	36	37	62
Switzerland and Spain/Italy	44	45	36	21
Spain/Italy	35	19	27	17
N	143	97	101	58

Cramer V=.19, P=.00 * Only the three main options are presented in the table. Other answers and missing values are not included. Data from 1994 PRI Survey.

going' between the home and host countries, while the older group (aged 60–64) is more inclined to stay in Switzerland.

A point of interest is that, among both Italian and Spanish ageing immigrants, the proportion of women who choose to stay in Switzerland after retirement (43 per cent) is much higher than that of men (26 per cent). Conversely, the return option seems more popular among men (35 per cent as against 21 per cent), while the proportions choosing to live part of the year in each country tend to converge (39 per cent for men and 36 per cent for women), as shown in Table 4.1. This discrepancy between men and women about their future living place shows that the subject has the potential to be a cause of friction and/or bargaining between spouses. As one Italian woman told us:

> 'My husband wanted to return to Screso one year after retirement. He didn't want to stay, not at all ... He didn't like life here. He always wanted to leave. We have paid one firm to build our house in Italy and my husband finished the construction. But I wanted to stay. Here, it is a city. I like cities. I had everything here: my son, my grand-children and I knew all the women from the general store where I have worked. There was no reason to go back. Here it is more home for me than in Italy, even if here it is not home.'

This kind of situation gives rise to serious consideration of the option to live part of the year in each country, a compromise between competing requirements if no particular desire or constraint prevails (Bolzman et al, 2001b). This compromise may also mean a postponement of the decision, a feasible solution for the youngest couples (aged 55–59), who are probably not yet familiar with certain problems that may hasten the choice, such as failing health or economic difficulties. Transnational arrangements would then be a way of coping with the retirement transition, allowing behaviour adjustments to ease the entering of a new period of life (Bures, 1997).

Criteria influencing intentions with respect to the place of residence

The choice of a future place of residence is the outcome of an assessment of the present and future situation according to various criteria related to access to resources and/or to identity issues. Those criteria include, for example, economic consideration of the comparative material advantages that may be expected respectively in Switzerland and in the country of origin, as well as the quality and accessibility of health services, relational criteria concerning the future social network and symbolic criteria concerning the recognition of the person as a full citizen. When ageing immigrants were asked to list, in the order of importance, what criteria they had in mind when considering a future place of residence, the following answers were given (several answers allowed; N=442 per item):

Proximity of children	63%
Quality of health services	45%
Cost of living	39%
Social life and friends	35%
Not feeling a foreigner	27%

We observed similarity between the ranking of criteria governing respondents' choice of post-retirement domicile and the values governing their life, the order of the replies being in fact very close[5]. This similarity lends weight to the theory that the question of returning home is the prism that reflects the immigrants' way of life before retirement and, more generally, the characteristics of their social integration and of the links they have maintained with their home country. I shall now explore the influence of key resources and criteria that appear significant for the respondents in making plans for their future: location of the family; economic situation; health condition; and cultural identification either with the host country, the home country or both.

Family criteria

Location of the family, and especially of children, appears to be a very important criterion when deciding choice of place of residence after retirement: only 11 per cent of those with more than half their kinship network living nearby consider returning to homeland as an option, compared to 40 per cent of those with less than a quarter of their kinship residing locally, as shown in Table 4.2. Moreover, when at least one child is living in the country of origin, 47 per cent of respondents are planning to return to the home country, while this is the case for only 22 per cent of parents whose children are all resident in Switzerland. However, among those having all their children close by, more than 40 per cent prefer the prospect of living partly in Switzerland and partly in the home country, whereas fewer of those who have at least one child in the country of origin are tempted by this solution (16 per cent).

Table 4.2: Intentions concerning future place of residence by location of family members * (% in column)

	Less than 25% nearby	From 25% to 50% nearby	More than 50% nearby
Switzerland	27	36	42
Switzerland and Spain/Italy	33	40	47
Spain/Italy	40	24	11
N	150	157	91

Cramer V=.17, P=.00, * Only the three main options are presented in the table

It seems to be the case that when there is a child living in the home country, there is a greater tendency to make firm decisions: this usually means return or possibly settlement in Switzerland. When all the children are in the host country, being near to them can be very important, but it does not preclude thoughts of moving between the two countries in the future, as this Spanish woman explains:

'I have two daughters. They are Swiss, but they feel themselves both Swiss and Spanish. But I think that their future is here. If I didn't have children I would leave for Spain to live in my house. But now, our future is here, we have our children here. We have attachments in Spain and in Switzerland. I would like to live in both countries.'

The situation is different when there are no children in the host country kinship network. Then the return option is more feasible. In this respect a Spanish immigrant told us:

> 'I would like to live in both places: in Switzerland, because I am living here for a long time and part of my roots are here. But I have also family in Spain and sometimes I feel lonely here, and my sisters and brothers in Spain, they need me because they are already quite old. I am planning to settle in Spain as soon as I obtain my retirement pension.'

Health criteria

Even if elderly immigrants are rather 'young old' in terms of demographic age, the PRI survey shows that Spaniards and Italians recruited to work in Switzerland in the 1950s and 1960s are, in later life, more likely than indigenous Swiss elders to encounter health problems or functional disorders. Moreover, these health problems in migrants often occur before the age of 65 (Bolzman et al, 2004), and most often after 65 in the indigenous population (Lalive d'Epinay et al, 2000). Researchers have called this phenomenon the 'exhausted migrant effect' (Bollini and Siem, 1995): immigrants arriving in Switzerland as healthy people (the most 'fit' emigrated and there was a further selection of the 'healthy' on arrival in Switzerland due to health checks at the border) are now exhausted, after 20 to 30 years of hard work and sometimes precarious legal and social conditions: they have aged prematurely. This is clearly related to the types of jobs occupied by immigrants of this generation. People who worked in the construction or cleaning industries are particularly affected: half of them experiencing significant health problems that led them to leave the labour market before the official retirement age.

The decision to return to the home country is relatively unaffected by the interviewees' assessment of their state of health. That assessment is decisive, however, in regard to the other two options: people in poor health are more likely to stay in Switzerland, whereas those who regard their state of health as fair or good tend to alternate between the two countries (see Table 4.3). The same kind of relationship between health and intention to return applies to persons in poor physical health (chronic disease, disability or important consequences of illness or accident) compared to those in good health or average health.

These observations suggest that, from the health point of view, the decision to live part of the year in one country and part of the year in

Table 4.3: Intentions concerning future place of residence by physical health situation * (% in column)

	Good health	Average health	Bad health
Staying in Switzerland	27	30	46
Living partly in Switzerland, partly in the home country	41	44	25
Returning to home country	32	26	29
N	203	82	107

Cramer V=.14; P=.00 *Only the three main options are presented in the table

the other has something in common with the decision to stay: these options, unlike the return option, are both connected with the physical and mental condition of the concerned person; the choice between staying or 'alternating' depends on the extent to which health problems force the person to stay, the tendency otherwise being to 'alternate'. As one Italian man explains:

> 'As long as I feel well, that my health allows me to do it, I would like to spend part of the year in my region in Italy. There we have our house, some friends, nice weather. But my children are here and it is important to be near them as much as possible.'

Thus, it appears that when ageing immigrants have to leave the workplace for health reasons and are forced to live with a disability pension until retirement, they tend to stay in the host country. This decision therefore appears less a choice and more a constraint, related to financial and health reasons. In this case, ageing immigrants nevertheless feel they have the right to be treated in Switzerland, after so many years of hard work during which they used much of their energy. These 'exhausted' immigrants estimate that their hard work legitimises their continued stay in Switzerland after retirement. In the words of a Spanish woman with ulcers, "I left my health here, we have the right to be treated here."

When work is interrupted for health reasons, the event may manifest as a passport to claim social citizenship rights. The notion, therefore, of 'vacancy', in terms of lack of residence legitimacy when economically inactive, as defined in the institutional theory, is seen by immigrants whose poor health can be attributed to past work as unreasonable and invalid.

Economic criteria

The economic dimension weighs heavily on the choice of future place of residence. To show this, let us take the interviewees' own assessment of their financial situation as an indicator. Two thirds of them consider their situation comparatively satisfactory; their tendency to return is lower than that of the other third that have economic problems (27 per cent compared with 39 per cent), while their tendency to alternate appears to be higher (43 per cent compared with 25 per cent). One third of the interviewees claim to be in financial difficulty. In terms of deciding upon a future place of residence, this has the effect of reducing sharply the proportion of those who intend to live part of the year in each country (25 per cent versus a sample average of 38 per cent), the others being divided between returning and staying on. For those persons in financial difficulty, the tendency to stay on in Switzerland is much stronger if they do not own property in the country of origin (see Table 4.4). As explained by a Spanish woman:

> 'I believe that if we could, we will all come back. But many of us stay here because we have not a real choice. If I had a house in Spain it would be different, but since it is not the case, with my retirement pension and without any state support it is not possible.'

Table 4.4: Intentions concerning future place of residence by economic situation and ownership of a house in the home country * (% in column)

	Satisfactory situation and housing in home country	Satisfactory situation and no housing in home country	Difficult situation and housing in home country	Difficult situation and no housing in home country
Staying in Switzerland	19	48	19	62
Living partly in Switzerland, partly in home country	48	34	36	9
Returning to home country	33	18	45	29
N	166	111	64	45

Cramer V=.36 ; P=.00 *Only the three main options are presented in the table

Ownership of a dwelling in the country of origin is not a factor that has any bearing on how the present economic situation is perceived: the percentage of owners is in fact the same among those satisfied and among the ones dissatisfied with their situation (three out of five). However, the way this asset is exploited at the time of retirement is not the same in the two sub-groups: although in both cases one person out of five intends to remain in Switzerland, despite being a property owner in the home country, half of the owners who are free of economic constraints prefer to 'alternate' while half of the more poorly off prefer to return (see Table 4.4).

Turning to the question of ownership of a dwelling in Switzerland, which represents a sizeable investment, it can be assumed that ownership has a certain symbolic value for immigrants, in that it reconciles the initially contradictory concepts of home and adopted country; in accordance with the sample average however, a third of those who own homes in Switzerland still plan to split their time between the two countries. This leads to the suggestion that living part of the year in each of the two countries is an expensive option, feasible only when one is relatively well off, but also that it provides a way of respecting the 'duality of resources and references' and of finding a third course to add to the stay-or-return dichotomy. With respect to this dichotomy, we have seen that the disabled show a greater-than-average tendency to remain in Switzerland, which is consistent with our observations about health factors. However, the only persons with economic difficulties whose attitude towards return stands out are the unemployed (5.2 per cent in our sample), who are strongly in favour of leaving Switzerland (53 per cent); this group presumably feels more keenly that the legitimacy of its presence in the host country is put into question (Sayad, 2001).

Cultural and symbolic criteria

The development of strong cultural and symbolic ties with the host country may favour either the decision to stay or to live part of the year in the host country and part of the year in the home country, while the keeping of symbolic ties with the home country may favour the return option. An analysis of the language of radio and TV programmes tuned into by ageing immigrants throws some light on the symbolic ties they have created with the host country (Portes and Rumbaut, 1990). It also provides an indication of the extent to which the country of origin is still present in immigrant's daily life, thanks to the numerous cable and satellite television channels available today to most of them. Three quarters of the interviewees watch Italian and Spanish TV programmes, with roughly the same proportion of each national group watching both channels (59 per cent for the Italians and 53 per cent for Spaniards). Roughly, the same proportion of each national group prefers to watch only its own-language programmes (23 per cent as against 17 per cent). We observed that the attitude towards return of those who watch TV programmes exclusively in mother tongue is different from that of immigrants who follow local-language programmes (whether or not they also tune into programmes in their native tongue); as expected, the first group shows a tendency to return that is much higher than average (41 per cent against an average of 27 per cent) and they are less ready to stay on or 'alternate'. In other words, a decisive factor is interest in and access to local-language media; acquiring it narrows the gap between intention to stay in the host country or to alternate between host and home country (see Table 4.5).

Table 4.5: Intentions concerning future place of residence by language of radio and TV programmes* (% in column)

	Local language only (French or German)	Home country language only (Italian or Spanish)	Local language and home country language
Staying in Switzerland	38	27	35
Living partly in Switzerland, partly in home country	42	32	42
Returning to home country	20	41	23
N	83	80	217

Cramer V=.13; P=.01 *Only the three main options are presented in the table

Cultural attachment is therefore a significant factor, as indicated by one Italian man:

> 'Society has not changed us. We have kept our habits. When we are outside we do like the majority here, but since we are at home we are again like in Italy. It is a piece of our country. We are just waiting for the retirement pension and then we will go back to our village. We still have family and friends there.'

Another indicator of immigrants' symbolic orientation towards the 'host' country is the acquisition or not of Swiss nationality by the 'second generation' (Bolzman et al, 2003). In our sample, 59 per cent of respondents have children who are still exclusively Italians or Spaniards, while 41 per cent have at least one child who became Swiss. Again, we observe here that the attitude towards return is more favourable among those whose children are all still foreigners, when compared to those who have at least one child who has become Swiss (32 per cent against 14 per cent). Proportions are inversed as regards the option of staying in Switzerland (30 per cent against 42 per cent), while the differences with respect to 'alternating' are slight. Thus, at the cultural and symbolic level, a strong orientation towards the home country is positively related to the return option, while the 'duality of references' goes hand in hand either with the option of living part of the year in the host country and part of the year in the country of origin, or with that of staying in Switzerland.

Social structures and their perception

As Table 4.6 shows, while Italians mostly choose the option of staying in the immigration country, Spaniards were more numerous in planning a return to the home country.

Table 4.6: Intentions about future place of residence by nationality (% in column)

	Italians	Spaniards	Altogether
Staying in Switzerland	35	21	30
Living partly in Switzerland, partly in home country	38	28	34
Returning to home country	18	40	26
Other choice	5	3	4
Doesn't know	4	8	6
N	268	174	442

Cramer V=.28, P=.00

Empirical evidence shows that these differences are not related to conventional explanations such as distance between the home country and the host country, or length of residence in the immigration country. Rather, those differences are related, to some extent, to the immigrants' relationships to their country of origin and to its social policies with respect to return, as well as to the ethnic community structure in the host country. Spaniards are more oriented towards the solution of permanent return because they have a better image of their home country than do Italians. This applies in particular to the health system and to elderly care in the country of origin. Elderly Spanish migrants also spend more time each year in their country of origin than their Italian counterparts, who prefer to stay in Switzerland because they have developed stronger community structures in the 'host' country than have the Spaniards. These social structures favour the Italians' collective integration over a considerable period of time. Moreover, integration has also been facilitated for them, because Italian is one of the four national languages officially spoken in Switzerland, even though the official use of Italian is mainly restricted to the canton of Ticino in the southern part of the country[6]. Thus, one needs to keep in mind that images of reality may constitute reality, and that contextual factors exert an important influence on decision processes. Ageing migrants intentions are moulded by their personal history in interaction with national policies towards them, both in the immigration country and in the home country (Warnes et al, 2004:314).

Concluding remarks

In this chapter I have explored empirical data detailing the intentions of Italian and Spanish immigrants in Switzerland as regards residence after retirement and significant criteria influencing their decisions, discussed in connection with two theoretical perspectives. The majority of respondents are either planning to stay in Switzerland, or to live part of the year in Switzerland and part of the year in their home country. Contrary to the outcome implicit in the institutional perspective, we observed that the permanent return option is somewhat less popular than the other two.

Literature on migration has already pointed out the existence of the transnational mobility of older migrants between two countries. In particular, studies on Northern European retirees in Southern European areas have heard evidence of this form of living arrangement (Williams et al, 1997; Casado-Diaz et al, 2004; Huber and O'Reilly, 2004; Rodriguez et al, 2004). But the extent of the phenomenon among former guest workers that came from Southern countries to a Northern country seems surprising. Moreover, this option is considered by people regardless of socioeconomic background. And this option of 'going back and forth' has been achieved and developed by many ageing immigrants in a context of potential or actual constraining legal regulations on this kind of mobility. This appears to be related to immigrants' need to experience borders as a form of continuity rather than as a barrier. And it is related to the development, through time, of a transnational way of life defined by cultural, symbolic, concrete and affective ties with both countries. This perspective has been highlighted in the theory of transnationalism.

I have explored on an empirical basis important criteria influencing ageing immigrants' views on the three main return options. Two important themes stand out as having a strong influence on intentions with respect to future place of residence: symbolic orientation and the amount of resources at migrants' disposal. The first concerns the cultural identity of elderly immigrants, ranging from a strong and almost exclusive reference to the home country to successful symbolic integration in the host country. The second theme centres on the amount of social and economic resources elderly immigrants may count on, particularly in the fields of income, housing, social support and health care services.

Consideration of these two themes shows that ageing migrants who choose the permanent return option have an overriding and strong symbolic orientation towards their home country, while those that choose one of the other two options are more symbolically oriented towards the host society, or towards what I termed the 'duality of references'. As regards amount of resources, this makes the difference between the two options of remaining in Switzerland after retirement and 'coming and going'. Those who are better off prefer to consolidate a transnational way of life and live part of the year in Switzerland and part of the year in Italy or Spain, while those who have less resources plan more often to stay in Switzerland, which appears to be contrary to the institutional theory perspective that those with a reduced economic role have a diminished legitimacy to remain in the host country. However, the option of returning for good to the native country seems to be independent from the amount of resources at hand.

Overall I have shown the complexity of the decision-making process when migrants deliberate options for country of residence after retirement. The classical binary distinction between staying and returning does not fit with more sophisticated models elaborated by migrants to establish links between their country of settlement and their home country (King, 2002). This binary distinction was probably adapted to a more sedentary conception of society, where mobility was perceived as an exception, as an abnormal temporary situation (Sayad, 1999). This was the basis of the guest-worker model. The fact that returning to the home land is the less frequent choice made by ageing Italian and Spanish immigrants in Switzerland indicates that this model is certainly becoming less a social obligation. In line with the transnational perspective, the circulation model is the emerging pattern, allowing migrants to keep in touch with both realities of significance, host country and native country. No wonder that the circulation model appears to be the most popular pattern among ageing immigrants, perceived as an ideal option when social, health and economic resources are available.

However, the circulation option raises the question that has been a subject of debate in some federal States, including the United States, as to who should cover the cost of health care or dependency care (Longino and Crown, 1990). Should it be covered entirely by the country of origin or should the country in which the person spent his active life contribute? As a matter of fact, because of their mobility, migrants raise a more general question as to whether social security, health and social care systems, premised on continuity in terms of space and time, are appropriate to the needs of a growing number of mobile individuals. This is a central question, one that may benefit from further consideration of older people's return migration intentions in the context of both institutional and transnational theoretical perspectives.

References

Arendt, H. (1981), 'Le déclin de l'Etat-Nation et la fin des droits de l'homme' (The decay of the nation-state and the end of human rights), in H. Arendt *L'impérialisme*, Paris: Fayard.

Baldassar, L. (2007) 'Transnational families and aged care: the mobility of care and the migrancy of ageing', *Journal of Ethnic and Migrations Studies*, 33(2):275–297.

Basch, L.G., Glick Schiller, N. and Blanc-Szanton, L. (1994) *Nations Unbound. Transnational Projects, Post-Colonial Predicaments and De-terriorialized Nation-States*, Langhorne, PA: Gordon and Breach.

Bollini, P. and Siem, H. (1995) 'No real progress towards equity: health of migrant and ethnic minorities on the eve of the year 2000', *Social Science and Medicine*, 41:819–828.

Bolzman, C. (1994) 'Stages and modes of incorporation of exiles in Switzerland: the example of Chilean refugees' innovation', *European Journal of Social Sciences*, 7:321–333.

Bolzman, C. (1996) *Sociologie de l'exil: une approche dynamique. L'exemple des réfugiés chiliens en Suisse* [Sociology of exile: a dynamic approach. The example of Chilean refugees in Switzerland], Zurich: Seismo.

Bolzman, C., Fibbi, R. and Vial, M. (1998) *Modes de vie et projets d'avenir des immigrés espagnols et italiens proches de la retraite* [Ways of life and the future plans of Spanish and Italian immigrants close to retirement] *PRI Research Report, National Research Programme 32 (FNS)*, Geneva: Institut d'étude sociales.

Bolzman, C., Fibbi, R. and Vial, M. (2000) *Les loisirs des personnes âgées immigrés: pratiques, besoins, demandes, Genève, Rapport de recherche* [Leisure activities of older immigrants: practices, needs, demands], Geneva: Institut d'étude sociales.

Bolzman, C., Fibbi, R. and Vial, M. (2001a) 'La famille: une source de légitimité pour les immigrés âgés après la retraite?' [The family: a source of legitimacy for older immigrants after retirement?] *Revue européenne des migrations internationales*, 17(1):55–78.

Bolzman, C., Fibbi, R. and Vial, M. (2001b) 'Der Ruhestand – eine neue Grenze für Migranten?' [Retirement : a new border for migrants?] *Zeitschrift für Migration und Soziale Arbeit*, 3–4:96–101.

Bolzman, C., Fibbi, R. and Vial, M. (2003) *Secondas-Secondos. Le processus d'intégration des jeunes adultes issus de la migration espagnole et italienne en Suisse*, [Secondas-Secondos. The process of integration of second generation Spanish and Italian young adults in Switzerland], Zurich: Seismo.

Bolzman, C., Fibbi, R. and Vial, M. (2006) 'What to do after retirement? Elderly migrants and the question of return', *Journal of Ethnic and Migrations Studies*, 32(8):1359–1375.

Bolzman, C., Poncioni-Derigo, R. and Vial, M. (2003) 'Switzerland' in N. Patel (ed) *Minority Elderly Care in Europe. Country Profiles*, Leeds and London: PRIAE.

Bolzman, C., Poncioni-Derigo, R., Vial, M. and Fibbi, R. (2004) Older labour migrants' wellbeing in Europe: The case of Switzerland, *Ageing & Society*, 24:411–429.

Bolzman, C., Hirsch-Durret, E., Anderfuhren, S. and Vuille, M. (2008) 'Migration of parents under family reunification policies. A national approach to a transnational problem. The case of Switzerland', *Retraite et société*, 2008:93–121.

Bond, J. (1990) 'Living arrangements of elderly people', in J. Bond, P. Coleman and S.M. Peace (eds) *Ageing and Society*, London: Sage.

Bures, R.M. (1997) 'Migration and the lifecourse: is there a retirement transition?', *International Journal of Population Geography*, 3:109–120.

Casado-Diaz, M.A., Kaiser, C. and Warnes, A.W. (2004) 'Northern European retired residents in nine southern European areas: characteristics, motivations and adjustment', *Ageing & Society*, 24:353–381.

Catani, M. (1983) 'L'identité et les choix relatifs au système des valeurs. Associationnisme immigré, projet familial et projet de vie' [Identity and choices related to value systems. Immigrants associations, family projects and life projects], *Peuples Méditerranéens*, 24:117–126.

Dietzel-Papakyriakou, M. (1993) *Altern in der Migration. Die Arbeitsmigranten von dem Dilemma: zurückkehern oder bleiben?* [Older people and migration. Migrant workers and the dilemma: return or stay?], Stuttgart: Enke Verlag.

Dietzel-Papakyriakou, M. (2001) 'Elderly foreigners, elders of foreign heritage in Germany', *Revue européenne des migrations internationales*, 17(1):79–99.

Guarnizo, L.E. (1994) 'Los Dominicanyorks: The Making of a Binational Society', *Annals of American Academy of Political and Social Science*, 533:70–86.

Guillemard, A.M. (1992) 'Salariés vieillissants et marché du travail en Europe [Older workers and labour market in Europe]', *Gérontologie et société*, 60: 66–80.

Huber, A. and O'Reilly, K. (2004) 'The construction of Heimat under conditions of individual modernity: Swiss and British elderly migrants in Spain', *Ageing & Society*, 24:327–351.

King, R. (2002) 'Towards a new map of European migration', *International Journal of Population Geography*, 8:89–106.

Lalive d'Epinay, C., Bickel, J.F., Maystre, C. and Vollenwyder, N. (2000) *Vieillesses au fil du temps. Une révolution tranquille.* [Old lives through time. A quiet revolution], Lausanne: Réalités sociales.

Le Gall, J. (2009) 'Le lien familial et la solidarité à l'épreuve de l'immigration. Le cas des musulmanes libanaises à Montréal' [Family ties and solidarity confronted to migration. The case of Lebanese Moslems in Montreal], *Les Politiques Sociales*, 3/4 :27–44.

Leser, M. and Seeberger, B. (1992) *Alter und Migration. Eine empirische Untersuchung an ungarischen Migranten in Basel*, [Ageing and Migration. An empirical study about Hungarian migrants in Basel], Basel: Basel and Bad Kissingen: published by the authors.

Longino, C.F. and Crown, W. (1990) 'Retirement migration and interstate income transfers', *The Gerontologist*, 30:784–789.

Oriol, M. (ed) (1984) *Les variations de l'identité* [The variations of Identity], Rapport final de l'ATP CNRS, Nice: IDERIC.

Peil, M., Ekpenyong, S.K. and Oyeneye, O.Y. (1988) 'Going home: migration careers of Southern Nigerians', *International Migration Review*, 22:4.

Piore, M.J. (1979) *Birds of Passage. Migration Labour in Industrial Societies*, Cambridge: Cambridge University Press.

Portes, A. (1996) 'Globalization from below: the rise of transnational communities', in W.P. Smith and R.P. Korczenwicz (eds) *Latin America in the World Economics*, Westport, CN: Greenwood Press, 151–168.

Portes, A. and Rumbaut, R. (1990) *Immigrant America. A Portrait*, Berkeley and Los Angeles: University of California Press.

Rodriguez, V., Casado-Diaz, M.A. and Huber, A. (eds) (2004) *Migración internacional de retirados en España* [International Migration of retirees in Spain], Madrid: Consejo superior de investigaciones científicas.

Sayad, A. (1991) *L'immigration ou les paradoxes de l'altérité* [Immigration and the paradoxes of 'the other'], Bruxelles: De Boeck-Wesmael.

Sayad, A. (1999) *La double absence* [The double absence], Paris: Seuil.

Sayad, A. (2001) 'La vacance comme pathologie de la condition immigrée. Le cas de la retraite et de la pré-retraite' [The vacancy as a pathology of the immigrant condition. The case of retirement and pre-retirement], *Revue européenne des migrations internationales*, 17(1):11–36.

Vatz Laaroussi, M. and Bolzman, C. (2010) 'Familles immigrantes et réseaux transnationaux: des articulations théoriques aux stratégies politiques' [Immigrant families and transnational networks: from theoretical links to political strategies], *Lien social et politiques*, 64:7–25.

Warnes, A.M., Friedrich, K., Kellaher, L. and Torres, S. (2004) 'The diversity and welfare of older immigrants in Europe', *Ageing & Society*, 24:307–326.

Williams, A., King, R. and Warnes, A.M. (1997) 'A place in the sun: international retirement migration from northern to southern Europe', *European Urban and Regional Studies*, 4:115–134.

FIVE

Caribbean return migration in later life: family issues and transnational experiences as influential pre-retirement factors

Dennis Conway, Robert B Potter and Godfrey St Bernard

Introduction

In this chapter we widen the scope of research enquiry into Caribbean return migration in later life and empirically examine the case of Caribbean pre-retirement and retirement return migration so that the behavioural dynamics of retirement return migration are explained more completely, if contingently. The migrant's flexibility of options is given more credence, family ties and obligations are shown to definitely 'matter' and transnational experiences and practices are additional influential determining factors for retirement-related return migration. In short, we seek to expand our understanding of the patterns and processes of lifecourse planning that underline retirement return migration in the contemporary Caribbean. In so doing, our account offers conceptual explanations that are more complex and flexible in terms of timing, motives and mobilities. First, however, the contextual background is forwarded, before proceeding with the identification (and examination) of the behavioural dynamics of Caribbean return migration in later life.

For the post-1948 'Windrush generation' of British West Indian emigrants (Peach, 1968; Lowenthal, 1972), return migration in later life has commonly been believed to be directly related to the timing of retirement in the overseas destination to which these now-elderly retirees initially emigrated; most frequently, the UK or North America – the US and Canada (Gmelch, 1992; Byron, 1999; Goulebourne, 1999). After all, many emigrated to seek better lives for themselves, their partners and children, while retaining a deeply-felt sense of belonging to the Caribbean homeland they left behind (Philpott,

1973; Fog Olwig, 2005). Also, many retained an intention to return, eventually, with retirement being a significant lifecourse event that prompted thoughts of a permanent return as a culmination of their overseas migration experience.

US-based research on 'amenity-retirement migration', versus 'assistance-migration' and 'spouse-absence migration' (Wiseman and Roseman, 1979; Litwak and Longino, 1987; Walters, 2000; Bradley, 2011), finds there are a variety of causes and reasons for such later-life migration decision making, though these authors were explicitly dealing with internal migration within the US[1]. Older movers in the US are found to be a heterogeneous mix of migrant types with decidedly different lifecourse trajectories, and varying familial/dependent relationships. The needs and motivations underlying this later-life migration of older people, therefore, are conditional on many differing situations and lifecourse transitions, so that the timing of such residential relocations is by no means generalisable and there are no definitive stages in the decision making that can be viewed as logical temporal steps. In short, the retirement date is more a referent for considering a move in later life, rather than the time at which this 'lifecourse transition' is most likely to be instigated.

Concerning the timing of a later-life move, retirement migration research in the US by Haas and Serow (1993) found that potential migrants had been actively considering retirement migration for over five years on average, while a minority among their respondents had chosen to migrate and then retire at a later date, after four or more years. More significantly, however, recent research points to a 'pre-elderly retirement transition' among US internal migrants in the 50 to 65 age cohort, whose patterns differ from those in younger and older age groups (Bures, 1997). As Bures sees it, changes in 'age-specific migration rates' in contemporary post-industrial societies – both in the global North and South – might be expected to widen and contextualise the pre-retirement and retirement transitions, so that this previously conceptualised, definitive lifecourse shift may in fact become much more flexible and indeterminate in terms of its timing. For example:

> [A]t the end of working life, a combination of factors, including continuation of the trend towards flexible retirement ages and changing family patterns, will result in a less concentrated but more substantial retirement peak ... [and] a growing proportion of pre-elderly adults can expect to live a significant number of years with few child- or job-related commitments ... Individuals may take their

longer life expectation into consideration as they evaluate
residential choices. (Bures, 1997:110–111)

So, it is this 'pre-retirement' decision making that this chapter explores,
for its empirical and contextual relevance to theory development of
later-life mobilities, and the ways in which it characterises some, but
not all, international/transnational return migrations to the Caribbean
in contemporary times. Beyond the 'bounded' geographical domain
in which US internal migration decisions in later life are undertaken,
Caribbean return migration in later life is very much affected and
conditioned by the contextually different international spaces, national
borders and 'home' and 'away-from-home' locales that both separate and
link migrants, partners and spouses, dependent children, extended and
lateral families and transnational friends (Conway, 2007). The particular
international or transnational geographies of the Caribbean diasporas
clearly distinguish and differentiate such circulations or return moves
from the patterns of internal retirement migration and later-life moves
within the US that underpinned extant theoretical discourses and
frameworks about elderly mobilities and immobilities.

For Caribbean overseas emigrants, who have retained an intention
to return to their homeland, or ancestral birthplace, return would be
expected to occur on cessation of work or completion (and termination)
of a career. Facilitating such a decision to move 'back home' would
be the acquisition of an occupational pension, and/or lump-sum
payments, and the achievement of earlier lifecourse accomplishments
that bring later-life satisfaction and senses of achievement. With the
security provided by regular fixed incomes, and with older people able
to look forward to a much longer life after the common retirement
ages of the mid-fifties and mid-sixties, return migration for elderly
emigrant cohorts in the Caribbean diaspora has become an increasingly
common practice (Plaza and Henry, 2006). Indeed, retirement return
was believed to be a major reason for such realisations of long-held
intentions, so that the return of elderly pensioners was expected to
bring the cycle of Caribbean international mobility to a successful
conclusion (Byron, 2000).

The timing of such retirement-influenced moves may not, however,
be so directly linked to the aforementioned lifecourse change
in occupational circumstances, as previously surmised. Though
retirement certainly may be one persuasive determinant for elderly
Caribbean emigrants to return home from overseas, other factors
may intervene, or pre-empt such a major decision. Among the many
influential determinants that should be expected to vary the timing

of the decision to return, or even postpone it are family obligations, generational ties and supporting efforts, partnership dissolution, divorce or widowhood. Then there are dependent children's maturation and subsequent migration decision-making to pursue their own career and partnering options, so that the older parent or parents find themselves as 'empty-nesters' and relatively independent again in terms of their mobility options. There are also family and individual family members' transnational experiences and practices that can intervene in diverse ways to influence migration potentials and prompt further mobility in pre-retirement and retirement lifecourse stages.

Among Caribbean elderly retirees, travelling to be reunited with elderly kin, siblings, and extended or lateral family members who had not emigrated, was commonly believed to strengthen their homeland yearnings and prompt thoughts of a return 'sooner or later'. However, this was often countered, or modified, by their equally powerful, strongly felt need to stay close to their immediate children who had emigrated with them, or been born overseas. This would interrupt extended family-reunification returns because these dependent 'next generations' had no intentions of leaving their new overseas homeland. Yet, when, or if, such 'next generation' children or siblings returned to their ancestral homeland, then this might prompt, or encourage a move of their elderly parents or siblings to return also and join them. Such close family ties and obligations clearly would influence the mobility propensities of all generations of Caribbean elderly during their later lives, and the ever-increasing life spans of these elderly movers' durations-of-retirement, then further extend the time frame and ensuing flexibility of movement options.

Caribbean return migration in later life: conceptual frames

The conceptual frames we see as influential to return migration decision making in later life are now presented, and their brief characterisations lend further support to our more complex and flexible explanations, which depart from definitive and predictable lifecourse stages determined by ageing time lines. We believe strongly, with a confidence bolstered by our own qualitative research on Trinidadian's return motivations and experiences in mid-career and mid-life (Conway et al 2008, 2009a, 2009b; Conway and Potter, 2009, 2012; Potter et al 2009, 2010) that later-life return migration is significantly influenced by family love and obligations, intergenerational ties, transnational practices and experiences. Family assistance-migration also features in the mix.

Significantly, 'coming and going' and 'returning and re-returning' feature among the options open to some elderly, first-generation Caribbean migrants as well as to their more youthful but now quite elderly 'next generations' who are contemplating a return home for a while, at least. And, a distinct contextual factor, amenity-migration, also characterises later-life mobility for some Caribbean returnees. In addition, note must be taken of the demographic extensions of the later-life time-period for ageing returnees, which also serve to modify the patterns and processes of lifecourse planning that underline pre-retirement transition practices and experiences, pre-retirement return migration, and retirement return migration in the contemporary Caribbean.

Caribbean conceptual frames

Family 'love'

Intergenerational ties and obligations between first-generation elderly parents who have returned – either as a pre-retirement relocation or a retirement relocation – and their transnational migrant offspring – now in later life in their fifties and looking towards retirement within the following two decades – prompt or strongly influence pre-retirement return migration of the 'next generations' – 1.5-generations, second and even youthful third generations (Conway and Potter, 2009). Elderly couples, or individuals who have experienced loss or death of their partner, may return to their ancestral homeland in the Caribbean to seek the companionship and familial assistance of their siblings and lateral-family kin, who had moved back earlier, or who had never left.

Like many others in contemporary societies who are afflicted by demographic pressures in their immediate-family relationships and partnership disappointments, Caribbean emigrants or prolonged sojourners are also equally prone to experience family divorce, partner-separation, the early deaths of husbands (or wives), or the return (or onward migration) of one or the other in such disrupted partnerships. Such lifecourse events may have direct and indirect effects on further migration decision making. And, when their dependent children are involved in the mix, then all sorts of options, including return migration, or staying abroad longer may be anticipated among Caribbean transnational families in mid-family formation, mid-career and even in later life.

Intergenerational family ties, and firmly held family obligations, further add to the variety of lifecourse transitions that immediate, lateral and extended families experience; including their 'mobilities'. Generational ties and intergenerational ties are reinforced by 'family love' and familial responsibilities to each other, and encourage transnational practices such as frequent telephoning (Vertovec, 2004), repetitive return visiting (Duval, 2004; Conway et al, 2009a), and return vacations to attend family reunions at Christmas, to participate in external- and lateral-family wedding celebrations, and attend funerals of 'dearly departed' loved ones (Sutton, 2004).

As the first generations of transnational migrants reach retirement ages and beyond, generational and intergenerational 'family ties that bind' also influence the migration decision making of their next generations as care givers, or dependents. If the first generation return to the Caribbean and age into their eighties and nineties, then health care issues loom as an obvious concern for them. The return migration of their grown-up children, often with their own immediate family responsibilities for their 'next generations', may be one option, but the multiple responsibilities will obviously complicate decision making, or at the very least make the issues at stake entangled with family emotions, and sensitive dealings of family ties, obligations and responsibilities. Again, we might expect various scenarios to play out in such entangled, intergenerational, familial support systems among contemporary Caribbean transnational families (Goulebourne and Chamberlain, 2001; Chamberlain, 2006).

Assistance-migration

Family obligations to care for elderly parents strongly influence later-life moves of their grown-up dependents, with a common practice being for widows and widowers who outlive their spouses moving into the home of their daughter, or married son. In the case of return moves of emigrants to the Caribbean that are 'assistance-migrations', the process may be reversed with 'first-generation' elderly emigrants returning home on retirement, and the next generations following them later. Alternatively, independent elderly parents or pairs of elderly parents who have returned to reunite with siblings who never left, or transnational siblings who have also returned after retirement, may have a sufficient social safety net and familial support network 'back home' for them to not need their next generations' assistance.

'Place attachment': long-held intentions to return 'sooner or later'

Pre-retirement return migration fulfils a long-held desire of the next-generations to eventually return to their national 'birthplace', or the ancestral home of their parent, or parents (Philpott, 1973; Conway and Potter, 2009). Stoller and Longino (2001) remind us that personal responsibilities and place ties intertwine so that circulations among family members build familiarity and security for later life adjustments, whether such moves are internal or international. McHugh and Mings (1996) conceptualised this as '[t]he circle of migration: attachment to place in aging' in which internal migrants in the US 'take journeys to and from home places ... in three phases – separation, experience and return – over varying time frames, ranging from a single annual cycle to recurring cycles over the lifecourse.' (McHugh and Mings, 1996:530). Developing a desire to return home to their ancestral homeland or that of their parent(s) could also be developed while overseas, could be encouraged and strengthened while making repetitive visits, or could be developed through transnational extended/lateral family links and the help and encouragement provided by transnational social networks.

Temporary circulation as a transnational strategy

Transnational migrants in later life may choose a 'va-et-vient' retirement strategy, where elderly overseas emigrants choose to share their time between the ancestral homeland and the overseas 'home away from home' (De Coulon and Wolff, 2006). Such 'coming and going' circulation in later life continues patterns undertaken earlier in life, learned by way of family or individual histories of repetitive visiting (Conway et al, 2009a). Acquiring dual citizenship via binational partnerships, birthright or permanent residency, among other institutional pathways in overseas territories also facilitates such temporary sojourns and is likely to 'arbitrate' decisions to return to the ancestral homeland both during pre-retirement, transition periods and in post-retirement (Conway et al, 2008). 'Making the best of both worlds' becomes part of their livelihood strategising, so that maintaining transnational ties between their homelands – 'homes' and 'homes away from home' – in the Caribbean and overseas is to be an expected strategy among Caribbean returnees in later life, whether at pre-retirement (forties and fifties) or retirement (65+) ages (Conway, 2007). By keeping their mobility options open for a 're-return' rather than settling 'back home' for good, elderly returnees are maintaining 'flexibility' in their future plans, and 'maximising freedom' (Thomas-Hope, 2006), particularly useful should health problems require attention that is available and better provided in the overseas home.

Amenity return migration

Amenity-migration among internal migrants in the US has been found to have a distinctive spatial pattern that follows a search, or searches, for attractive climate and leisure amenities (Haas and Serow, 1997). Retirement, loss of a spouse, varying degrees of disability, health and adequate incomes, are lifecourse events and contexts that are expected to influence later-life decisions to move to 'amenity-rich places' in later life (Haas and Serow, 1993; Walters, 2002). Caribbean pre-retirement and retirement return migration, therefore, will be obvious variants of this amenity-seeking behaviour, because the tropical and subtropical island environments of the returnees' homelands are often perceived to offer superior climate and leisure opportunities, which may be enjoyed in later life, as a 'satisfying' decision, if not necessarily an optimal, final one.

Supportive and qualifying trinidadian 'narratives': variety reigns

The 2004/2005 snowball-sample of returning Trinidadians that we interviewed[2] (including two Tobagonians) consisted of 40 respondents, who were identified as 'returning nationals' or 'citizens by descent'[3]. Most were returning from the UK, Canada and the US in mid-career and mid-family stages of their lifecourse, in their forties and fifties. No returnees who had been forced to return, such as US deportees, were included, so the majority of our sample returned voluntarily. More than half of our sample of returnees acknowledged that one or both of their parents lived in Trinidad at the time they themselves returned. A few now-elderly parents had preceded them as 'first-generation' returnees who had left Trinidad and Tobago for Britain and North America during the 1950s and 1960s, and who had returned in later life on retirement, or earlier in anticipation of retirement. Several other elderly parents had never left Trinidad for any appreciable length of time, but many of our respondents' siblings had, with some returning in pre-retirement too. Indirectly, these first-generations' pre-retirement and retirement experiences are referenced in this chapter through the life-stories of their offspring – our respondents – who we actually interviewed.

Of those we interviewed, nine were second generation, seven one-and-a-half (1.5) generation, and twenty-four 'prolonged sojourners' (labelled as 'Sojourner' in Table 5.1). Second generation returnees have been born abroad and are returning to the country of one or more of their first-generation emigrant parents or parent; the one-and-a-half generation are returning to the birthplace they left as children accompanying their emigrant parents or parent; and the 'prolonged sojourners', who were also born in Trinidad and Tobago are returning after they emigrated independently as youths in their late teens and early twenties seeking further education, work opportunities or better opportunities. We include the latter as a significant 'return cohort', because their stays abroad commonly exceed 12 years – indeed, the mean and median for the whole snowball sample of returnees is 17 years – so they all have had plenty of time to acquire the metropolitan and cosmopolitan traits of transnational experience before returning in their thirties, forties and fifties (Conway et al, 2009b). Table 5.1 'identifies' the migration pedigrees and birthplaces of the respondents we quote in this chapter; names have been changed to ensure anonymity.

Table 5.1: Demographic and migration attributes of 'quoted respondents'

Pseudonym	Age at interview	Cohort	Place of birth	Country returned from
Elton	47	Sojourner	Trinidad	USA
Charles	57	Sojourner	Trinidad	Canada
Julia	31	Sojourner	Trinidad	UK
Sandra	35	Sojourner	Trinidad	USA
Garth	45	Sojourner	Trinidad	USA
Ernest	53	1.5 generation	Trinidad	UK
Monica	39	Sojourner	Trinidad	Canada
Carol	41	Sojourner	Tobago	UK
Vera	41	1.5 generation	St Vincent	UK
Laura	38	Sojourner	Trinidad	USA
Catherine	34	2nd generation	Canada	Canada
Sonora	40	1.5 generation	Trinidad	USA

Although none of our respondents were in the age cohorts usually associated with retirement (the post-65 years cohort), we believe an examination of this data set contains 'narratives' that can be drawn upon to substantiate some of the hypothetical modifications to later-life migration decision making offered in this chapter. Quotes drawn from our respondents' 'narratives' and life stories are used to answer a series of questions about their experiences and practices on return, which pertain to their return decision making, and to their pre-retirement transitions that are already occurring or will follow during their later years. We frame the constructs, with reference to the various influences that have helped determine our respondents' return decision making while they are in mid-career and mid-family formation. In doing so, we fully embrace Chamberlain's (2006) convincing theoretical and methodological arguments on why Caribbean family 'closeness' and 'family love' are abiding themes among the contemporary generations of transnational family members, both within and beyond the region (also see Chamberlain, 2005), and why intergenerational obligations invariably feature in family decision making among extended and lateral families during their intertwined lifecourse transitions, particularly in pre-retirement and retirement. Saliently, important events like international moves are firmly remembered and become embedded in Caribbean peoples' life stories, and the resultant comparative, transnational cultural contexts reinforce such memories and recall. Methodological robustness is therefore assured by this qualitative maxim (Chamberlain, 2006).

More specifically, we examine our Trinidadian transnational respondents' self-expressed motives and reasons for their 'return migration in later life' in which the return and presence of their elderly parents features prominently for several among our sample. We also seek a better understanding of the ways our Trinidadian transnational respondents are already thinking ahead, anticipating and planning their future, while keeping their options open, flexible and contingent on 'how t'ings turn out'.

Return for several of our respondents turns out not to be a final permanent relocation, but more a temporary 'coming and going' or a 'va-et-vient' pre-retirement re-return. Worthy of note is that all but 10 of our respondents' elderly mothers were alive in Trinidad at the time of our interviews. Their elderly fathers were not in such abundance 'back home', however, there being only twenty still alive and residing in Trinidad, and nine in retirement elsewhere – two in Canada, the UK and the US, and one each in Venezuela, Jamaica and St Vincent. A few of our respondents' elderly parent couples had divorced and gone their separate ways, with one consequence of this being a widening of these Trinidadian respondents' transnational social fields and the formation of binational family allegiances, which either hindered return to the twin island nation or prompted it.

Return migrants' own 'migration-stories' on later-life decision making

Drawing selectively from our 2004/2005 sample of respondents, we highlight the commonalities in experiences, practices and behaviours that characterise their later-life transitions, their decision making and pre-retirement adjustments to life 'back home'.

Though variety occurs more often than singular generalisations, several general commonalities can be garnered from the respondents' 'stories'. We, therefore use our respondent's own words (though not their real names, which are replaced by pseudonym) to empirically demonstrate the features (and factors) of influence and substance in their adjustments on return to Trinidad and Tobago. First, we explore several sub-themes in respect of 'family obligations and family love'; we then examine a number of 'flexible strategies' as regards 'coming and going'.

Family obligations and family love

In this particular section we are especially interested in how 'family matters' feature in their decision making. We focus on the possible influence of concerns for immediate family members, and links with a parent or parents, grandparents, siblings, aunts and uncles among the relatively youthful Trinidadians in our interviewed sample.

Parental reinforcement of the desire to return

Three of our respondents – Elton, Charles and Julia – indicated they had always harboured a desire to return; all citing their parents as influential in this respect. Charles also indicated that in addition to his long-held desire to return, he felt Trinidad was also the best place for his children to be brought up. After spending 19 years in the US, Elton (47 at time of interview) stressed that his parents' influence during his upbringing was a major reason why he had returned:

> 'I grew up in a background where my parents always feel committed to government and the Public Service, so I think that was the environment and they always talking about serving, and if everybody leave, they talk about the brain-drain and all this kind of thing. So that, from very early, it was always an option for me to return to Trinidad.

So that, although I had spent some time working there ...
the option was always in my mind to return to Trinidad.'

Elton's mother was especially influential in providing guidance and
assistance in developing his life skills, and social consciousness, as well
as providing him with care and affection and family love:

'Well, in my home, my father was a teacher, my mother was
a housewife ... . But she was the one who was influential
in everything we did home, you know, support wise ... .
And today I still do the same thing – that giving – I try to
show my children the same thing.'

Returning from Canada after acquiring higher education and skills,
Charles was another who stressed the major role his family played in
assisting him to return home to Trinidad, and also felt very strongly
about his social obligations and ties to his homeland, so that return for
him was always a question of when, not if:

'Well, it has always been my desire to work in Trinidad, to
live in Trinidad, to bring up a family in Trinidad because
all I knew was Trinidad and even with my experience in
the metropole, I still felt I had a bonding to Trinidad, the
home of my birth. I feel to myself that I am a patriotic
citizen; I really love my country and even though I find the
life in Canada was more amenable for advancement and
opportunity, yet, I still had that yearning to be back once
I had qualified.'

Returning from the UK after 12 years abroad, Julia also commented on
her parents' guidance and assistance, but was adamant that her parents
were not so much demanding that she return as helpful and concerned
in their family support:

'Kind of half and half ... I think in their hearts they wanted
to have their child home with them, to spend time with
them and that kind of stuff. On the other side, in terms of
guiding me, they were not so sure in terms of me coming
home, whether it was a good thing for me to be coming
home or not in terms of what I want, professional or career
wise, that kind of thing. They weren't so sure that it was a
good idea for me to come home, and on the other hand

they wanted their daughter to come home and spend time with them ... For the past year of me being here in Trinidad I have been living with them. So they have been that kind of support where I don't have to go out and find somewhere else to live.'

Family assistance-return

Additionally, two of our respondents, Garth and Ernest, insisted that they had returned in response to parental needs: such as elderly fathers or mothers seeking their son's or daughter's return, or problems such as illness that necessitated a return of the migrant or his or her spouse to help look after an elderly or sick parent. Garth returned from the US after 24 years away. His return was motivated, in part, by amenity considerations for his later life and in part by his dad's illness. He put it this way:

> 'I did intend to retire [in the US] and go to Florida, so I figure I should just get a head start and come to Trinidad. I am in my forties and I would finish my career here when I retire. ... My dad was sick last year, so when that happens you start thinking – family is kind of important, even though my kids were there [in the US], I figured that my Dad needed me around more than my kids at that time ... the kids are at an age now where I likely can be away from them for an extended period ... So the fact that they are at a decent age now made the decision easier for me.'

Ernest returned after a persistent campaign by his ageing mother to have him, his Trinidadian spouse and their three children (her grandchildren) come back home from the UK. In part, this 'parental pressure' was because her three daughters had left for the States leaving her alone, and in part because she missed her only son. It took 10 years of temporary visits, and a heavy dose of emotional arguments before Ernest's mind was made up, and he brought his family 'back home':

> 'I talked it over with some of my friends and many of whom had ideas that they were gonna come back to Trinidad anyway shortly, and we talked about it a lot, and it took quite a long time, it took the best part of ... maybe 10 years before we came back ... [in between] we came to Trinidad five times.'

Ernest didn't think returning and adjusting to life back home in Trinidad was easy even after taking so long to decide, so he has kept his options open to re-return to the UK once his children have 'left the family nest'.

Family warmth in a comfortable climate

With their ancestral roots and family in tropical Trinidad, a few of our returning respondents would mix rationales for return, by adding Trinidad's favourable and warm environment as an incentive to quit the cold of North America and the UK and join their family. Returning from Canada after 19 years, Monica had this to say about the decisive influence of family, especially her dad; coupled with the additional benefit of escaping the Canadian winters for the Caribbean tropics:

> 'I guess you can say after spending 19 years abroad in a very cold country, and most of my family being back in Trinidad, that was the compelling factor for me to come back. My family was here, and I got a little bit tired of the cold weather, I wanted to be back in the hot weather.'

Trinidad's societal warmth and hospitality, in extended families and in schools, as well as Trinidadians' expressive and sincere 'love for children', came through as an important contextual consideration for several child-rearing couples, who had returned. Also important in a number of cases was the availability of transnational friendship and support networks, influencing interest in moving between the respective countries.

Flexible strategies: transnational 'va-et-vient': 'coming and going' in later life

Transnational migrants in later life may choose a 'va-et-vient' retirement strategy, instead of a permanent and final return to their ancestral homeland (de Coulon and Wolff, 2006). Building upon experiences acquired while undertaking repetitive temporary circulations between the ancestral homeland and the overseas 'home away from home', such 'coming and going' circulation in later life continues patterns undertaken earlier in life, learned or habitually practiced by way of family or individual histories of repetitive visiting (Conway et al, 2009b). Some returnees will seek to maintain flexible options for the future, whether during pre-retirement transitionary stages, or at later-life retirement ages, which involve a re-return, a move back for a while, or other equally indeterminate choices. Others might choose to return for good, and forego any further flexible ambiguity or uncertainty. Still others keep their later-life options open, in part because two decades or more of unfettered elderly mobility is at least a realistic demographic possibility for the most healthy. There is evidence, also, that the acquisition of dual citizenship via binational partnerships, birthright or permanent residency, among other institutional pathways in overseas territories, does appear to facilitate 'cross-border mobility, the maintenance of patterns of temporary circulations (Conway et al, 2008), and, 'va-et-vient' temporary circuits of return and re-return.

Significance of dual citizenship and binational identities

Dual citizenship and binational identities, respectively, are formal and personal acquisitions (and valuable products or outcomes) of transnational experiences and practices, so that they feature as influential factors in later life and mid-career determinations in returnees' lifecourse decision making. Two of our respondents' 'migration-stories' demonstrate this.

Catherine is a second-generation returnee with a dual, 'binational' identity, because she was born in Canada – her mother's birthplace – then raised in Trinidad – her father's birthplace. When her Canadian mother divorced her Trinidadian husband, Catherine accompanied her estranged mother to Canada. Catherine, therefore, grew up in Canada, married a Canadian, but retained her love for her father's family and visited Trinidad a few times despite the feuding between her parents. Her firm ties and positive feelings towards Trinidad and her Trinidadian extended family are explained this way:

> 'I think what I wanted, in moving back, was to come home, because Trinidad has always been my earliest experience and memories and my childhood was spent here. So it will always feel like home. That was a part of it. Facing the prospect of having my own children was a big motivator to examine how I wanted to raise my children and where I would want to raise the children ... And I considered the values of the community I had experienced within Trinidad to be a very positive set of values – values about community, about sharing responsibility for each other's children, about looking out for each other, not only in the family but the whole extended family. Trinidadians keep

this huge extended family; everybody is your auntie and uncle. You know, you have cousins and they are not even related to you. I find that very heartening. I find that is a very warm and supportive environment in which to raise children. So that was a big motivator and finally the fact that I have older relatives in Trinidad and I don't want the time to slip away before it's too late for me to spend more time with them. They are retiring and they need more support at home. So I came back to spend more time with them. … My long term goal is I should never have to say no to one country or one lifestyle or one part of my family, and cut them out of my life the way I had to for the first 10 years after moving away. So my long term goal is I should be able to call Trinidad home and call Canada home.'

Sonora is a 1.5-generation migrant who returned to Trinidad from the US with her American husband and bi-national children after 22 years. She had been raised by her grandmother and aunt in Trinidad. Then, when Sonora was 10 years old, the whole family relocated to the US, where she grew up, got advanced degrees and built her career. Her reason for moving back was inexplicably unique, as she explains:

'The reason I came back was that after living in the US for a while, even though I was having a great time, I came back at around the age of nineteen or something – and sort of rediscovered Trinidad. And I promised myself that one day I will return. I have no idea why I said that; I have no idea why I was committed, but I told myself one day I would return and actually that was the sort of inspiration [for how] I discovered international development.'

Sonora insisted that she and her husband were pragmatists in comparison to some of her Trinidadian relatives who had returned and been disappointed:

'We visited together many times deliberately to acclimatise ourselves … So we kind of knew what we were coming back into, because we have relatives who came back. They came back; they retired and they had this fantasy of coming back and falling back on the retirement money from the States and build their house and come back to realise that

Trinidad is not that beautiful place they left. So I think there is a huge difference between that sort of fantasy and taking a more pragmatist view … We just felt we'll come back; we'll give it a couple of years and after that, if we stay, we stay. If we didn't want to stay, we'd leave. So, no real commitment. It's now been six years later and we're still here and still not committed one way or the other. We just stay because we love it.'

Concerning her immediate family's future migration options, Sonora pragmatically evaluated the usefulness of her spouse and children's dual identity:

'I think if I was here and my husband was not a foreigner, I probably would not have held on to my US papers but, because he is, I feel we need to maintain his options and now I am part of his options and our children are part of that option. So, yes, we have to maintain our options because at the end of the day, that's his home and my second home and because it has been such a great experience over there. I really have nothing to complain about the US you know. When you think about it, we didn't run away from there, we ran to here. We love here, but if we have to go back tomorrow for whatever reason I will embrace that as well, because we need to maintain those options. … We prefer Trinidad, we really do – but we got to keep the options open; you never know.'

Alternatively, some are 'home to stay'

One of our respondents did not follow the practice of other transnational returnees to keep their options for more mobility in later life open and flexible (also see Thomas-Hope 2006). Elton, who featured earlier in this examination of Trinidadian returnees' migration-stories, eschewed dual citizenship to come back home 'for good':

'Nah, nah, I ain't going nowhere. I had a green card and all that kind of thing and I choose to give it up … because … well because of the stipulations when you go in they want to know why you was out so long … I am coming back home. I am Trinidadian. Every opportunity I had to come home I would come. The time away from home was just for developmental reasons. In a way you have to, you know, thinking about coming back home to help Trinidad and Tobago ... bring this country to developed country status.'

Although Elton's return reasoning is altruistic and nationalistic, he certainly views this pre-retirement move back home as a final one, so that his later-life years in retirement during the decades that follow will also be spent 'back home'. This is opposite to the more flexible transnational options others among our respondents prefer, with 'nationalism' sentiments trumping transnational pragmatism in this case.

Conclusions

In this chapter, we have widened the frame of return migration decision making during the later-life stages of older people to incorporate pre-retirement, transitionary experiences into the theoretical explanations of later-life return migration in the Caribbean and elsewhere. Our empirical observations drew upon selective quotes from returnees' narratives and migration life-stories which detailed the transnational experiences of a sample of Trinidadian return migrants who had returned to their ancestral twin-island home nation in mid-career and mid-family formation stages, in their forties and fifties. Notably, return intentions among most of our respondents were developed early in life, with repetitive visiting being a relatively common practice.

Return intentions might have been at the heart of later-life moves 'back home', but the role of family obligations and family love also featured as prominently, both as indirect and direct influences on return decision making – its timing, its reasons, its family-strengthening consequences, its family bonds. For the majority of returnees, one or both of their parents lived in Trinidad at the time they decided to go back. Most, therefore, returned with the knowledge that family and relatives would be available to provide them with all kinds of support, help and assistance as they adjusted to the first months of return – the most stressful period for such 'newcomers'; a fact that has implications for policy in taking into account the inter-generational character of return migration.

This essential supporting role was built upon long-held traditions of Trinidadian, Tobagonian (and Caribbean) family obligations and family love, both within immediate families, among family-generations and disbursed through extended and lateral families of 'tanties' and 'uncles' (Plaza, 2001; Sutton, 2004; Chamberlain, 2005; Fog Olwig, 2005). Children's wellbeing and educational progress also featured prominently as a rationale for returning nationals as mothers and fathers consider and eventually undertake a return home to the twin island nation of their birthplace, or that of their parents.

Social linkages featured prominently as partial reasons, but in addition, success and satisfaction with employment, professional advancement and job satisfaction meant a lot too, in terms of considering returning, staying, or only staying for a while. Enjoying life to the full during later-life transitions, both before and after formal retirement ages, does not prevent returning nationals from undertaking meaningful work, rewarding vocational activities, professional services fitting their qualifications and volunteering in community services. Hence, the adjustment transitions that our respondents are undertaking are within the 'life-path' of the more elderly, later-life stages that our 30+, 40+ and early fifties respondents are moving towards as they age.

In summary, it would appear that Bures (1997) has it right concerning the increasing flexibility and contingency of later-life behaviours, including return migration decision making, where there is a wider 'window' for pre-retirement and retirement mobility, where longer durations of life as ageing elderly retirees can be expected. We would take exception to only one of Bures' (1997;110–111) claims, which concerns her idea that elderly and pre-elderly adults might be expected both to have fewer child- and fewer job-related commitments as they evaluate residential choices. In our Caribbean case, Trinidadian returnees might also behave as 'empty-nesters' and might not seek regular employment on return at retirement ages. However, during pre-retirement and in mid-career and mid-family stages of their lifecourse, they have both deep parental and familial commitments to their children and firm commitments to furthering their careers on their return.

Family love and family obligations run deep in the majority of our returnees' reasoning for returning and succeeding 'back home'. Flexibility and variety in timing of such choices cautions us to not make such definitive associations, as if retirement and later life are devoid of social agency, of transnational praxis and are without new (or continuing) career, or work goals.

With some pre-retirement returnees looking forward to retirement and 'staying for good' in Trinidad or Tobago, their transnational family network, whether back home or remaining overseas, is likely to continue as a valuable source of familial support and 'love', of health assistance and impromptu necessary social resources – which could involve temporary visits overseas as long as the older person's physical capabilities are not diminished to the point of preventing air travel.

Continued access to pensions acquired during careers abroad facilitates transnational flexibility in later life. Returnees' use of home-equity loans and bequeathed estates to purchase a 'second home', or even 'assisted living accommodation', adds to the transnational migrants' freedom to contemplate future moves 'back and forth' in later life. This can occur even if such mobility is most likely temporary, or transitory, rather than another permanent relocation to a penultimate or final 'place of rest'.

From a policy-point of view, the return of professionals with strong ties to their ancestral homeland, and the needed skills and experience has been heralded as a 'brain gain' to partially offset the 'brain drain' of previous cohorts of emigrants (Hugo, 2003; Conway and Potter, 2007). Caribbean public-private policies aimed at attracting more highly skilled professionals with the right experiences, entrepreneurialism and social commitments will need to be sensitive to the central roles that transnationalism and family ties and obligations play in making the return home an attractive option for such sought-after, returning nationals. Aggressive policies of recruitment and enticement are most probably not going to be effective, unless family love and obligations and transnational flexibilities and 'freedoms' are fully recognised and incorporated into their planning. After all, as Carnegie (1982) noted three decades ago, migration – whether a return move, a temporary circulation, or a re-return – is most effective for all concerned when it is both voluntary and 'strategically flexible'.

References

Atkinson, P. and Flint, J. (2001) 'Accessing hidden and hard-to-reach populations: Snowball research strategies', *Social Research Update*, 33 (Summer):1–4.

Bradley, D.E. (2011) 'Litwak and Longino's developmental model of later-life migration: evidence from the American Community Survey', *Journal of Applied Gerontology*, 30(2): 141–158.

Bures, R.M. (1997) 'Migration and the lifecourse: Is there a retirement transition?' *International Journal of Population Geography*, 3:109–119.

Byron, M. (1999) 'The Caribbean–born population in 1990s Britain: Who will return?' *Journal of Ethnic and Migration Studies*, 25:285–301.

Byron, M. (2000) 'Return migration to the eastern Caribbean: comparative experiences and policy implications', *Social and Economic Studies*, 47:155–188.

Carnegie, C.V. (1982) 'Strategic flexibility in the West Indies', *Caribbean Review*, 11(1):11–13, 54.

Chamberlain, M. (2005) 'Language, identity and Caribbean families: transnational narratives', in J. Besson and K. Fog Olwig (eds) *Caribbean Narratives of Belonging: Fields of Relations, Sites of Identity*, Oxford: MacMillan Caribbean, pp 171–188.

Chamberlain, M. (2006) *Family Love in the Diaspora: Migration and the Anglo-Caribbean Experience*, New Brunswick, NJ: Transaction Publishers.

Conway, D. (2007) 'Caribbean transnational migration behaviour: reconceptualizing its "strategic flexibility"', *Population, Space and Place*, 13:415–431.

Conway, D., Potter, R.B. and St Bernard, G. (2008) 'Dual citizenship or dual identity? Does "transnationalism" supplant "nationalism" among returning Trinidadians?' *Global Networks*, 8(4):373–397.

Conway, D., Potter, R.B. and St Bernard, G. (2009a) 'Repetitive visiting as a pre-return transnational strategy among youthful Trinidadian returnees', *Mobilities*, 14(2):249–273.

Conway, D., Potter, R.B. and St Bernard, G. (2009b) 'Returning youthful Trinidadian migrants: prolonged sojourners' transnational experiences', in D. Conway and R.B. Potter (eds) *Return Migration of the Next Generations: 21st Century Transnational Mobility*, Aldershot: Ashgate, pp 161–183.

Conway, D. and Potter, R.B. (2007) 'Caribbean transnational return migrants as agents of change', *Blackwell Geography Compass*, 1(1):25–45.

Conway, D. and Potter, R.B. (2009) *Return Migration of the Next Generations: 21st Century Transnational Mobility*, Aldershot: Ashgate.

Conway D. and Potter, R.B. (2012) 'Transnational urbanism in Port of Spain: Returning middle-class urban elites', *Urban Geography*, 33(5):700–727.

De Coulon, A. and Wolff, F.-C. (2006) 'The location of immigrants at retirement: stay/return or "va-et-vient"?' *IZA Discussion Paper, No. 2224*, Bonn, Germany: Institute for the Study of Labor.

Duval, D.T. (2004) 'Linking return visits and return migration among Commonwealth Eastern Caribbean migrants in Toronto', *Global Networks*, 4(1):51–67.

Fog Olwig, K. (2005) 'Narratives of home: visions of "betterment" and belonging in a dispersed Caribbean family', in J. Besson and K. Fog Olwig (eds) *Caribbean Narratives of Belonging: Fields of Relations, Sites of Identity*, London: Macmillan Caribbean, pp 189–205.

Gmelch, G. (1992) *Double Passage: the Lives of Caribbean Migrants and Back Home*, Ann Arbor, MI: University of Michigan Press.

Goulebourne, H. (1999) 'Exodus? Some social and policy implications of return migration from the UK to the Commonwealth Caribbean in the 1990s', *Policy Studies*, 20(3):157–72.

Goulebourne, H. and Chamberlain, M. (2001) *Caribbean Families in Britain and the Trans-Atlantic World*, London: Macmillan Caribbean.

Haas, W.H. III and Serow, W.J. (1993) 'Amenity retirement migration process: a model and preliminary evidence', *The Gerontologist*, 33(2):212–220.

Haas, W.H. III and Serow, W.J. (1997) 'Retirement migration decision making: lifecourse mobility, sequencing of events, social ties and alternatives', *Journal of the Community Development Society*, 28(1):116–130.

Hugo, G. (2003) 'Circular migration: keeping development rolling?' *Migration Information Source*, Washington, DC: Migration Policy Institute. Available at: www.migrationinformation.org/feature/print.cfm?ID=129

Litwak, E. and Longino, C.F. Jr. (1987) 'Migration patterns among the elderly: a developmental perspective', *The Gerontologist*, 27:266–272.

Lowenthal, D. (1972) *West Indian Societies*, Oxford: Oxford University Press.

McHugh, K.E. and Mings, R.C. (1996) 'The circle of migration: attachment to place in aging', *Annals, Association of American Geographers*, 86(3):530–550.

Peach, C. (1968) *West Indian Migration to Britain: A Social Geography*, Oxford: Oxford University Press for the Institute of Race Relations.

Philpott, S. (1973) *West Indian Migration: The Montserrat Case*, London: Athlone Press.

Plaza, D. (2001) 'Ageing in Babylon: elderly Caribbeans in Britain', in H. Goulebourne and M. Chamberlain (eds) *Caribbean Families in Britain and the Trans-Atlantic World*, London: Macmillan Caribbean, pp 219–234.

Plaza, D.E. and Henry, F. (2006) *Returning to the Source: The Final Stage of the Caribbean Migration Circuit*, Jamaica, Barbados and Trinidad and Tobago: University of the West Indies Press.

Potter R.B., Conway D. and St Bernard, G. (2009) 'Transnationalism personified: young returning Trinidadians, "in their own words"', *Tidschrift voor Economische en Sociale Geografie*, 100(1):101–113.

Potter, R.B., Conway, D. and St Bernard, G. (2010) '"Racism in a melting pot?" Trinidadian mid-life transnational migrants' views on race and colour-class on return to their homes of descent', *Geoforum*, 41:805–813.

Stoller, E.P. and Longino, C.F. Jr. (2001) '"Going home" or "leaving home"? The impact of person and place ties on anticipated counterstream migration', *The Gerontologist*, 41(1):96–102.

Sutton, C.R. (2004) 'Celebrating ourselves: the family reunion rituals of African-Caribbean transnational families', *Global Networks*, 4(3):243–257.

Thomas-Hope, E.M. (2006) 'Maximizing migration: Caribbean return movements and the organization of transnational space', in D.E. Plaza and F. Henry (eds) *Returning to the Source: The Final Stage of the Caribbean Migration Circuit*, Mona, Jamaica: University of West Indies Press, pp 167–187.

Vertovec, S. (2004) 'Cheap calls: the social glue of migrant transnationalism', *Global Networks: A Journal of Transnational Affairs*, 42(2):219–224.

Walters, W.H. (2000) 'Types and patterns of later-life migration', *Geografiska Annaler B*, 82(3):129–147.

Walters, W.H. (2002) 'Later-life migration in the United States: a review of recent research', *CPL Bibliography, Journal of Planning Literature*, 17(1):38–66.

Wiseman, R.F. and Roseman, C.C. (1979) 'A typology of elderly migration based upon the decision making process', *Economic Geography*, 55(4):324–337.

.

SIX

'We belong to the land': British immigrants in Australia contemplating or realising their return 'home' in later life

John Percival

> Though earth holds many splendours,
> Wherever I may die,
> I know to what brown country
> My homing thoughts will fly
>
> *My country* by Dorothea Mackellar

Introduction

Dorothea Mackellar's poem, of which the above is the final verse, was written when she was homesick in England, far away from her birthplace in Australia. It is an iconic and romantic rendition, which evocatively recalls the pastoral landscape of England before rejoicing in Australia's more rugged geography and the poet's love for this homeland. The poem was given to me in Australia by one of my British born respondents, who, like many featured in this chapter, recognised its underlying sentiments, most particularly those enshrined in the final verse, although in their case 'homing thoughts' were to a more lush and less brown country.

During the course of my social gerontology research and my social work practice over the years, I have occasionally heard older people talk of a heartfelt desire to return to their place of birth or childhood before the end of their life. A vague interest in this phenomenon grew as I myself became older, but was only fully ignited when two unexpected events took place, in quick succession. The first was a visit to Sydney, Australia, the city of my birth and early childhood, to present a paper at a gerontology conference. Although not having set foot in that country for over 30 years, on leaving the airport and travelling though the city I suddenly, and unexpectedly, had an overwhelming feeling of being 'home'. The second relevant event was a chance sighting of a message posted on a BBC website, from an English woman who had watched a TV programme about post-World War Two emigrants to Australia, of which she was one. Her message read, 'I am too British to change my nationality and never will regret coming back [after 30 years]. As the years went on, my dread was that I would die before returning.'

I subsequently decided to send a letter to the editor of a major Australian newspaper, inviting interested readers to contact me with their views on return migration in later life. Over the following two months I received 50 replies (email and letter) from older people who originally emigrated to Australia in the 1950s, 1960s and 1970s, replies that typically provided biographical accounts and personal reflections that testify to the importance and complexity of this subject, and its apparent profound influence on respondents' current wellbeing and future life plans. Those who initially contacted me spoke of their interest in return migration as something that had significantly increased following retirement, when they had more time to reflect on their priorities in their third age and beyond. In this respect, correspondents spoke of their identity with, and yearning for, their native place, referring to the culture, history or landscapes that they missed, as well as for reconnection with important family members in Britain. It was also clear from emails and letters that profound feelings were involved when considering the subject of return migration, as well as elements of puzzlement, continuous deliberation, and difficulty sharing thoughts and feelings with close family in Australia. Indeed, one or two respondents thanked me for providing an opportunity to 'crystallise' their thoughts, as one put it. An illustrative and representative selection of this early correspondence follows:

> 'When I return [from the UK] I cannot look at photos I have taken, I miss it so much. It seems to be like a magnet, calling me back ...' [Mrs JF]

> 'Since going back to my homeland and spending time with my sister I've become torn ... It seems the older I get the more I think of where I've come from.' [Mrs JT]

> 'Having raised a family of three, we are now grandparents as well, seven grandchildren. We are seriously considering returning to our country of birth to spend our remaining

years there. The reasons for that desire are somewhat obscure to ourselves, and nearly impossible to explain to those that we love.' [Mr H]

Encouraged by the range of heartfelt responses, and the rich collection of issues and reflections that were emerging, I engaged in further correspondence with many of these respondents, and eventually embarked on a month long visit to Australia, in 2010, to learn more about their reasons for thinking about return migration; the different factors that influence decision making; and perspectives on future strategies. I carried out in-depth interviews with 13 respondents in New South Wales, as well as one interview with the secretary of the Australian Irish Welfare Bureau, who had also written to me. I also interviewed a married couple, and one single person, who returned to live in the UK during the course of our contact. Relevant characteristics of these 16 older people are shown in Table 6.1:

Table 6.1: Interviewee characteristics

Pseudonym	Age at interview	Years in host country	Marital status	Location of children (if applicable)
Richard Bunyan	63	38	Divorced	N/A
June Castle	67	30	Widow	Australia
Dot Chivers	72	51	Divorced	N/A
Jane Dougal	66	64	Married	Australia and UK
Elizabeth Foster	63	45	Divorced	Australia
Valerie Harris	67	38	Widow	Australia and USA
Christopher Hitchins	84	50	Married	UK
Maisie Lawton	71	58	Widow	Australia
Jill Lewis	68	44	Married	N/A
Brian Linton	55	27	Married	Australia
Margaret Mills	68	44	Widow	UK
Anne Milsom	74	51	Widow	Australia
Wynne Morris	65	N/A	Married	Russia
Peter Morris	71	42	Married	Russia
Lorraine Salisbury	57	34	Divorced	Australia
Sandra Wilson	69	59	Widow	Australia

Throughout interviews I used a semi-structured topic guide as the basis for 'co-equal dialogue' (Gubrium and Lynott, 1983:37), an approach that assists research participants develop narrative accounts, which would seem relevant and important in this study and which offers the prospect of rich, detailed data that large migration studies often lack (Peace et al, 2006). This approach enabled the tailoring of interviews to individual circumstances, taking into account the 'virtual' discussions that had already taken place and the details previously provided, and probing a wide range of potential reasons for return as well as respondents' present and past links with their country of origin. Generally, the topic guide included questions that sought to learn about respondents' reasons for emigrating; subsequent moves; trigger factors affecting motivation to return to country of origin; issues involved in decision making as regards return migration; consideration given to (re) adapting to daily life on actual/prospective return; and, for those who had returned to live in the UK, the implications of their deliberations and experiences for other prospective returnees in later life.

In the course of carrying out these interviews, themes emerged that helped develop and shape my understanding of the original correspondence data. These emerging themes in turn led to my progressive and regular re-formulation of the questions I put to respondents, an approach to ethnographic analysis supported by, among others, Spradley (1979, 1980), whose work on searching for patterns and relationships between categories of meaning, or 'cultural domains', informed my content and thematic analysis. The data and its analysis revealed a number of important concerns and preoccupations experienced by respondents, including: ambiguous national identity and meanings attributed to 'home'; changes in family ties and competing responsibilities; lifecourse events and personal priorities as older people; emotional and practical challenges and the development of return migration-oriented strategies; advice and support requirements and their resources and policy implications.

The material that makes up the remainder of this chapter is organised into areas of discussion indicated by these prominent themes. The word 'return' is mainly used in this chapter to refer to permanent return migration, but where it refers to temporary visits of some kind, this use will be distinguished. This chapter makes regular use of extracts from interviews, to help illuminate important perspectives, experiences and feelings. Respondents' names have been changed to protect confidentiality and respect individual anonymity. Unless otherwise indicated, extracts are taken from transcripts of face to face interviews.

Home(s) and 'that magnet in the beak thing'

Many 20th century emigrants to Australia went there for secure and better paid employment, but not all respondents emphasised this as their prime motivation. A number referred to their spirit of adventure and search for fun as a prime reason, whereas, for others, Australia presented new life chances:

> 'We came over and got married, and started our life here in Australia, which has been great, has been wonderful, and for my children has been absolutely brilliant. I've seen them do things that I would never have got the chance to do in England, and they're just second nature things here, just the way things are done, horse riding, silly things like that. Where I come from in England people that ride horses are posh ... they [daughters] just had a really good education, they've had a good life, done lots of things, both travelled overseas.' [Lorraine Salisbury]

Positive experiences of settling, child raising, career building, and maintaining a good life style in the host country were regularly aired by respondents, but they also talked of a defining and abiding identification with their country of origin. In this respect it was not unusual to hear respondents refer to an almost 'organic' connection that draws them back to their homeland. Richard Bunyan, like most respondents, has spent over half his life in Australia. He told me:

> 'Australia is a great country but it has never been my home. Your country of birth, it's home, it's something that's in your soul, I think ... I'm English and I'll never be anything else.'

This innate sense of home was vividly emphasised in a number of discussions. Valerie Harris speculated on the possibility of "genetic memory" and a "human homing instinct", comparable to that of the salmon, which exert a strong 'pull' back to place of birth. An important reason for such a pull appears to be an affinity for homeland that strikes an inner chord and resonates with something deeply personal. Jill Lewis spoke to me of a profound, deep-seated feeling that "we belong to the homeland", that "we are part of it", an insight shared by Jane Dougal, who was careful not to romanticise this affinity with native place:

> 'I'm not talking about the green fields and all that, it's beautiful and all of that, and moves me terribly, but the thing that really strikes me is the way in which the [older] settlements in England have grown out of the soil, the buildings are made out of the local material ... I feel as though the land speaks to me there.'

This sense of belonging and organic grounding in the homeland is, perhaps an example of the framework put forward by Rowles (1983), when he argued that older people's identity with, and attachment to, environmental roots involves physical as well as social and autobiographical dimensions. Another example is provided by respondents who spoke of their country of origin as the preferred and most natural final resting place. Some had left instructions that their ashes should be scattered in meaningful locations. Lorraine Salisbury told me that she had asked her daughters to make sure some, if not all, her ashes are returned to England, and explained how this corporeal sense of "going back to where you originated" achieves some kind of permanent reconnection with home. Although Jane Dougal moved to Australia at the age of two, shortly after the end of World War Two, she has felt over many years a "yearning to go home before I die". In our interview, Jane went on to explain that she has told her Australian husband "I don't want to die here. I really want to go back to the soil I know." For most respondents, this knowledge of the land of their native place is less experiential and more intuitive, a point strongly made by June Castle, another respondent who returned to live in England during the course of my study:

> 'You can't really think completely logically because you're just in, you're following this sort of magnetic pull, which is very hard to talk about, to talk yourself out of once it's got hold of you. ... It's organic, actually that's the word, it really is ... it's beyond sentiment, it's beyond church bells over the meadows ... it's more profound ... you know in your bones it's not just sentiment, it's much more than that ... a cellular thing really.'

Interestingly, June told me that this "magnetic pull" did not negate her sense of attachment to Australia, her home for 30 years, a place where her links are "forged forever" and to which she has "deep joy" in knowing that she can again go back. Such enduring links with the host country raise another related aspect of migrants' attachments to place, that of their hybrid nature, which can give rise to a sense of dual identity or, contrariwise, no firm sense of attachment or belonging in either host or home country.

'Two lives in a parallel universe'

An early correspondent, Lorna Stanford, said in an email:

> 'I feel that I don't belong anywhere any more. My UK friends and family consider I have an Australian accent and outlook now, but Australians would laugh at that notion.'

During our interview, Jane Dougal was philosophical about dual connections when she said that for most migrants "belonging is illusory" as their "roots are torn up". Two respondents cited writers who have something to say on this subject. Bob Charles emailed to let me know about the Australian writer Martin Boyd, who once termed the dilemma facing the migrant as 'geographical schizophrenia', a condition Bob said is well understood by migrants, as "for most of our lives we are wrestling with who we are and where we belong". Dot Chivers also sent me an email, following my interview with her, to mention a novel she had found interesting, concerning an Australian of Greek heritage travelling through Europe, seeking the Europe of his father's stories. Dot considered how this scenario typifies the migrant, in that however they try to adapt to their new country, the majority find it impossible to cut the ties with their past. Dot reasoned that "It is the fortunate person who can live entirely in the present and the future with no looking back." Wynne Morris hinted at the Janus-like duality in migrants' lives when she talked of the "yo-yo" effect when describing dual attachments and the regularity of travel between home and host countries that can ensue. Such travel can bring both joy and heartache, as Jane Dougal suggested when she acknowledged how, after her yearly or biennial visits to England, she feels deflated having to "turn round and go back". Positive aspects of such regular return may include their potential to reinforce self-identity (Basu, 2007) and it is not surprising, therefore, that negative consequences may follow when this affirmed sense of self is again denied.

Sometimes, this sense of uncertain attachment was explained as a result of social exclusion in the host country. George and Fitzgerald (2012) suggest that immigrants' identity is affected, to some extent, by their outsider status, which can persist despite decades spent in the host country. This was certainly the experience of respondents in Australia who mentioned the unsettling effect of always being referred to as a 'pom' [derogatory term for English immigrant] as well as irksome comments about their English accent and behaviour that accentuated difference and non belonging. Such behaviour made Peter Morris "more determined to come back", and led Lorraine Salisbury to consider herself "an outsider", even after 32 years in Australia. I return later in this chapter to a fuller consideration of social inclusion and the context of cultural orientation.

Only a minority of respondents, however, considered such dual attachments to be detrimental, and many derived some comfort from knowing they had 'two homes', an issue I come back to later when discussing respondents' return strategies. Valerie Harris suggested that this sense of a having a niche in two countries may continue after the final move back to the home country, a point symbolically represented, I thought, by Valerie's placement on her kitchen wall of two large maps – one of the US, where she lived for 38 years, and one of Australia, the home country to which she has returned – shown in the photo below.

Valerie with two maps on the kitchen wall

Respondents indicate that migrants can hold a sense of 'love' for both host and home country, which does not necessarily diminish when thinking of return and is part of the tension and complexity of dealing with emotional aspects as regards return. But attachment to country of origin can prevail and assume special importance in later life, not least in regard to family (re)connections and care issues.

'Family connections definitely play a big part'

Family ties to the home country

The presence of family in the home country, and an abiding bond with them, can exert a strong attraction for people in or approaching older age. Brian Linton still has a "very big network of friends in the UK", who he has kept in touch with throughout his 27 years in Australia, and who he considers will be friends "at the end". Lorraine Salisbury values her siblings' availability when she visits family in England, and emphasises the comfort of knowing "my sister is there to go shopping with, my brother, he was available to go to the karaoke with", contact that enhances Lorraine's quality of life, as "my social life improves".

Many respondents echoed these sentiments and emphasised the importance of their relationships with siblings who remained in the home country. This was most pronounced with those who were divorced or widowed, or without children, factors that appear to assume particular significance for migrants in later life. Dot Chivers has no children, and told me that her brother and sister, also in Australia, have no interest in going back, because they have children and grandchildren on whom their lives are centred. Dot went on to say that because she does not have children "I'm looking backwards to where I came from rather than where I'm going. I think having no children is why I keep in contact with all these friends."

Respondents with children but who are widowed or separated from a spouse may consider that their attachment to siblings exerts a stronger pull, as suggested by Lorraine Salisbury:

> 'I have many friends [in England] who for varied reasons are single like myself. My sister is married to a man many years older than herself and has no children, so it is reasonable to assume she will also be alone at some point. It seems to make sense to me to return and live the rest of my life with her.'

Sandra Wilson, who emigrated to Australia in 1951, told me that since her husband had died 10 years previously, she has been thinking about return more seriously. Sandra went on to say that after a busy life working and raising children, and seeing them settled, she had realised that "life is short and it's best to make the most of it". Maisie Lawton reflected on the time when her husband suffered a major stroke, "which started me thinking, what will I do, where will I go?" Jill Lewis, whose husband was recently seriously ill, has started to think about returning to England as a likely option:

> 'If he [husband] predeceases me, and he's just had the most mammoth health scare ... I will probably come back to England ... my sister [in England], who is now a widow, wants to move into some kind of sheltered housing, so we talked a lot about that. I've got family [in England], I've got cousins, and not having children myself I suppose it makes members of one's family more important.'

Those without siblings or extended family in the host country could also long for connection with family available to them in the home country. Before her return to England, Wynne Morris emailed me to say that her husband Peter "has no family here and is very aware time is running out and wants some quality time with his brothers, sisters and their families [in England]".

An additional family connection with homeland is when their children, having travelled to Britain to tour the countries and explore Europe, decide to stay for extended periods, or, in some cases, settle. This reverse flow of family migration presents another reason for respondents to make extended visits or permanently return. Jane and Robert Dougal's two sons now live permanently in London, and yearly house-swops enable the couple to maintain regular contact, as well as provide a welcome opportunity to look into the practicalities of their own, now likely, permanent move back to England. Valerie Harris, an Australian who lived in the US with her American husband for 38 years, decided to return to her homeland largely because she missed her American born daughter, who had enjoyed family visits to Australia and had decided to settle there. Valerie told me that many members of her large Australian family had been out to see her in the United States, and together with return visits she and her children made to Australia, relationships developed that cemented bonding, to the extent that Valerie's daughter subsequently opted to move there permanently.

The death of Valerie's husband was the final event that triggered her own decision, one year later, to return to live again in her home country.

Caring responsibilities

As well as ongoing relationships with siblings and extended family, caring responsibilities may lead to extended return visits to the homeland, during which family relationships there can be re-established or strengthened. Richard Bunyan returned to England when his father required care at the end of his life, and stayed for seven months. Lorraine Salisbury spent 12 months in England caring for her ailing mother, then tending to the practical and emotional needs of her bereaved father. Valerie Harris travelled home to Australia from the US every year so as to see her ageing mother. At this stage Valerie had not taken the decision to return for good, but at the back of her mind was the concern that "every time you say goodbye you don't know if it's the last time. It's very difficult." Jill Lewis was brought up by her unmarried aunt, who was the most significant family person in her life. Jill told me how she would return to England every two years to see her aunt, something she could afford to do as she was earning good money. As her aunt grew older, and became more frail, Jill made a decision to move back to England for good, and bought a house there; however, a relationship she had formed with an Australian developed, and when they married, and he said he wished to return to Australia, Jill acquiesced.

The vulnerability of older people who are so distant from potential family carers is a challenge to care-giving across national borders, as documented by Baldassar (2007), chiefly in the context of younger care givers. However, when distant care givers themselves are getting older, particular difficulties arise. In an email I received from Ellie Birch, the daughter of an elderly British couple who had returned from Australia to England, Ellie said she would advise older people against return, explaining that her parents, in their eighties, have brothers and sisters in the UK who are not much younger than they are and would not therefore be able to take on the responsibility of looking after them if they became too ill. Ellie and her sister, who both live in Australia, are late middle aged and "dread the day when one of our parents falls ill".

While the presence of family in the home country can wield a strong attraction, the continued presence of family in the host country can exert an equal or stronger pull to remain there and render plans for return to the homeland unrealistic, particularly when caring obligations are factored in. Claudio Bolzman, in Chapter Four of this volume, refers to the importance of childrens' location to post-retirees' decisions regarding residence, and such considerations occupied the minds of many of my respondents, who nonetheless struggled with the implications. Jill Lewis evoked likely questions her stepdaughters and step-grandchildren would ask about why she would want to leave them to return to England, and said "those questions are hard to answer". For Anne Milsom, the emotional closeness of her long-standing friendships in Australia preclude any serious thought of return, as "you don't actually want to walk off and leave them".

Caring responsibilities, in particular, can make return impossible. Elizabeth Foster had intended to make an extended visit to England, with a view to possible permanency, when her childen finally became independent, but explained how events took a different turn when her un-partnered daughter had a baby and Elizabeth became the "second parent". Now that her grandchild has turned two, Elizabeth feels she is "getting to the point now where maybe I can have another go". Such accounts of family bonds and caring responsibilities, in home and host country, also provide examples of how family connections can give rise to competing claims, reinforcing the possible tensions involved in migrants' dual attachments.

Family bonds and competing claims

Dot Chivers went to live in Australia, at the age of 21, encouraged to do so by her 32-year-old brother, who had already emigrated there. As a schoolchild in England, Dot had been thwarted in her ambition to go to university and study medicine, instead having to leave school at 16 and work, to support her mother who had been widowed three years previously. When she was free to decide her own future, Dot appreciated the encouragement and guidance her older brother provided, and continues to be thankful to him, to the extent that she now feels obliged, not for the first time in her life, and at the age of 72, to put her own plans on hold, and defer returning to the UK in order to support her 82-year-old brother in his old age. Competing personal and family priorities can therefore affect migrants throughout their lives, indeed may be characteristic of such lives. A detailed example of the complexities involved in balancing competing claims is provided by Lorraine Salisbury, who describes the weakening and strengthening of particular family attachments as she ages, and how these interact with her changing personal circumstances and priorities:

> 'I have two daughters, and four grandsons, and the thing that keeps me here is the grandsons, not the daughters; the

siblings pull me back more than the daughters keep me here ... my daughters have their husbands, their families, their lives, and whilst they include me in that, it's their little world. My sister has her husband and her life, but it's different, and I [also] think it is that generation thing, that she [sister] understands me and they don't.'

Lorraine had previously told me, in email correspondence, that when she visited England she enjoyed her sister's company, missed her on her return to Australia, and was contemplating the possibility of going to live with her when her sister's older husband eventually dies. In our interview in Australia, Lorraine continued on this subject, explaining that she could envisage growing old with her sister, enjoying a much fuller social life than the one available to her where she currently lives, given that some of her former close friends had moved, died, or were seriously ill. Other friends had become less close, the result, Lorraine believes, of her absence for a year when she was in England caring for her mother. Lorraine was convinced that she would be better off socially in her home country:

'I'd have this social network that I could build on again, and not be lonely. I've a wonderful life here in Australia, but I'm lonely [and] as I get older I get less energy to want to go out and do things, and being female you don't.'

However, the arrival of grandchildren had put such contemplation on the back-burner, not that this resolved Lorraine's personal companionship needs. Furthermore, the bond she was developing with her grandchildren had started to remind Lorraine of, and alert her children to, the sacrifices involved in leaving family behind to pursue personal ambitions abroad:

'Now that we have grandchildren in the mix that's changed things, changed how I feel about whether I could go home, not changed me wanting to but changed whether I could. ... And it's like a backwards, forwards, tearing, pulling. [However] it wasn't until my daughters gave me grandchildren I realised what I'd done to my mum, how my mum must have felt when I brought Joanne to Australia. ... And [when] I spoke to both the girls about it [idea of living in England], the eldest one said, "How dare you consider leaving him [grandson] behind and leaving me to explain where you've gone," and the youngest one said to me, "You must do what you feel you have to do mum, I want you to be happy. But you need to know that how you felt about nana all those years – every time nana got sick you worried, every time nana was upset you were upset, you wanted to be there in England to help – I will feel all of that when you're in England." And it made me stop and think, do I really want her to feel all of that?'

Lorraine Salisbury with grandchildren

A further example of the emotional charge that seems to underpin migrants' competing family claims is that of a couple who have actually followed through return migration plans. Prior to their return to England, Wynne Morris, who is Australian, informed me that she and her English husband Peter had reached this decision despite conflicting emotions and demands:

> 'We have decided to make the 'big move', even though it means leaving my elderly parents to cope alone [but] it also means Pete's emotional wellbeing will improve and we will see our daughter more often. [I] have had months of little sleep, tears, stress, enormous guilt, but ultimately I had to decide: husband or parents.'

Since Wynne and Peter have returned, Wynne's father in Australia has died and she has gone there to help her 91-year-old mother, who has "early dementia", prepare for the journey to England, where Wynne will be able to care for her more easily.

These accounts of strong family bonds and connections across the globe, and competing loyalties affecting migration decisions, suggest that those studies predicting how older people's future migration will be characterised by 'substitution of family-oriented to individualistic lifestyles' (Longino and Warnes, 2005:543) may not have fully recognised the complexities involved, certainly in respect of return migration. While my respondents were mindful of a need to secure good quality of life following any return they might, or had, put into effect (relevant strategies are discussed in due course), more often their desire to return was driven by personal priorities particularly important to them as older people, including lifecourse considerations, cultural orientation, emotional factors, and the resolving of past troubles.

Personal priorities as older people

Lifecourse considerations

The arrival of retirement can, of course, be an important watershed in people's lives, an occasion for contemplation of future goals and priorities. As such, retirement can be an event that triggers thoughts of return to homeland, "before it's too late", as Dot Chivers remarked. In our interview, Dot expanded:

> 'While I was working I was quite happy living in Australia, with several trips back to the UK for holidays, but since retiring the desire to return to live in England has been at the back of my mind constantly ... you've got time on your hands to think more and you want to do things. I'm interested in history, archaeology, and there's nothing here [in Australia] older than 200 years.'

Dot now has time to research her family tree, which also draws her to England and emphasises her long standing connections there:

> 'I have my family tree on my father's side going back to 1470 and on my mother's side almost to the Doomsday Book, and would love to get back to the land of my ancestors ... I have joined that ancestry.com [online resource] ... I've

started putting the family tree in ... [but] it is very difficult to do the research from across the world and it is one of the reasons I would like to return to England for an extended period even if it wasn't permanently. I want to know who I am, how do my ancestors make me what I am, why am I the way I am you know, why do I have the character that I have?'

Dot Chivers is not alone as regards respondents' interest in making sense of their lives by re-connecting with family or ancestral roots and early life experiences, a further example of how important it can be to construct meaningful narratives in later life (Bengston et al, 2005; Biggs, 2005; Coleman, 2005), not least through return visits to native place (Basu, 2007). Richard Bunyan is also interested in personal heritage, partly because he was adopted, and now that he is retired is planning return to England, so as to explore family connections as well as a possible final return there. In addition to retirement, another important lifecourse event influencing some respondents' migration plans is their decrease in parenting responsibilities, which can accentuate other imperatives, as the following two extracts clearly demonstrate:

'I think once the children were grown, really had flown the nest, I think that was when it really hit home ... that feeling that I've completed my biological role and so now you orient differently, you orient, I think really you orient towards death. It may be a very long way away but you turn your head towards home.' [Jane Dougal]

'It was a very good time [to return] because no-one was dependent on me and I wasn't dependent on anybody ... suddenly you see, nothing's stopping you ... and also [there] is the feeling, am I ever going to get old and regretful, I should have done it.' [June Castle]

The changing body in older age may also react differently to temperature, a factor raised by respondents who were finding the Australian heat more difficult to cope with, preventing a good night's sleep and draining energy during the day. While agreeing that Australian summers could be unbearable, a minority of respondents expressed doubt they could once more cope with British winters in older age.

Cultural orientation

Basu (2007) has proffered the idea that older people may yearn for a simpler life than they currently experience, hence their interest in looking back to earlier times and associated places that seem to offer a more calm, comforting foothold in life. This perspective has some purchase as regards respondents' changing cultural interests, as the following extract from my interview with Richard Bunyan illustrates:

> 'Australia is a young country, I was a young guy [when I emigrated], it was great. Now this is still a young country and I'm an older guy, and I love the British way of life, or the English way of life .... there's still a respect there [in England], when you stop at the crossing if you're driving, they still tip their hat or wave, they don't here. That's just one thing, and there's many things like that, this is a far more aggressive country.'

However, reconnection with one's roots can also be a way of emphasising prevailing cultural priorities that are at odds with those found in the host country, a cultural dissonance raised by a number of respondents, including Jane Dougal, who has published a novel based on an extended return visit she made to the English Lake District. Jane told me of the profound importance to her of language and public cultural debate, aspects if life that are "central to my culture, my spiritual life, my social connections". Jane went on in our interview to explain that in her opinion there is limited public intellectual life in Australia and a narrowly defined popular culture, heavily dominated by a "huge focus on sport". Jane favourably compared the number and range of newspapers in Britain to those in Australia. This view was shared by Tom O'Casey, secretary of the Australian Irish Welfare Bureau, who informed me that many of the British and Irish immigrants he is in touch with, people who have worked in the local steelworks a great part of their lives and are now retired, "just don't culturally connect. ... The [dominant sporting] culture in Australia is a very difficult culture for a lot of people to connect to."

Indeed, cultural variety and its importance was often voiced in the context of contrast between host and home country. Anne Milsom had been impressed when visiting England by "the availability of art galleries, museums, libraries, parks and gardens, and historic places to visit". A big attraction of return to England for Brian Linton, a 55-year-old school teacher considering early retirement, is its proximity to

Europe and the cultural vibrancy found there, which he favourably contrasted with the rather insular and parochial cultural interests available in his adopted home town in Australia.

Emotions involved when thinking of home

Thomson's (2005) study of post-World War Two British immigrants in Australia refers to homesickness as a particular driving force towards homeward return, one that can be 'constant' while fluctuating in intensity. Thomson emphasises that the intensity or existence of homesickness is not simply a matter of looking back but is bound up with perspectives and feelings rooted in the present day. Current feelings and constant deliberation about return were certainly at the forefront of my respondents' accounts. For example, thoughts of returning to the homeland can be a surprising reaction to a pressing problem or stressful event, such as a spouse's sudden illness, a time when Jill Lewis "found myself speaking out loud. What I said, quite surprised me, it took me aback, I said, 'I want to go home.'" Many respondents talked of the constancy of their thoughts about returning to the homeland, which could be emotionally draining, as suggested by Elizabeth Foster and Lorraine Salisbury in the two extracts below:

> 'Oh it's [thinking of return] always there, it's always at the pit of your stomach, a missing actually.'

> 'I am depressed, lonely, miss my family, have a lack of interest in my work, become reclusive and generally want to be back in the UK.'

The constancy of these strong feelings can lead to an overwhelming desire to be back in the home country, which, in the case of one of my respondents, led to a rather rash return. Chris Hitchins told me how, at the age of 84, he had suddenly felt a great urge to return to the south of England before he died, and had quite spontaneously booked a flight and taken off. This was a disastrous episode, as he had not really planned where he would stay or how he would live when in England, and he quickly found himself adrift. He then realised how much he missed his wife, who speedily had to put into effect her husband's flight back to Australia. Chris explained how this "sudden brain storm" had crystallised for him the realisation that he had left his return migration "too late". Constant thoughts about return migration can also affect motivation to maintain friendships in the host country, as suggested by Brian Linton, who told me how he has been "tending to wean my way off ... purposely been weaning my way off people [friends in Australia]. Just in case I do [return]."

However, thinking about return migration did not necessarily translate into discussing the subject with friends, or even family, and respondents sometimes admitted to their difficulty in expressing or sharing their thoughts. Elizabeth Foster found that return migration is "not really something that you can articulate with other people", for fear that she would be castigated as a disloyal and complaining 'pom'. June Castle similarly finds it hard to talk in depth to people about return, saying "you don't talk about these things and certainly in no depth to people ... there's no way ... it's a completely foreign thing [to people] ... and so you talk in small little gobbet bites." This difficulty in communication can even take place between husband and wife. Only during my interview with Peter and Wynne Morris, following their return to England, did Wynne learn of her husband's past reluctance to tell her of his true feelings:

> Wynne: 'Is that why it was so hard for you to decide about buying a house [in Australia], because you knew it'd be [putting down] roots?'

> Peter: 'Yes'

> Wynne: 'My God! Pete's usually quite good about important decisions, not like me, and I remember, practically a whole day, he would not make the final decision about signing the papers ... it's revelations today, I'm just realising how long you didn't want to be there.'

When I interviewed Brian Linton in Australia, I did so in the school where he teaches. Brian said this was preferable to his home, as his Australian wife does not share his desire to move to England, as she is firmly rooted in Sydney, where her large family is based and whom she badly missed when they spent time in England some years previously. Brian's growing interest in return migration is therefore a difficult subject to broach. In our interview, Brian said "Whenever I bring it up, she's not very happy, she says, 'Look, I don't want to go back to England.'"

The tendency for thoughts about return migration to provoke strong feelings and emotional reactions is very apparent when considering how decisions may be influenced by a need to resolve distressful past experiences, as shown in two particular extracts included in the following section.

Helping resolve past sorrow

The autobiographical dimension of place attachment is important to 'sustaining a sense of personal identity', not least in respect of ability to project into past places 'imbued with a temporal depth of meaning' (Rowles, 1983:305). The relevance of this connection, between person, time and meanings associated with place, became apparent during my interviews with two particular respondents. June Castle has returned to live in England after 30 years in Australia. One year on, she has had time to reflect on some of the reasons that influenced her decision, including some deep-seated concerns. In our interview in England she explained:

> 'I went [to Australia] following a divorce and I took my two young sons with me. They were born here in England ... I felt quite irrationally I was kicked out of my home country, England, by a wayward husband, in the sense of a divorce ... and if I leave [this time] it's going to be on my terms, if I leave England again, it's going to be on my terms ... it's a sort of settling of an old internal argument ... a way of reclaiming your birthright ... you want to know that you've really genuinely paid your dues to England and if you do say goodbye to England it's on really good terms, not how it was when I said goodbye to England 30 years ago.'

In returning to England, June left her two, independent, sons in Australia, and said that her belief that she can now leave England on her own terms has made her realise that being reunited with them may prove to be her priority.

Margaret Mills also experienced a 'yearning' to return to England, and had become unsettled after visiting her son who lived there, but her way to resolve troublesome emotional experiences in her past life was to build on neighbourhood friendships and a sense of belonging in her local community in Australia. It was clear when she met me, as I stepped off the country bus, that Margaret had great pride in her adopted home town. As we walked to her house, Margaret took time to show me streets and houses where she had connections, naming friends and local acquaintances, and giving me a potted history of her life there over the past 19 years. We went to the park, which Margaret visits every day to feed the possums, and called in at the art gallery, where Margaret volunteers one day a week. During our interview, Margaret told me that her emigration to Australia 44 years previously had been her husband's idea, as he 'was always looking for better things'. Unfortunately, the marriage deteriorated as her husband became abusive, and Margaret had to put up with various moves over which she had no control. When her husband was killed in a plane crash, Margaret could have returned to the UK but was fearful of her husband's family there, who had signalled their desire to be involved in her children's lives, something that Margaret could not countenance. As a result, Margaret continued to live in Australia, and settled in her current town, where familiarity and everyday interactions appear to be providing the anchor that was missing from her life for so long. As Margaret put it, "It wasn't until I moved to [town name] I could really be myself."

Many British post war emigrants to Australia have settled well (Hammerton and Thomson, 2005), but for most of my respondents the desire to pull up the anchor that had rooted them in their host country was a persuasive and sometimes forceful one. Whether or not an individual could make the decision to return depended, to a significant extent, on resources and practical considerations.

Resource and relocation issues

Sufficient funds are decisive when considering possible timing of return to the home country. Richard Bunyan said he was awaiting a lump sum, related to past work, and would not be able to return without it. Lorraine Salisbury regretted that she was now too old to build a sufficiently large 'nest egg' and would have to postpone retirement and depend on the Australian Government to supplement her retirement income. Many respondents said they were concerned at the perceived higher cost of living in the UK, which could not be afforded. As well as financial concerns, there are a range of practical matters that may affect relocation to the homeland:

> 'The main deterrent for me is the logistics − finding somewhere to live, organising pensions, bank accounts, investments, finding a new doctor etc. ... it's all these little things ... it's knowing where to go, can I afford to rent over there, I mean rent's bad enough here but from the magazines and things I get, I think it's quite expensive, isn't it, to rent over there? It all seems too difficult.' [Dot Chivers]

Respondents who had returned to their homeland after decades away did find the relocation challenges difficult. For Wynne Morris, the "physical side of it and the mental strain" were significant, not helped by pension complications and disputes. Valerie Harris emphasised the challenges presented by "basic things like getting a credit card ... getting back in the banking system, and health system". June Castle had been back in England twelve months when I met her, and had reflected on the pressures and processes involved in the move:

> 'I can certainly see that there is a need for a lot of hand-holding for people who [return] who are either on pensions or approaching pension age ... there's going to be quite a lot of financial sorting out ... there's going to be pensions ... you've got pension credits ... they're going to [have to] know the tax obligations here ... even just simple things like there's a million phone companies, and perhaps there was only one when you left but ... Gas and electricity. It's all these things ... they've got to establish themselves with all these completely confusing things ... it will be just like a completely disintegrated jigsaw at first because it's so different.' [Jane Castle]

Jane went on to advocate a relocation service for older return migrants, along the lines of that often provided to young business executives moving home, but adjusted to suit this different market. In addition to reflecting on such practical issues, respondents could expect to face challenges in adapting to life in the home country. Changes in the homeland can take people by surprise if they have not returned for some time, which appeared to be the case for many immigrants worked with by community worker Tom O'Casey, who "came back with a feeling that they didn't know anybody and it wasn't the same place ... the place was full of strangers". For those, like Lorraine Salisbury, who had been able to fund regular return visits, the home country held no surprises, as "I've seen the changes, I know what to expect kind of thing." However, as Lorraine went on to tell me, changes in society at home are not the only ones a migrant has to come to terms with, as an individual's personality is also likely to have evolved. Lorraine explained that she no longer has the British reserve, being more outspoken and less shy, attributes she quickly had to develop as an immigrant in Australia and which she now values, although they seem less appreciated, by family and the public at large, in England. Even final return to the homeland can require adaptation and adjustments, as Wynne Morris explains:

'After finally settling in the house and, I guess, "stopping" at last, I became depressed. Felt alone and displaced. Couldn't see my parents. I realised friends would have their own busy lives and increased families, but I think we have been away so long, some forgot we are back. I realised then that I had to do more.'

Wynne told me that she now volunteers in an art gallery and is planning to do additional voluntary work, with under 16s who have been excluded from school. All this suggests that putting return migration into effect has to be carefully thought through and strategically planned.

Future strategies

Given the likely changes in the homeland, and the changes in the individual migrant, respondents thought it sensible to spend time 'testing the water'. Some thought they would return for "three or four months and see what it's like, see if we can live there again" [Dot Chivers]. During a period of very stormy weather throughout the UK, I received the following email from Maisie Lawton, who I had met the previous year in Australia:

'I'm in Shetland at the moment, trying out three months of the worst weather, to see if I can hack it here. I'm strongly thinking of moving to Scotland but I want to make sure that I'm not indulging in a fantasy.'

June Castle similarly wanted to experience the realities involved with return to homeland, to be "really grounded", by living in England, buying a house, and "giving it one hundred per cent". Sandra Wilson had not taken such a major step but had spent six months working as a live-in carer in England, to get an understanding of daily life from the perspective of a native resident. It was also common to hear respondents talk of having a foot in two worlds, a strategy that enables them to divide their time between host and home country:

'Ideally I would love to stay six months in Scotland/Europe and six months here. I intend to sell my house, buy my daughter's unit – she wants a bigger place – and with what cash is over, and providing my health remains in good shape, do just that.' [Maisie Lawton]

In similar vein, Jane Dougal told me of her plans to sell her large house and buy a small apartment in Sydney, should she wish to spend time there, and then buy a place in England, to enable her return.

It can also be important to consider a trial period in the home country, rather than definitive return, thereby reducing possible pressure to enter into premature commitment as well as build in opportunity for reflection and compromise. Building in such room for manoeuvre is important to Brian Linton, whose Australian wife does not share his enthusiasm for life in England. However, Brian is uncertain what would happen when the envisaged year's trial ends, if his wife insists on coming back to Australia and he wishes to remain in England; as Brian told me in our interview, "that's the Rubicon I have to cross". June Castle had been reflecting on her first year back in England prior to our interview, and said that her emotionally driven urge to be back in her home country, which she likened to a "magnetic pull", was giving way to "a more balanced view" of her priorities, something she could not have achieved without taking the step of actually returning. June added that she was "becoming more analytic ... referring to it [return to live in England] as my experiment".

Concluding remarks

In considering 19th-century emigration from Britain to Australia, Richards (2005) argues that the idea of return, whether for or against, was always present in people's minds, right up to death. Indeed, he argues, some spent most of their time weighing the pros and cons of return. The account set out in this chapter provides contemporary evidence of strikingly similar preoccupations, some respondents having always kept in readiness the return fare to Britain, and many regularly contemplating the prospect of return. Richards suggests that such preoccupations arise from a mentality of mobility, but I suggest this is not the whole story, given the long period of residence, and stable lives in the host country, of my respondents. Furthermore, many respondents value their time in Australia and the opportunities and life style it has provided over the years, to them and their family members. At the same time, they harbour a strong, sometimes overwhelming, and often perplexing desire to return to their country of origin. This chapter has shown that although nostalgia may form a part of migrants' yearnings for home, there are a myriad of personal, social and cultural factors that impact on older migrants' return deliberations, involving both practical and emotional challenges.

Baldassar's (2007) contention that migrants are involved in a wide range of 'transnational' activities also resonates in this chapter, in respect of respondents who spoke of visits to the UK to take part in activity holidays, heritage tours, short-term work opportunities, as well as to visit, or sometimes care for, relatives. We have also learned that transnational visits can help respondents determine and structure strategies to trial permanent return migration, or split their lives between home and host country. Whether or not such strategies are considered, followed through, and work out, will of course depend on individual circumstances but this chapter as a whole highlights how the desire to return to country of origin reveals priorities and challenges of particular importance to the ageing migrant, and is a complex subject that can be difficult to discuss with close friends and family.

The availability of support and advice from interested but independent parties would seem important. Rutter and Andrew (2009) suggest that older people returning to live in the UK may have particular difficulties with housing and benefit entitlements, and it is certainly true that respondents raised worries and uncertainties in this respect; one of my earliest pieces of email correspondence included the disarmingly simple question: 'Would I be entitled to a UK pension?' As Rutter and Andrew go on to show in their report, there is information available on financial aspects of migration and return migration, although much of this does not reach older people, an issue they believe local older people's forums, Age UK (the largest charity working with and for older people in the UK) and the British Legion (the leading UK service charity working with veterans of all ages and their families) should look into and try and help with.

On the basis of material contained in this chapter, a case can be made for a relocation-type service for ageing immigrants, to assist older people who are struggling with the physical, emotional and practical challenges that can be involved in return migration. For example, Age UK, the British Legion, local older people's community forums in the UK, and also UK local (regional) government social services (welfare) departments, could work in unison to develop publicity and protocols that focus on the information and advice needs of older return migrants. Australia based organsations such as BAPA (British Australian Pensioner Association) and COTA (Council on The Ageing) are well placed to provide prospective returnees to the UK with practical advice, for example about ways in which their Australian and UK pensions might be affected, and also information about sources of support or counseling that enable expression of feelings that may be difficult to share with close family members. Although migrants, such as those who feature in this chapter, were often adventurous in their original decision to emigrate to Australia, and may remain resourceful characters, it is also the case that their experiences and needs as ageing immigrants make return migration a complex and compelling subject, one with which older people can struggle without sufficient help.

Acknowledgements

I am deeply indebted to the hospitality and openness of respondents in Australia and England, and their continued interest in, and patience with, my research endeavours. I sincerely hope I have done them justice in this chapter and look forward to their further thoughts. I am also grateful to the Open University's Faculty of Health and Social Care for financial assistance with interview transcription costs.

References

Baldassar, L. (2007) *Families Caring Across Borders. Migration, Ageing and Transnational Caregiving*, New York: Palgrave Macmillan.

Basu, P. (2007) *Highland Homecomings: genealogy and heritage tourism in the Scottish diaspora*, London: Routledge.

Bengtson, V.L., Elder, G.H. and Putney, N.M. (2005) 'The Lifecourse Perspective on Ageing: Linked Lives, Timing and History', in M. Johnson (ed) *The Cambridge Handbook of Age and Ageing*, Cambridge: Cambridge University Press.

Biggs, S. (2005) 'Psychodynamic approaches to the lifecourse and ageing', in M. Johnson (ed) *The Cambridge Handbook of Age and Ageing*, Cambridge: Cambridge University Press.

Coleman, P. (2005) 'Reminiscence: development, social and clinical perspectives', in M. Johnson (ed) *The Cambridge Handbook of Age and Ageing*, Cambridge: Cambridge University Press.

George, M. and Fitzgerald, R.P. (2012) 'Forty years in Aotearoa New Zealand: White identity, home and later life in an adopted country', *Ageing & Society*, 32:239-260.

Gubrium, J.F. and Lynott, R.J. (1983) 'Rethinking Life Satisfaction', *Human Organization*, 42:30-38.

Hammerton, A.J. and Thomson, A. (2005) *'Ten Pound Poms': Australia's Invisible Migrants*, Manchester: Manchester University Press.

Longino, C.F. and Warnes, A.M. (2005) 'Migration and older people', in M. Johnson (ed) *The Cambridge Handbook of Age and Ageing*, Cambridge: Cambridge University Press.

Peace, S., Holland, C. and Kellaher, L. (2006) *Environment and Identity in Later Life*, Maidenhead: Open University Press.

Richards, E. (2005) 'Running home from Australia: intercontinental mobility and migrant expectations in the nineteenth century', in M. Harper (ed) *Emigrant Homecomings. The return movement of emigrants, 1600–2000*, Manchester: Manchester University Press.

Rowles, G. (1983) 'Place and personal identity in old age: observations from Appalachia', *Journal of Environmental Psychology*, 3:299–313.

Rutter, J. and Andrew, H. (2009) *Home Sweet Home? The nature and scale of the immigration of older UK nationals back to the UK*, London: Age Concern and Help the Aged.

Spradley, J.P. (1979) *The Ethnographic Interview*, New York: Holt, Rinehart and Winston.

Spradley, J.P. (1980) *Participant Observation*, New York: Holt, Rinehart and Winston.

Thomson, A. (2005) '"My wayward heart": homesickness, longing and the return of British post-war immigrants from Australia' in M. Harper (ed) *Emigrant Homecomings. The Return movement of emigrants, 1600–2000*, Manchester: Manchester University Press.

SEVEN

Diasporic returns to the city: Anglo-Indian and Jewish visits to Calcutta in later life

Alison Blunt, Jayani Bonnerjee and Noah Hysler-Rubin

The city of birth as a focus of return

The city is a central focus of research on diasporic resettlement, with studies of urban cosmopolitanism and/or multiculturalism alongside work on urban policy, employment, the built environment, consumption, and cultural and artistic practice. Less attention has been paid, however, to the city as a site of diasporic return. While research on return visits and return migrations is diverse and wide-ranging, including historical research on migrant homecomings (Gowans, 2001; Harper, 2005; Wyman, 2005) alongside more contemporary research on first- and second-generation returns (King and Christou, 2010), the repatriation of refugees (Hammond, 2004) and 'heritage tourism' (Basu, 2007), most of this work has focused on returns to the nation and/or 'homeland'.

Ideas about the 'homeland' as a site of return have been central not only to well-established and critiqued notions of a diasporic 'myth of return' (Brah, 1996; King and Christou, 2010), but have also informed a wide range of research on return in practice. Ideas and practices of return to a 'homeland' are often bound up with, and articulated through, understandings about shared ethnic and other identities, genealogical connections, personal and inherited memories, and attachments to place and landscape (Baldassar, 2001; Thomson, 2005). A wide range of work explores the challenges of return, particularly in terms of how ideas about home, ethnicity, identity and culture might become unsettled and uncertain alongside the difficulties of reconciling a remembered and/or imagined past with life in the present (Kibria, 2002; Bunkše, 2004; Christou and King, 2006; Tsuda, 2009). While much of the literature on return migration focuses on the significance of generation more than age (Kibria, 2002; Christou and King, 2006; Tsuda, 2009), other work focuses on particular groups such as those of working age (Potter et al, 2005; Conway and Potter, 2009). Research on return *visits* rather than permanent migrations spans work on particular age groups (including Dwyer, 2002, on young British Asian women visiting Pakistan) and across different age groups and generations (including Baldassar, 2001). Less work, however, has focused specifically on return visits by migrants in later life.

This chapter is about return visits by retired members of two minority communities from Calcutta. Through its focus on the Anglo-Indian and Jewish communities and their migration to London, Toronto and Israel since 1947, the chapter has two main aims. First, in contrast to research that focuses on the nation and/or 'homeland,' we explore the city as a destination for diasporic return. Second, unlike research that concentrates on particular ethnic groups that become minorities *after* migration and expect to feel an ethnic 'affiliation' on their return to the 'homeland' (Tsuda, 2009:3), we study two communities that were minorities *before* migration.

Reflecting these aims, the chapter addresses the following questions: how and why does the city figure in narratives of return for both communities? How might members of two minority communities return in different ways to the city of their birth? How does a focus on minority returns to the city complicate ideas about the 'homeland' as a site of return and unsettle assumptions about ethnicity, diaspora and return? What are the meanings and experiences of return for those visiting in later life, particularly in understanding urban and community change? Before situating our chapter in relation to broader debates about cities, diasporas and returns, we begin by introducing both communities and the importance of Calcutta as a site of community history and identity.

Anglo-Indian and Jewish Calcutta

Like most imperial and trading cities, Calcutta grew through the migration of a wide range of people from other parts of India and beyond. Jewish, Chinese, Armenian and Parsi communities lived in Calcutta alongside Marwari, Punjabi, Gujarati, Tamil, Bihari and Oriya communities (for more on Calcutta's minorities, see Banerjee et al, 2009 and Chatterji, 2009). For Anglo-Indian and Jewish Calcuttans, the city was in different ways already diasporic, shaped by connections to a range of other places, particularly Britain, Iraq and Israel. As a community of mixed descent, tracing its origins to a European paternal ancestor, many Anglo-Indians in British India imagined themselves to be living in an imperial diaspora, with attachments to Britain as 'fatherland' and India as 'motherland' (Blunt, 2005). The former capital of India was the largest and most permanent site of residence for Anglo-Indians before independence, and it continues to be a key site of Anglo-Indian memory, imagination and attachment (Andrews, 2005; Blunt and Bonnerjee, forthcoming). Before large-scale migration around the time of Independence and up until the 1970s, the community lived in particular neighbourhoods in central Calcutta and attended the same schools, churches and clubs. An estimated one third of the community has migrated since independence, first to London in the 1940s and 1950s, and then primarily to Toronto and Perth in the 1960s and 1970s. While some Anglo-Indians continue to migrate from Calcutta today, most left around the time of independence because they felt uncertain about the future of the community in the 'new India,' and then in the 1960s and 1970s when many lost their reserved jobs in certain fields of work. Today there are up to 30,000 Anglo-Indians in Calcutta and the community has become increasingly dispersed from central neighbourhoods (Blunt, 2005).

Despite its varied socioeconomic status, the Jews in Calcutta were, and are, a close-knit community. The community remains concentrated around Canning Street and Royd Street, where a number of organisations and institutions were established, including three synagogues, the Jewish Girls School, the Jewish Ezra hospital, and charitable institutions such as the Jewish Women's League. Calcutta Jews began to migrate to London in the 19th century, and did so in larger numbers after independence, seeking better economic and social opportunities. Since the 1970s, the Calcutta Jewish community in London has worshipped at two main synagogues: Gan Eden in Stamford Hill and the Lincoln Institute in Golders Green. The foundation of the state of Israel in 1948, and the 'right of return' for Jews across the diaspora, also saw the large-scale migration of Calcutta Jews to join other Baghdadi Jews in Jerusalem, Ramleh and Ramat-Gan. Although the community in Calcutta is very small today, memories of, and attachments to the city have become increasingly important across the wider diaspora, as shown by the publication of histories and memoirs (Musleah, 1975; Ezra, 1986; Hyman, 1995; Ray, 2001) and a range of other cultural practices and representations, including *Calcutta Kosher*, a play first performed in London in 2004 (Kali Theatre Company, 2004).

Both Anglo-Indian and Jewish communities occupied an ambivalent space between the British and the Indian, and as minorities in both colonial and postcolonial Calcutta shared particular areas in the city. They socialised with each other and share a common nostalgia for a past Calcutta when there were more of them in the city. In this chapter we explore return visits by both communities to trace how shared memories of the city are bound up with narratives of community identity, continuity and change. Before focusing on return visits to Calcutta by former Anglo-Indian and Jewish residents, we situate our argument within wider debates about diasporic return.

Cities, diasporas and returns

A growing body of work on return has come to focus on different scales and sites of attachment to particular places and landscapes as a way of exploring grounded identifications with, and articulations of, a wider sense of belonging – and not belonging – in the 'homeland' (for more on homeland belongings, see Abdelhady, 2008 and Hage, 1996).

In his research on return visits by Caribbean migrants in Toronto, for example, David Timothy Duval describes them as 'one manifestation of the numerous social conduits between former homelands and new homelands' (2005:249). And yet, as he shows, the connections between different homelands might be experienced most directly on a range of smaller scales than the nation: 'Some may feel nationalistic ties, while others may identify, first and foremost, with a smaller unit of association – a village, district, part of town, or a family home and neighbourhood' (2005:254). This builds on the pathbreaking work by Loretta Baldassar (2001) on return visits between Perth in Western Australia and the village of San Fior in north eastern Italy (also see Salih, 2002, on Moroccan women living in Italy; Dwyer, 2002, on visits to Pakistan by second-generation British Muslim schoolgirls, and Kibria, 2002, on 'homeland trips' for second-generation Chinese and Korean Americans). As Baldassar vividly describes, the idea of *campanilismo* – 'which might be translated literally as 'bell-towerism' (2001:110) – refers to local identity, and 'is a useful conceptual tool in the comprehension of both the migrants' attachment to their home town and their ethnic identification in the host country' (2001:323). But while rooted in a particular home town, such attachments also stretch far beyond and 'can expand or contract along provincial, regional or national lines depending on the context' (2001:323). Other research has shown the importance of landscape in understanding diasporic returns and homing desire (Brah, 1996; Thomson, 2005; Horst, 2005).

While such research reveals the importance of different places and landscapes in shaping return visits and return migrations, less work has focused specifically on the city and the extent to which it is an important and distinctive site of diasporic return as well as resettlement. Important exceptions exist, however, including David Ley and Audrey Kobayashi's work on the 'hyper-mobility of transnational citizens' between Hong Kong and Vancouver, 'for whom the two sides of the Pacific are part of a single life world' (2005:123). As Ley and Kobayashi show, such transnational mobilities disrupt ideas about return migration that imply a circular movement 'with its own logic of arrival, assimilation and closure' (also see Conway et al, 2008).

Other work challenges the extent to which return migration implies 'assimilation and closure,' as shown by Anastasia Christou and Russell King's research on the return migration of second-generation Greek-Americans to Athens (2006). Crucially, the city itself makes the process and experience of return complex and ambiguous. They identify 'a potentially confusing conflation of certain aspects of rural and urban Greece: the Athens which is the participants' present location, and the rural and seaside idyll of leisure time and prior holiday visits' (2006:824). As a central part of this, returning to a city now inhabited by other migrants unsettled the perceived possibility of returning to an 'authentic' Greek homeland and culture. Indeed, as Anastasia Christou explains in Chapter Nine in this book, homeland return for some can almost be an 'exile,' since prior constructions of homogeneity in the homeland are ruptured by immigration and other changed elements of social structure.

This chapter focuses on the city as a distinctive site of diasporic return for members of two minority communities who were in different ways already diasporic before they left Calcutta. Doing so, we seek to widen debates about ethnicity, diaspora and return to encompass the experiences of minority communities, to consider the ways in which the city rather than the 'homeland' might be understood as a site of return for such communities, and to analyse the ways in which diasporic returns to the city are experienced and understood in terms of wider narratives of urban and community change. This chapter also contributes to debates about urban imaginaries in India specifically and across South Asian diasporas more widely. Most closely tied to the concerns of this chapter, Mark-Anthony Falzon's research on Hindu Sindhi migration to Bombay foregrounds attachments to the city rather than a 'primordial homeland' as a 'cultural heart' (2003:662, 665), and as a site of return for Sindhis across a wider diaspora, materialised through practices revolving around patronage, investment, consumption and religion. Additionally, this chapter builds on wider work in the Diaspora Cities project[1] including Shompa Lahiri's (2010, 2011) research on the translocal mobilities of Brahmos between London and Calcutta and research on attachments to the city as home more than the nation as 'homeland' for Anglo-Indian and Chinese Calcuttans living in London and Toronto (Blunt and Bonnerjee, 2013).

Diasporic methodologies

This chapter draws on semi-structured individual and group interviews with 63 Anglo-Indians in Calcutta, London and Toronto and 58 Jews in Calcutta, London and a range of cities in Israel including Jerusalem, Ramleh and Lod. Most interviewees were aged over 55 and reflected migration at different periods of time, particularly to London in the late 1940s and 1950s and to Toronto since the 1970s, for Anglo-Indians, and to London and Israel over the post-independence period for Jewish Calcuttans. The interviews with Anglo-Indians were conducted in English, the main language of the community, and those with Jewish Calcuttans were conducted in English or Hebrew. Discussion about return visits to Calcutta formed part of wider interviews that spanned migration histories, memories of Calcutta, and community life in the wider diaspora.

The research aimed to study the importance of the city rather than the nation and/or 'homeland' for many people living in diaspora, to investigate the effects of migration on culture and identity for minority communities and to explore the connections between cities as sites of departure and resettlement. Seeking to move beyond not only 'methodological nationalism' in transnational and diaspora studies (as critiqued by Wimmer and Glick-Schiller, 2002) but also 'methodological territorialism,' whereby cities are often understood as contained entities in comparative urban studies (Ward, 2010), the research sought to draw out a range of 'interconnected trajectories – how different cities are implicated in each other's past, present and future' (Ward, 2010:480).

Interviewees were recruited through personal contacts, community organisations and snowball sampling. Alongside interviews, ethnographic research was carried out in participants' homes, restaurants and at community events and religious festivals, including the International Anglo-Indian Reunion in Toronto in 2007, Anglo-Indian Christmas celebrations in Calcutta, and services attended by Jewish Calcuttans in London and Israel. In this chapter we focus on the memories and experiences of migrants in later life to explore the ways in which return visits are articulated and understood in relation to urban and community change over time. Some members of both communities have migrated more than once, often first to London and then to Toronto for Anglo-Indians, and in both directions between London and

Israel for Jewish Calcuttans. In the rest of the chapter, we interweave narratives from both Anglo-Indian and Jewish Calcuttans who live in Calcutta, London, Toronto and Israel, drawing out similarities and differences in narratives of return both to the city and to the community.

Urban returns

Anglo-Indian and Jewish Calcuttans return to the city in a variety of ways. Most returns take the form of one-off visits: often, for Anglo-Indians, to celebrate Christmas and New Year in the city; others return more regularly, particularly if they have family or work ties to Calcutta. While a small number of Anglo-Indian and Jewish Calcuttans would like to move back to Calcutta more permanently, usually remembering communal support and social life in contrast to feelings of isolation and loneliness when growing older abroad, very few do so in practice. Some Anglo-Indian and Jewish Calcuttans would like to visit but are unable to do so because of ill-health or a lack of resources, whereas many choose not to return to Calcutta and sometimes visit other places in India for the first time instead. In this section we explore the ways in which decisions to return, and not to return, are shaped by ideas about the city as home more than the nation as homeland.

Returning to the city, often after many years away, is an emotional affair, with many Anglo-Indians in particular describing their visit as a journey home. Emily and her husband Richard, for example, returned to visit Calcutta after 40 years living in London. Emily explained that she had never wanted to return, but listening to people talking about Calcutta at the South London Anglo-Indian Association had awakened a yearning to do so. She said that "when the plane landed at Dum Dum airport, I really had tears in my eyes. ... This is where I was born and where I grew up." While there is often a wider cultural attachment to India, for Anglo-Indian Calcuttans the city as the place of birth was the emotional home. This interplay between the idea of home, nostalgia and roots is evident in Richard's sentiments about returning to Calcutta:

> 'I feel that nostalgia is something which comes with age. A 30 year old doesn't know the meaning of nostalgia. In the first six months I was in London, I would have gone back if I had the opportunity. But after that it settled and I never had the yearning. But after all these years I have the desire to go back. When we went back, we loved it. The smells, the memories, the sounds. ... Our children are not

much interested about India right now, but maybe when
they grow older they will want to know about their roots.'

(See Lahiri, 2011, for more on sensual memories of the city).

For Richard, his initial desire to return to India was strong but short-
lived, and he describes a different and more recent nostalgic yearning
to return, "which comes with age." While Richard was talking about
India more widely, he also invoked Calcutta as a site of diasporic return
through specific memories of the city and urban life. Describing the
nostalgia that took him back to the city, he said that "when we go back
to Calcutta it's not like we go back as tourists ... we go back for the
memories." Such memories are closely tied to a sense of belonging to
Calcutta rather than India more widely.

Ideas about belonging to Calcutta are often articulated through
attachments to the city as home, both in terms of genealogical 'roots'
and the material spaces of urban dwelling, which span the domestic
home and urban neighbourhood as well as the wider city (see Blunt
and Bonnerjee, 2013, for further discussion). For Peter, an Anglo-
Indian who lives in Calcutta, Anglo-Indians come back to the city
"because generations have lived here – their fathers, grandfathers,
great-grandfathers and mothers did things around the city, so it still
draws them ... it's the roots that are here." The sense of roots evoked
by Peter implies genealogical inheritance and cultural affinity, which
can combine as personal priorities in later life, as Percival points out
in Chapter Six.

In the years before and after independence, many Anglo-Indians
had a complex and ambiguous sense of belonging to both India as
motherland and Britain as fatherland (Blunt, 2005). But for many
of those who emigrated to Britain and elsewhere – as well as for
those who remained in India – a cultural identification with India
has become stronger over the years. Sharing memories of India and
expressing pride in being an Anglo-Indian have been particularly
important for older community members and are manifested through,
for example, school and international reunions and community events
marking World Anglo-Indian Day; a wide range of societies and
websites; the popularity of genealogical research; and the importance
of fundraising and welfare work to help poor Anglo-Indians in the
subcontinent (Blunt, 2005).

Despite a growing identification with India, the city (and, for
many Anglo-Indians, the railway colony) remains a more concrete,
located and personal site of attachment and belonging. Unlike Emily

and Richard, many Anglo-Indian Calcuttans return to the city with their children and grandchildren to show them important places in their family history. Joan, who now lives in London, described one of her friends returning "not for the sake of nostalgia, [but] because their children were interested to see where their parents' homes were, where their schools were." Similarly, David, who migrated to Toronto in 1972, took his son back to Calcutta for a visit and explained their sentiments on returning:

> 'In the heart, [those who left Calcutta] always say, you know, "we left Calcutta, but we left our heart and soul in the city," because even today, there's a charm, a wonderful charm about Calcutta; something that will never change. And I feel so blessed, and my son too went to experience it. My son saw the same thing. And you know what, he loved it. But guess what he loved about it? He loved the people. He loved the hospitality, the warmth.'

These feelings are echoed by Patricia, who lives in Calcutta and was involved in organising a short trip to the city after the World Anglo-Indian Reunion held in Bangalore in 1998.[2] As she said, "If it is their hometown, there is a strong attachment. There is something about Calcutta – the warmth, the food, the togetherness, that they don't find anywhere else."

Fewer Jewish Calcuttans than Anglo-Indians return for occasional visits, mainly because the community in Calcutta is now very small and there is a sense that it has relocated particularly to London and Israel. But those Jewish Calcuttans who do return to the city usually do so on a more regular basis than many Anglo-Indians. Some community members return on a regular basis either for paid or philanthropic work. Sam, who now lives in Israel, returns most years and works in a Jewish bakery for two to three months, for example, whereas Benny, a prominent figure in the Calcutta Jewish community in London, has been returning regularly for the last 25 years:

> 'I go back every three years ... most of our friends now are Indian ... we just go and see the people that we know, people that we worked with and we know from our childhood. Also I work with a charity. It's not a Jewish charity. ... I lost my son in Calcutta ... and in his name we put a fixed deposit [to fund a hospital]. ... I also have

connections with Muslim charities, I try to help them whenever we can.'

In contrast to those Anglo-Indian and Jewish Calcuttans who return on a regular or occasional basis to the city, many others choose not to return. For Linda, an Anglo-Indian living in Toronto, "there would be a sadness that I would not recognise anything. ... I will not know anybody and I will see a lot of poverty that will affect me very much." Helen, a Jewish woman who has lived in London since 1970 has also chosen not to return to Calcutta: "My friends have asked me to go back but I don't think I want to go. Too much has happened. You know it's a different country, the people have become different." Such perceived changes include higher levels of urban poverty, particularly within the Anglo-Indian and Jewish communities, more begging on the street, and anxieties about health and hygiene. As Eli explains, for example, "My wife for a start doesn't like to go back for one reason and that reason is not the poverty so much as the cleanliness, the hygiene is not so good. I mean the food and all wouldn't appeal to my wife." In contrast to others who return to Calcutta with their children and grandchildren, Nelson, a prominent figure in the Jewish Calcuttan community in London, has never returned, unlike his children: "My kids have gone but they didn't like it at all ... the beggars have multiplied tenfold."

Although ideas about the city more than the nation as homeland were important for both Anglo-Indian and Jewish Calcuttans returning to the place of their birth, other narratives of return beyond the city have been important for both communities. Historically for Anglo-Indians, contested ideas about Britain as 'home' and/or 'homeland' – often embodied by the figure of a European forefather – were prominent in debates about the place and future of the community in independent India (Blunt, 2005). Although many Anglo-Indians imagined themselves to be returning 'home' when they migrated to Britain after independence, they often found life there unfamiliar and unsettling when they arrived (Blunt, 2005). Such ideas of Britain as a site of return were widely discussed around the time of independence, but are far less important for Anglo-Indians today.

In contrast, the idea of Israel as a site of return has been significant for Jewish Calcuttans since the foundation of the state in 1948. Migration patterns are complex, with some Jewish Calcuttans in our research settling in Israel, others living there for a time before moving to London, and others living in London before moving to Israel. The idea as well as the practice of return to Israel is important for Calcutta Jews in both Calcutta and London. For Mike, who left Calcutta as a child and lived in Israel before settling in London, "When Israel was created in 1948, all the Jews of Calcutta said, 'Next year in Jerusalem …'", While Dan remembered that "The only subject that interested us [in the late 1940s] was that of Zionism and Israel." Many like Elias from London expressed the desire to 'make Aliya' – to return to Israel: "We love Israel, I'd run and stay in Israel tomorrow if I could get the chance … that's our homeland. That's where all Jews want to finish up." As an example of someone who has 'made Aliya,' Ernie migrated to London and visited a friend in Israel in 1956: "And he invited me to his home and I came to his home and I fell in love with Israel. And I said I'm going to come live here one day. And I came – three years later I was here, with my wife and daughter." Although the city more than the nation is important for Anglo-Indian and Jewish Calcuttans when they return to India, other sites of return beyond the city, and particularly Israel for Jewish Calcuttans, exist across a wider diaspora.

City and community

In contrast to most research on return visits and migrations, Anglo-Indian and Jewish Calcuttans were members of minority communities before they left their place of birth. Members of both communities emigrated in large numbers after independence. While both communities are much smaller today, there are far more Anglo-Indians than Jews in the city. Both Anglo-Indian and Jewish organisations and institutions continue to exist but now take different forms: the three synagogues are no longer open for worship; two schools remain Jewish in name, but they are now attended by pupils from other communities; churches, clubs and schools once dominated by Anglo-Indians are now more diverse in their membership; and community organisations are increasingly involved in philanthropic work for each community. While the very small Jewish community continues to live in particular streets in the central city, many Anglo-Indians have moved away from central neighbourhoods to places like Picnic Garden in east Calcutta.

In this section, we explore the ways in which returns to the city are also, in different and sometimes contested ways, returns to the community. In particular, we address the ways in which diasporic returns to the city by Anglo-Indian and Jewish Calcuttans in later life are experienced and understood in terms of wider narratives of urban and community continuity and change.

For most Anglo-Indian and Jewish Calcuttans who visit Calcutta, key points of return include public and often iconic sites alongside more personal places of memory. June, an Anglo-Indian who has lived in London since 1958, has returned to Calcutta twice and visited "New Market ... Nahoum's [a Jewish bakery in New Market] ... the barley sugar place." For Noel, places such as New Market, the Victoria Memorial and the Botanical Gardens have become like a "pilgrimage ... [where] if you don't go, something is incomplete." Visiting both public and personal places of memory is evocative and emotional. Matilda, for example, described her feelings when visiting the synagogue where her family used to pray: "What I remember of the holiday was – my synagogue was open. Now they've closed it. ... And we went there and I went up to sit where I used to sit. And I, I was crying. I was crying like a baby." Her husband recalled a similar reaction when visiting New Market: "Wherever she went she used to cry ... as we were approaching the New Market, the smell of the flowers hit her and she started moaning. And I said, what's wrong? 'The flowers, the flowers! They're making me nostalgic.'"

Remembering the city as home was viewed by many Anglo-Indian and Jewish Calcuttans in terms of nostalgia (for more on nostalgia, see Blunt, 2003; Walder, 2010), and reflected a disjuncture between attachments to the wider city as home and the difficulties of finding home-like places in the city today. For many Anglo-Indian and Jewish Calcuttans, the difficulties of returning to their former homes were poignant and emotional. Donald, an Anglo-Indian who has lived in London since 1954, described the unfamiliarity of his home:

> 'We went back to our house, our home. When we were away, many of our friends who went to Calcutta took photographs of our house. When I first saw it, I could not recognise it. ... I knew the address, but I could not recognise it.'

For Susan, who left Calcutta when she was 17, "I still dream of going through each room in my house, either at night, if I can't sleep, and I picture every room, and I remember opening every drawer. ... I have been back four times and I just can't wait to go again." When she returns, "I knock on the door and they show me how it has changed and I stand there and cry."

While such accounts reveal the difficulties of returning to one's former home, particularly after a long period of time (in a different context, see Bunkše, 2004), urban neighbourhoods and the wider city were significant points of return, with specific buildings, locations and practices evoking memories of Anglo-Indian and Jewish Calcutta. Such sites and practices revolved around family, friends, religious worship, school, work and food and, together forged a sense of community identity and sociality. Returning to Calcutta at particular times of year – notably, for many Anglo-Indians, to celebrate Christmas and New Year – involves participating in wider community events in the city and provides a clear contrast for many with life in London or Toronto. For example, Lionel, an Anglo-Indian who lives in London, returns to Calcutta most years for Christmas and New Year, "because they know how to enjoy themselves … over here, nothing." Eating particular foods at Christmas, notably cakes from Nahoum's, the Jewish bakery in New Market, is important for resident and returning Anglo-Indians. But throughout the year, reliving past memories of the city through eating particular foods, such as Calcutta Chinese food, kati rolls and barley sugar, was closely associated with restaurants, street stalls and New Market more than domestic homes (also see Lahiri, 2011).

Visiting particular shops and restaurants also often felt more familiar than returning to former homes in the city, and can be important sites of encounter and recognition. Charles, for example, is an Anglo-Indian who has lived in London since 1955. He returned to Calcutta in his seventies, and went into a shop where his mother used to take him to buy clothes. An elderly man at the back of the shop asked him "You are from Ripon Street, aren't you? … I remember your mother bringing you here as a child," and Charles was profoundly surprised to be recognised after almost 50 years: "My heart stopped beating for a while you know."

Urban neighbourhoods and the wider city are also – like former homes – sites of change. For Sarah, a Jewish Calcuttan now living in London: "things are not the same as they were in India. The spit and polish has gone out … It's standards. And these big clubs have gone down. The Bank Club has gone down. The Calcutta Club has gone down." For Jewish Calcuttans in particular, not only has the community significantly diminished in size, but communal places are now often closed or neglected. Salomon, for example, described visiting the Jewish cemetery in Calcutta, an area frequented by dogs, which caused him to be ashamed that members of his family are interred there. For Salomon, the decline of the cemetery was part of what he perceived as a wider urban decline since independence, resulting in an ability to live in Calcutta "the way I used to live as a child".

The disjuncture between the past and the present of both the city and community is reflected by Agatha, an Anglo-Indian living in London:

> 'We still cling to what we used to be, what you like a place to be, what it meant to you. And it is quite a rude awakening if it is so glaringly different or isn't there at all.'

For Agatha and for many other Anglo-Indian and Jewish Calcuttans, the links between 'what *we* used to be' and 'what you like a *place* to be' bound personal and community memories to particular neighbourhoods as well as the wider city. Narratives of urban change were thereby closely intertwined with narratives of community change. A clear distinction was drawn by a number of Anglo-Indian and Jewish Calcuttans between the 'old' and 'new' city, with implications for older returnees. As Agatha's husband Donald explained:

> 'one should look at it as a city out of time with itself, it's being overrun by modernity, so nobody's got time for the old. This is how I explained it to myself.'

Daniel, a Jewish Calcuttan living in London, describes:

> 'just the feeling of being there, just to visit and come back to my road with a group of friends it brings back memories. But they've ruined Calcutta. ... Calcutta has become so neglected, un-repaired. The roads are not repaired. Mind you there's a new Calcutta being built, by the way. ... Old Calcutta is very, very dilapidated.'

Alongside narratives of urban decline and the juxtaposition of 'old' and 'new' Calcutta, many Anglo-Indian and Jewish Calcuttans described continuity as well as change in each community and their experiences of the city. Such continuities revolved around the warmth and friendliness of other Calcuttans and the ability to live in comfort while visiting. Morris, who first migrated to Israel and now lives in London, describes his positive experiences of return:

> 'We go to clubs, we know everyone at the top ... so it's luxury for us, always VIP treatment wherever we go, restaurants, you name it, the Indians all want to be our friends so we have a better, nice feel about it. Who cares about me in London?'

Similarly evoking a sense of status, recognition and familiarity, Bradley describes visiting the Grail Club: "the bearers ... they know us so well ... he watches us from the bar ... he comes ... he's got soda in his pocket ... whiskey in his hand. ... he does it exactly the way you want it." Both Bradley and his friend Lionel feel that the quality of life for Anglo-Indians is better in Calcutta than in London, and in this context others talked of friendship, warmth, comfort and hospitality. Sarah, a Jewish Calcuttan from London, returns regularly and stays with a friend, which she appreciates, because "I am alone here. And I'm very fond of her."

Both in clubs and when visiting friends or family, Patricia (an Anglo-Indian who lives in Calcutta) explains that "They revel in the comfort of having someone do the things for them," in contrast to their lives in diaspora (see Blunt, 2005, for more on domestic work after migration for Anglo-Indians). But for others returning to Calcutta, not only is there a clear disjuncture between the past and present, but also between the community that stayed in Calcutta and those who migrated. Thomas (an Anglo-Indian who lives in Toronto) was distressed at seeing the poverty experienced by many Anglo-Indians who remained in the city, and his vivid memory of these encounters reveal the ways in which the familiar can be experienced as unfamiliar on return, reflecting the temporal disjuncture between the past and present as well as the social disjuncture between many members of the community in Calcutta and across the wider diaspora.

Many Anglo-Indian and Jewish Calcuttans choose not to return to the city because of the level and visibility of urban poverty. For many of those who visit Calcutta as well as those who choose not to do so, philanthropic support for their communities serves in many ways as a figurative return, whereby they attempt to ameliorate the poverty experienced by many who remained. Reflecting the complex and multi-layered returns to both the city and the community, Erwin, a Jewish Calcuttan who lives in London, described his feelings about a recent visit to Calcutta: "Hated it, but I loved it ... I hated what it's become but I loved being back there."

Conclusions

Through its focus on return visits by Anglo-Indian and Jewish Calcuttans in later life now living in London, Toronto and Israel, this chapter has explored the importance of the city more than the nation and/or 'homeland' as a site of diasporic return. While a growing body of work on return has come to focus on different places and landscapes of memory and attachment, little work has concentrated on the city as a site of return. At the same time, a wide range of research has revealed the ways in which ethnic identities come to be unsettled on return, but little work has explored the dynamics of return for those who were minorities before as well as after migration. Little research has also focused on return visits by migrants in later life.

Through our examination of two minority communities from Calcutta and their diasporic returns to the city, we have made two main contributions to broader debates not only about return but also about the connections between cities, communities and diasporas and about the meanings and experiences of return in later life. First, a clear distinction was drawn by Anglo-Indian and Jewish Calcuttans about returning to the city as a former resident and visiting other parts of India as a tourist. While some chose to return to Calcutta for occasional or more regular visits, others chose to visit different places in India for the first time, and viewed this less as a return visit than a holiday. Narratives of genealogical roots and cultural inheritance bound members of both communities, whether or not they chose to return, to Calcutta more than India, revealing the importance of the city as home. Second, diasporic returns to the city by Anglo-Indian and Jewish Calcuttans were experienced and understood in terms of wider narratives of urban and community continuity and change, particularly in relation to community practices and the built environment.

For members of both communities, key points of return included public and often iconic sites alongside more personal places of memory. While visiting former homes was often difficult and emotional, other places in the wider city, including particular neighbourhoods, streets and restaurants, were important in shaping narratives of the wider city as home. Particular practices, notably community sociability for Anglo-Indians in clubs and at Christmas and New Year and, for both communities, visiting New Market, other shops and eating particular food, bound experiences of the city to memories of community life. The Jewish community in Calcutta is now very small and community sites and practices are in decline, and the larger Anglo-Indian community is now more dispersed away from the central city. In different ways, returns to the city were also, often in unsettling as well as affirming ways, returns to the community.

The continuities and change of both communities were also mapped onto the wider city, with comparisons between the 'old' and 'new' Calcutta reflecting not only wider changes in the built environment but also the place of both minorities within the city. For both Anglo-Indian and Jewish Calcuttans, returning to the city rendered it both familiar and strange, reflecting a series of disjunctures not only between the past and present of both the city and each community but also between both communities in Calcutta and across the wider diaspora. The history and identity of both communities were intimately bound up with the city.

While we have focused on two particular communities from Calcutta and the similarities and differences between them, our arguments have wider implications for studying cities, diasporas and returns. Cities themselves are already diasporic, shaped by multiple histories of migration and resettlement. The study of return visits and return migrations should not only consider the city as an important site of return, but should also focus on communities who were minorities before as well as after migration. Doing so not only complicates ideas about the 'homeland' as a site of return but also unsettles assumptions about ethnicity, diaspora and return.

Acknowledgements

This chapter is a revised version of a paper published in the special issue of *South Asian Diaspora* on 'South Asian Cities and Diasporas' (A. Blunt, J. Bonnerjee and N. Hysler Rubin, 2012, 'Diasporic returns to the city: Anglo-Indian and Jewish visits to Calcutta,' 4 (1): 5–43) and is reproduced with kind permission of Taylor and Francis (www.tandfonline.com). We would like to thank Ajaya Sahoo, editor of *South Asian Diaspora*, the two reviewers, and John Percival for their very helpful comments. The research was funded by The Leverhulme Trust as part of the wider project on 'Diaspora Cities: imagining Calcutta in London, Toronto and Jerusalem.' We would like to thank Shompa Lahiri for her work on this project too, and also the audience at the Annual Conference of the Royal Geographical Society (with Institute of British Geographers) in 2011 for their very helpful questions and comments.

References

Abdelhady, D. (2008) 'Representing the homeland: Lebanese diasporic notions of home and return in a global context', *Cultural Dynamics*, 20(1):53–72.

Andrews, R. (2005) 'Being Anglo-Indian: practices and stories from Calcutta', Unpublished PhD thesis, Palmerston North: Massey University.

Baldassar, L. (2001) *Visits home: migration experiences between Italy and Australia*, Melbourne: Melbourne University Press.

Banerjee, H., Gupta, N. and Mukherjee, S. (eds) (2009) *Calcutta Mosaic: essays and interviews on the minority communities of Calcutta*, New Delhi: Anthem Press.

Basu, P. (2007) *Highland Homecomings: genealogy and heritage tourism in the Scottish diaspora*, London: Routledge.

Blunt, A. (2003) 'Collective memory and productive nostalgia: Anglo-Indian home-making at McCluskieganj', *Environment and Planning D: Society and Space*, 21:717–738.

Blunt, A. (2005) *Domicile and Diaspora: Anglo-Indian women and the spatial politics of home*, Oxford: Blackwell.

Blunt, A. and Bonnerjee, J. (2013) 'Home, city and diaspora: Anglo-Indian and Chinese attachments to Calcutta', *Global Networks*, 13(2): 220-240.

Brah, A. (1996) *Cartographies of Diaspora: contesting identities*, London: Routledge.

Bunkše, E. (2004) *Geography and the Art of Life*, Baltimore, MD: Johns Hopkins University Press.

Chatterji, A. (2009) *Ethnicity, Migration and the Urban Landscape of Kolkata*, Kolkata: K.P. Bagchi and Company.

Christou, A. and King, R. (2006) 'Migrants encounter migrants in the city: the changing context of "home" for second-generation Greek-American return migrants', *International Journal of Urban and Regional Research*, 30(4):816–835.

Conway, D. and Potter, R. B. (eds) (2009) *Return migration of the next generations: 21st century transnational mobility*, Aldershot: Ashgate.

Conway, D., Potter, R. B. and St Bernard, G. (2008) 'Dual citizenship or dual identity? Does "transnationalism" supplant "nationalism" among returning Trinidadians?', *Global Networks*, 8(4):373–397.

Duval, D.T. (2005) 'Expressions of migrant mobilities among Caribbean migrants in Toronto, Canada', in R.B. Potter, D. Conway and J. Phillips (eds) *The Experience of Return Migration: Caribbean perspectives*, Aldershot: Ashgate, pp 245–261.

Dwyer, C. (2002) '"Where are you from?" Young British Muslim women and the making of "home"', in A. Blunt and C. McEwan (eds) *Postcolonial Geographies*, London: Continuum, pp 184–199.

Ezra, E.D. (1986) *Turning Back the Pages: a chronicle of Calcutta Jewry*, London: Brookside Press.

Falzon, M-A. (2003) '"Bombay, our cultural heart": rethinking the relation between homeland and diaspora', *Ethnic and Racial Studies*, 26(4):662–683.

Gowans, G. (2002) 'A passage from India: geographies and experiences of repatriation, 1858–1939', *Social and Cultural Geography*, 3:403–423.

Hage, G. (1996) 'The spatial imaginary of national practices: dwelling-domesticating/being-exterminating', *Environment and Planning D: Society and Space*, 14:463–486.

Hammond, L.C. (2004) *This Place will Become Home: refugee repatriation to Ethiopia*, Ithaca, NY: Cornell University Press.

Harper, M. (ed) (2005) *Emigrant Homecomings: the return movement of emigrants, 1600–2000*, Manchester: Manchester University Press.

Horst, H. (2005) 'Landscaping Englishness: the postcolonial predicament of returnees in Mandeville, Jamaica', in R.B. Potter, D. Conway and J. Phillips (eds) *The Experience of Return Migration: Caribbean perspectives*, Aldershot: Ashgate, pp 207–223.

Hyman, M. (1995) *Jews of the Raj*, London: Hyman Publishers.

Kali Theatre Company (2004) *Calcutta Kosher*, London.

Kibria, N. (2002) 'Of blood, belonging and homeland trips: transnationalism and identity among second-generation Chinese and Korean Americans', in P. Levitt and M.C. Waters (eds) *The Changing Face of Home: the transnational lives of the second generation*, New York: Russell Sage Foundation, pp 295–311.

King, R. and Christou, A. (2010) 'Cultural geographies of counter-diasporic migration: perspectives from the study of second-generation "returnees" to Greece', *Population, Space and Place*, 16:103–119.

Lahiri, S. (2010) 'At home in the city, at home in the world: cosmopolitanism and urban belonging in Kolkata', *Contemporary South Asia*, 18(2):191–204.

Lahiri, S. (2011) 'Remembering the city: translocality and the senses', *Social and Cultural Geography*, 12:855–869.

Ley, D. and Kobayashi, A. (2005) 'Back to Hong Kong: return migration or transnational sojourn?' *Global Networks*, 5(2):111–127.

Musleah, E.N. (1975) *On the Banks of the Ganga: the sojourn of Jews in Calcutta*, North Quincy, MA: The Christopher Publishing House.

Potter, R.B., Conway, D. and Phillips, J. (eds) (2005) 'The experience of return migration: Caribbean perspectives', Aldershot: Ashgate.

Ray, D. (2001) *The Jewish Heritage of Calcutta*, Calcutta: Minerva Associates.

Thomson, A. (2005) '"My wayward heart": homesickness, longing and the return of British post-war immigrants from Australia', in M. Harper (ed) *Emigrant Homecomings: the return movement of emigrants, 1600–2000*, Manchester: Manchester University Press, pp 105–130.

Salih, R. (2002) 'Shifting meanings of "home": consumption and identity in Moroccan women's transnational practices between Italy and Morocco', In N. Al-Ali and K. Koser (eds) *New approaches to migration? Transnational communities and the transformation of home*, London: Routledge, pp 51-67.

Tsuda, T. (2009) 'Introduction: diasporic return and migration studies', in T. Tsuda (ed) *Diasporic Homecomings: ethnic return migration in comparative perspective*, Stanford, CA: Stanford University Press, pp 1–18.

Walder, D. (2010) *Postcolonial Nostalgias: writing, representation, and memory*, London: Routledge.

Ward, K. (2010) 'Towards a relational comparative approach to the study of cities', *Progress in Human Geography*, 34(4):471–487.

Wimmer, A. and Glick-Schiller, N. (2002) 'Methodological nationalism and beyond: nation-state building, migration and the social sciences', *Global Networks*, 2(4):301–334.

Wyman, M. (2005) 'Emigrants returning: the evolution of a tradition', in M. Harper (ed) *Emigrant Homecomings: the return movement of emigrants, 1600–2000*, Manchester: Manchester University Press, pp 16–30.

EIGHT

Returning to 'roots': Estonian-Australian child migrants visiting the homeland

Brad Ruting

Introduction

As we have seen in previous chapters, ageing migrants can yearn to go back to their homeland. In many cases, having been separated by large physical distances and periods of time, this feeling tends to grow stronger and stronger (Baldassar, 2001). Some eventually move back to the homeland but the large majority do not. Rather, they engage with its emotional pull by making return visits, journeying back and forth between their country of birth and country of residence (Baldassar, 2001; Stephenson, 2002; Coles and Timothy, 2004). These trips are an important way of maintaining connections to the homeland, and building new ones.

This chapter explores the role of homeland visits for Estonians that migrated to Australia as children and are now around retirement age. There was a large wave of emigration from Estonia during the Second World War and many of those who left settled in Australia (Tammaru et al, 2010). Cut off from their homeland, which had become incorporated into the Soviet Union, they made new lives and many became, to a large degree, Australian. A significant number of them migrated as children and have lived most of their lives in Australia (Salasoo, 1986). But in the early 1990s, the situation changed. Estonia regained independence and many of these child migrants found it possible to visit Estonia. They went to seek out long-lost relatives and return to their 'roots', and even to form new relationships with Estonia, while maintaining their lives and family relationships in Australia. This chapter examines their experiences: Why did they visit Estonia? Why do they keep going back? How do these visits affect their identities and their lives?

The history

Estonia is a small country of around 1.3 million people in north-east Europe. In 1940, during the Second World War, it became absorbed into the Soviet Union and remained under the 'Iron Curtain' until regaining independence in 1991. Around this time, fear of repression, persecution or deportation to Siberia by Soviet authorities led to large-scale involuntary emigration, with thousands of Estonians fleeing to the West. Many lived temporarily in displaced persons camps in Germany and Sweden before ending up in the United States, Canada, Britain, Australia and elsewhere (Tammaru et al, 2010). After the war, around 6,000 Estonians resettled in Australia (Tammaru et al, 2010), mainly in Sydney, Melbourne and Adelaide.

Small 'Estonia House' cultural centres had already been established in these cities by earlier migrants and expanded considerably in the post-war period (Salasoo, 1986). Migrants and their children formed social groups for dancing, sport, summer camps, church services and language schools, and an Estonian-language newspaper has been published weekly in Sydney since 1949. As is the case in a number of diasporas (Brah, 1996; Cohen, 1997), many migrant parents attempted to maintain cultural memories, practices and their native language in their children, in the hope that one day Communism would fall in Estonia and they could move back 'home'. During these first few decades, it was often considered too dangerous or expensive to visit Estonia, and very few made the journey – those who did reported that while it was possible to visit from the late 1960s, Soviet authorities heavily restricted and monitored the movements of tourists. Some visitors also feared persecution.

As the years went on, there was gradual decline in participation and engagement in Estonian cultural events and activities in Australia. Conditions in Estonia made it difficult to maintain connections to relatives and others there, and meant that little information (or new migrants) made it to Australia. Moreover, Estonian communities were small and many migrants found it relatively easy to integrate into Australian society – some families did not want or need to involve themselves in migrant social groups or were put off by politicised discussions at events (Pehk, 2007).

By the time of the 2006 census, around 1,900 Australian residents were born in Estonia and a further 6,300 claimed Estonian ancestry (Australian Bureau of Statistics [ABS], 2007). The majority of these are the post-war migrants and their descendants – there has been relatively little emigration from Estonia to Australia since. Following Estonian independence in 1991 a growing number of them have made visits to Estonia, either to return to their place of birth or to experience their ancestral homeland. Visits have been particularly popular among those who migrated to Australia as young children – many visited for the first time when aged in their forties or fifties, and some continue to journey there aged into their seventies. This has been facilitated by a more favourable political situation in Estonia and reductions in the cost of international travel. Such visits have become a key part of how Estonian-Australians relate to, and form connections with, their homeland.

The research

There is a growing body of research on migrants that visit their homelands, sometimes multiple times, while keeping their everyday lives rooted in their country of residence (for example, Smith and Jackson, 1999; Lomsky-Feder and Rapoport, 2000; Stephenson, 2002; Duval, 2003; Oxfeld, 2004). This is part of a broader phenomenon of 'diasporic travel', where individuals or families journey to places of significance in their ethnic or migratory histories, including to the place they consider their homeland (Ruting, 2012). This can also encompass, for example, the children and grandchildren of migrants making a trip to the ancestral homeland (Baldassar, 2001; Carter, 2004; Ruting, 2012), or 'roots tourists' seeking out their ancestral origins in a distant land (Basu, 2007). Diasporic travel blends together migration and tourism across time and space, linking together, both physically and metaphorically, contemporary migrant or migrant-descended populations with their ancestral homelands, kin and cultural or ethnic origins. In the process, the diasporic travellers might revive old connections, form new ones, strengthen their sense of identity, or encounter the unexpected.

This chapter focuses on Estonians that migrated to Australia as children – those who are often termed the '1.5 generation', usually defined as having migrated under the age of 12. Many are now aged in their sixties and seventies and have made one or more journeys to visit Estonia. The chapter examines why many of them made such journeys and the experiences that they had there. There have been few studies that have touched on return visits by people later in life (Smith and Jackson, 1999; Baldassar, 2001), and almost no examination of migrants that were exiled from their homeland as children. The effect that exile can have on identities and cultural practices in the diaspora has been widely studied (Brah, 1996; Cohen, 1997). However, only a handful of studies have examined visits by exiles and their descendents to a homeland that they had long been cut off from (Smith and Jackson, 1999; Kelly, 2000), or that they could not visit due to government-imposed restrictions (King and Vullnetari, 2006). Much is left to be understood about the experiences of migrants who return to a country that they were born in but have been separated from for many years.

Estonian-Australians offer a useful case study. This research was based on surveys (paper and online) and interviews with Estonian-born people who migrated to Australia as children. Sixteen interviews and 31 surveys were conducted for these '1.5 generation' Estonian-Australians, most of whom migrated when very young and remembered almost nothing about their early lives in Estonia. Almost all were aged in their sixties or older – for example, 84 per cent of survey respondents were aged from 65 to 74, with a further 6 per cent aged 75 or above. Further, as I am of Estonian ancestry myself (third generation) this allowed me, at times, to establish valuable rapport with respondents. Interview respondents are referred to in the text with a pseudonym. Most respondents have visited Estonia three or more times, usually with their spouse or children, and stayed with relatives where possible (Table 8.1). Most visits occurred during the 2000s when many respondents had reached retirement.

Table 8.1: Frequency of visits to Estonia by generation, survey sample (missing responses excluded)

Number of visits	0	1	2	3 to 5	6 to 10	10+
Number of respondents	2	4	2	13	6	3

'Like touching with your roots'

A number of factors compelled Estonian-Australian child migrants to visit their homeland later in life. In many cases there was a desire to see and experience a small, distant country that was part of their parents' identity and stories, and which had been a focal point in many social activities when growing up. A major reason was to meet with relatives in Estonia. Many respondents had known their relatives only as young children and had lost contact since migration, with rare letters to their parents often the only source of contact for many years. But through visits, they could re-establish family relationships after the trauma of war, displacement and disconnection from the homeland. The desire to seek out Estonian relatives – or details of parents' lives in Estonia – was often triggered by particular life events, such as a parent dying, an onset of a feeling of mortality (often around middle age), retirement, or children finishing school (allowing time to undertake genealogical research). For others it was triggered by Estonia regaining independence or by a relative attempting to make contact. Some respondents took the task of discovering and meeting relatives with great seriousness:

'I'm now searching, doing family history searches, family tree searches. And I'm finding out missing things from the family story that my parents didn't know, especially because my Mum was adopted out, and my relatives in Estonia don't. know. I found their relatives they didn't know about.' [Priit]

These were also journeys of self-discovery that enabled respondents to establish a stronger sense of self. Researching family histories almost inevitably resulted in a trip to Estonia, or a strong compulsion to make a visit, especially when living relatives could be communicated with. These respondents had an urge to trace their 'roots' and engage with their homeland:

'It is a pilgrimage. It is something, it's almost you need to do, it's almost like touching with your roots because your parents have come from there as well.' [Helve]

Along with an innate compulsion to visit relatives, many respondents also felt a sense of curiosity about Estonia, a distant country that was in some sense a part of them, but about which they knew little. Many wanted to visit to find out how much Estonia had changed, and to experience its transition to a capitalist democracy (a curiosity also felt by some Russian migrants to Israel when visiting Russia (Lomsky-Feder and Rapoport, 2000)). Several respondents 'just had to go' as soon as they had the time and money to make the trip:

'[I went] to meet the relatives, but it was more than that too. I mean it was just to, just to be back there, to re-establish that connection that we had never lost. That emotional connection is always there. … It was just kind of self evident that we'd go.' [Jaan]

'I guess it was always the feeling that I needed to go, I wanted to go. I just wanted to see, wanted to connect.' [Krista]

'My entire life I'd associated entirely with Estonia, and just saw myself as trapped on a prison island, basically, of

> Australia. So I'd always wanted to go there, but because of the political situation, the financial situation, the family situation, education, I couldn't. It was just impossible. So I went in 1983 because that was the first time I could actually afford to go.' [Martin]

Moreover, the compulsion to visit Estonia arose both out of a desire to engage with the landscapes, buildings and places of memories, as well as to engage with ideals of the homeland that offered reassurance, cultural identity or forms of social engagement. Indeed, in many cases the stories told by parents, and migrant social activities, played an important role.

A defining feature of many diasporas and migrant groups is the reproduction of narratives of 'return' to the homeland, coupled with a desire for eventual and permanent return (Safran, 1991). However, migrants are often caught in a 'perpetual suspension' when return is undesirable – generally because material living conditions are better in the country of residence or because conditions in the homeland are never quite right for return migration (Skrbiš, 1999:51). These 'myths of return' can become a key influence on cultural memories and values that are transmitted to children through stories, social practices and migrant institutions (Skrbiš, 1999). They can also motivate these children to visit the homeland (Baldassar, 2001; Christou and King, 2010). To some extent, respondents maintained an awareness of Estonia and their exile from it due to these processes. This led many to visit there later in life to experience the land that meant so much to their parents. But in some cases, parents had suppressed painful memories of exile and the homeland they had left behind:

> 'I started to ask my mother a lot of questions. I really wanted to know about my father ... I was often getting the same stories again, but there were other things I wanted to know, in between. I wanted a fairly coherent and well sequenced narrative in my mind, but that never happened ... I wanted to start to make sense of it all, and wanted to know more about Estonia.' [Krista]

For respondents in such situations, missing information tended to reinforce their desire to visit Estonia, as a way of filling in the gaps.

'A very moving experience'

Visiting Estonia was a poignant experience for most respondents. Living in Australia and having little connection with Estonia itself for a long time often resulted in marked differences between what was expected and what was actually encountered. While almost all respondents had expected that Soviet occupation would have altered significantly the society and built landscape of Estonia, many still felt shocked when they first visited. Distant memories and the stories of parents and family friends had shaped expectations about what Estonia would be like, yet the reality of being there led, at times, to initial feelings of estrangement or alienation. One respondent found that going back to Estonia put her previous conceptions of it into stark contrast with the reality of a homeland that had changed markedly:

> 'I expected to be absolutely overcome with emotion, and I was disappointed that all that was missing. I didn't feel anything. I landed and I thought I'd be like the Pope kissing the ground … [But] I thought, this has got nothing to do with me … I thought [Estonian folk-hero] Kalevipoeg is sure to be waiting for me at the airport and take me off to a picnic … It didn't feel like [a homecoming], unfortunately. I would have loved that feeling.' [Pille]

Such impressions tended to be most pronounced for the small number of respondents that visited Estonia while it was still under Soviet occupation (pre-1991), who were generally those with stronger sentiments towards their homeland and had the means to visit. Going back to Estonia while it was under the Iron Curtain was sometimes a shock as restrictions on tourist movement, Soviet architecture, and sometimes hostile social relations, led to alienating experiences. Travellers were only allowed to stay in designated 'In-Tourist' hotels, all of which were located in Tallinn (the capital), and were forbidden from staying overnight with relatives or venturing out of Tallinn without special permission. As in other contexts, migrants' contact with their families in the homeland and ability to rekindle personal connections was highly constrained by the government (King and Vullnetari, 2006). Respondents also felt marked out by their 'Westernness' and stood out because of their appearance or the way they talked:

> 'Moving around was really weird, and you stood out like a sore thumb everywhere. People are suspicious of you, they

don't want to touch you or communicate with you or smile or exchange eye contact or anything, in case someone could construe that as communicating with someone from the West. ... So there was kind of a frustration as well as this elation and joy and immediate home recognition, and stuff like that.' [Priit]

As reported elsewhere, experiences of visiting the homeland are not always as positive or enriching as might have been expected beforehand: return can highlight social and linguistic change (Kelly, 2000; Lomsky-Feder and Rapoport, 2000; Baldassar, 2001; Duval, 2003), or compel the renegotiation of ethnic or national belonging. That said, other respondents expressed surprise that Estonia actually existed, having long thought of it as a kind of 'fairytale land' and an ideal of their parents, rather than an actual place where real people lived. Added to this was a sense of curiosity and discovery, of being in a place to which they had a strong connection:

'It was a mix of emotions, but mainly sort of joy, a sense of unreality I suppose, finally being there. I didn't remember Tallinn of course ... I was just a little bit too young [when I left], so the whole sort of notion of Estonia was a slightly mythic thing, just the stories you'd heard from parents and teachers and the books.' [Jaan]

First impressions aside, a more important part of visiting Estonia was meeting relatives. Most respondents had relatives there and travelled to meet them, in most cases for the first time since childhood (or the first time ever). Emotions were often overwhelming, with many feeling a sense of inclusion and that their trips felt like a reunion or a homecoming, a way of re-establishing kinship ties across great spatial and temporal divisions:

'You know that they're family, but you don't know them, so that's pretty emotional. And even to get close to them in that short time is pretty amazing. ... It's great just to see the faces, the family traits – like who do they take after?' [Helve]

However, meeting relatives could also be unsettling. Some respondents felt awkward, that while they were blood relations, vastly different life experiences and little contact with each other had resulted in different worldviews and few things in common, and thus little to talk about:

'There was an old lady in old clothes from another time, another era ... both of us recognising this bond, glowing and eyes shining, and not knowing quite what to say, or to ask, or to offer. But still there was an awkwardness there, because [of] this churned up mix of other place, other world, other people, and blood. ... They'd obviously prepared for months before, or whatever, because they knew we were kind of coming. ... Wanting us to receive, to eat, to consume, to touch, to use, you know, to offer whatever they can. And you being conscious that this was your role as well, to do that.' [Priit]

Despite this awkwardness, most respondents were welcomed and accommodated by their Estonian relatives, who often invited them to stay in their homes, drove them around the country and prepared meals for them, sometimes at substantial financial cost. This was coupled with an obligation to accept relatives' hospitality, as has been observed elsewhere when migrants visit (Baldassar, 2001).

Visits also frequently involved reconnecting with places, in a general sense by seeing the Estonian landscape and old town of Tallinn, and more specifically through visiting the houses, farms or graves of relatives or ancestors. Indeed, attachments to particular places are often a fundamental part of migrants' longing for the homeland (Baldassar, 2001; Weingrod and Lei, 2006) and images of homeland landscapes or towns are often displayed in houses and other spaces in the diaspora as important referents for the homeland (Basu, 2007) or as 'ethnic shrines' that foster ongoing familiarity with the homeland (Kelly, 2000, p. 71). In some cases, houses and farms were still owned and inhabited by living relatives. In others, the location of former houses was not always known. Some respondents arrived at these houses to find them bulldozed, destroyed during the Second World War, replaced with other buildings, or occupied by strangers. Whatever the state of physical structures, the experience tended to evoke emotions:

'It's a very moving experience to be ... in the house where generations of your family have been born and there you are. ... It's just a very, very good feeling. A very strong feeling ... You'd go to the cemetery and see all these people, and they're all your relatives and ancestors. So you do have a sense of them, and of the history.' [Martin]

'[We went to what] was basically the birth area, the cradle area, of my relatives. I saw the house that was built on the block that [my cousin's] mum was born in, and next door was the block where her father was born. It was just something I'd always wanted to see. ... It was maybe emotional I'd say.' [Laine]

Houses were visited to see, smell and touch the places where parents or grandparents had grown up (or where one was born), the places from where the family's identity and source of nostalgic longing was derived. These sites became destinations of pilgrimage, even when they had been reduced to rubble or it was not possible to go inside houses. Graves became markers of family history and sites of ancestry. And more generally, the landscape and natural environment evoked emotions. Visiting was thus an important way through which respondents explored their origins and formed their own sense of place as they attached their identities to particular places in the homeland.

'My roots are there'

Many Estonian-Australians who visit Estonia have done so multiple times. Some visit whenever they travel to Europe, and some travel to Estonia especially on a regular basis, in some cases, for up to several months at a time. This contrasts markedly with much of the post-war era, during which Estonian migrants in Australia were cut off from their homeland for an extended period, and were generally unable or unwilling to visit Estonia.

Respondents' activities in Estonia changed over multiple trips. Typically, the first few visits consisted mostly of meeting relatives. Later visits tended to involve spending less time with relatives and more time travelling around Estonia for sightseeing, or dedicated to particular activities. Some respondents even formed friendships with people in Estonia or visited particular cultural events such as singing festivals. But while repeat visits were sometimes made for specific reasons, many respondents could not always say exactly what kept drawing them back:

'There's sort of a sense of a mission still [to Estonia], a sense that you've got some sort of obligation not to lose the entity.' [Jaan]

'My roots are there, that's for sure. It's, well, my identity in a way. ... For a long time I've struggled with this ... [Estonia]

is this tiny little jewel that is so rich. And problematic –
because it carries the heritage. But it's part of my heritage
… And I think part of knowing who I am is tied up with
Estonia … I just want to explore more this Estonian thing.'
[Krista]

Repeated trips also provided 'snapshots' of the homeland, allowing
individuals to immerse themselves in Estonian society (and language)
while witnessing and experiencing the social, economic and physical
changes to Estonia as it developed from a centrally-planned economy
to a capitalist democracy. Frequent visits to Estonia were also ways
to reconnect with places where respondents, or their parents or
grandparents, grew up and were separated from, and to reinforce
Estonian ethnic identities. But most respondents, no matter how often
they visited Estonia, did not want to move there permanently. Mainly,
they perceived that their quality of life would be less satisfactory than
in Australia: lower real wages and pensions, a very cold climate, an
inferior healthcare system and a less certain political future. Personal
factors were also important, such as respondents' age, fluency in the
Estonian language, and their various attachments to Australia in the
form of friends, family and property. In most cases, respondents said
they would move to Estonia if one or more conditions were different,
mainly in terms of having fewer family commitments in Australia:

'I go back and forwards because it's a compromise. If I
have to live here, I have to go there every year. … As soon
as [my] family commitments are resolved, I will be on the
next plane out.' [Martin]

'If I lost my wife … I could conceive of the possibility of
actually moving there and living. Not with any sort of
commitment until the end of time, but I'd consider [it].'
[Priit]

As such, these respondents keep alive the 'myth of return' by becoming
more engaged with Estonia but finding reasons not to move there.
Rather than seeking to change the conditions that keep them firmly
in Australia, they make regular visits to their homeland to resolve their
longing for it, and as a way to find a sense of belonging and solace within
their ethnic identity. Strong yearnings for the homeland, as envisioned in
ideologies and myths of return, become translated into temporary visits,
allowing them to embrace the homeland while avoiding the practically

difficult (and often undesirable) act of return migration (Kelly, 2000; Lomsky-Feder and Rapoport, 2000; Baldassar, 2001; Stephenson, 2002; Weingrod and Lei, 2006). These visits are symbolic ways through which respondents could return 'home' without having to sever important familial and social connections with Australia.

Repeat visits also form part of a broader picture of transnational engagement – the social, economic and political connections that migrants create which span the borders of nation-states (Basch et al, 1994). These connections allow migrants to locate themselves in two societies at the same time, allowing ongoing involvement in the homeland while living outside of it. Physical visits are a core part of this co-locating process (Baldassar, 2001; Stephenson, 2002; Duval, 2003). For Estonian-Australians, transnationalism has emerged relatively recently. Estonian independence in the early 1990s was followed by phone calls and letters (no longer censored by Soviet authorities), and the rapid growth of information technologies and the internet has led to increasing use of email, instant messaging and internet telephone calls. This has been coupled with emigrants and their descendants claiming Estonian passports. This was done for a mixture of instrumental and emotional reasons, but mainly instrumental (cf, Weingrod and Lei, 2006):

> '[I got the passport for] practical reasons ... and it's certainly emotional too. If I wanted to work over in Europe for a few years, I could do that. And I did it for my sons as well. It was more for them than for me. It was nice for me, but better for them.' [Helve]

One important factor is that Estonia has been a member of the European Union since 2004, allowing passport-holders to live or work in much of Europe. Some respondents also said that claiming a passport made it easier for their children to do the same. To a lesser extent, passports were a way for respondents to engage with their cultural heritage and ethnic identity, as symbols of Estonian identity and a way to assert a personal connection with Estonia, even though possessing a passport did not necessarily make them feel more Estonian. And yet, when asked if they had to give up a passport, which one it would be, almost all respondents said unequivocally that it would be their Estonian one: they valued their Australian citizenship more.

This emerging transnationalism is partial, stronger in some ways than in others. For some respondents, communication with relatives or others in the homeland was only sporadic, such as sending occasional emails or Christmas cards. And economic relationships tend to be weaker still, based around property ownership (some Estonian-Australians have inherited, reclaimed or purchased property in Estonia), rather than remittances or business investment. Nevertheless, and in contrast to earlier, post-war times when migrant institutions played a significant role, engagements with Estonia are personalised and individual, allowing migrants to interact directly with their homeland in their own way – including through visits.

'It's like I've got two homes'

Visiting Estonia also had important repercussions for respondents' identities, senses of belonging and notions of 'home'. For some, visits were a homecoming, a symbolic repatriation with the place that they and their families had been exiled from. Such sentiment did not always emerge while visiting and was sometimes felt much later:

> 'It means that I too have a homeland, somewhere. That really, basically, there is somewhere where I belong. ... When we sing the [Estonian] national anthem, I'm definitely very tearful. So no matter how much I protest that [visiting Estonia] meant nothing for me, I suppose it does. That you know, for us people, there is a home too.' [Pille]

Travelling to Estonia was also a way to gain a better understanding of childhood experiences and transitions and, having grown up as an Estonian in Australia, also to provide a greater sense of appreciation of parents' efforts to maintain Estonian traditions and the language. However, a key aspect in feeling a sense of belonging in Estonia was being able to speak and understand the Estonian language. The majority of respondents said that this was the key factor in being considered truly 'Estonian' while visiting. The ability to speak Estonian also engendered feelings of being more strongly attached to the country, and hearing it spoken there elicited strong feelings of belonging and sentimentality among some respondents. This evoked a feeling of being 'at home'. Some respondents also explained how language was the main factor that distinguished *väliseestlased* ('foreign Estonians') from *kodueestlased* ('home Estonians'):

> 'It all depends on whether they speak the language. If you don't speak the language Estonians don't regard you as

Estonian. ... You can't be Estonian without having that
connection with the language.' [Merle]

Estonian-speaking respondents were conscious that their use of
language differed from that of *kodueestlased*, since the language had
evolved differently in the homeland to the diaspora. Very few claimed
to speak Estonian flawlessly. Most found differences, or had difficulties,
with grammar, vocabulary, nuances and jokes. While they may have
been comfortable speaking Estonian with their parents about everyday
things, they sometimes felt unable to express themselves in a more
complex manner, especially to strangers. Some had also been told by
relatives that they had developed foreign accents, or that they spoke
a very 'old' form of Estonian. Their language marked them out as
different, instantly inscribing them as *väliseestlased*:

> 'They said I spoke a very old fashioned sort of Estonian
> that hadn't progressed! And my Godmother said that of
> my mother's Estonian too, and she wrote and told her the
> new words.' [Riina]

> 'I don't think there were very many misunderstandings. It's
> just that you don't pick up nuancing. ... And also you can't
> share jokes. ... So if you're in a language situation like this,
> you can be seen to be just kind of dull. ... There is that
> missing connection.' [Priit]

More broadly, some respondents felt a sense of being alienated or of
not belonging, especially those with few known relatives or those
less fluent in Estonian. For others, while there was often a sense of
enjoyment when meeting relatives, and a welcoming attitude from
them, there was typically never a complete sense of attachment or a
complete understanding of Estonia and its people. There were also
many reminders that Estonia is, in many ways, a 'foreign' country, with
contrasting life experiences compared to people in Australia, legacies
of communism, and different social structures. Indeed, they may have
experienced 'the disjunctive condition of being a 'foreigner' in the
ancestral homeland' (Stephenson, 2002:411) that can be felt after
returning from a long time of absence. Regardless of whether they
were born in Estonia, or how many times they had visited, they were
still *väliseestlased*.

Several respondents professed to having confused identities,
particularly if their experiences of Estonia did not match memories,

parents' stories or prior expectations, or if they felt unable to comprehend what it meant to be Estonian as a child (such as possessing cultural and linguistic traits different to other children). Visiting Estonia did not feel like a homecoming; Estonia was not the place of childhood memories. Yet visiting did become a way to negotiate identities and senses of belonging. Estonia was a kind of cultural or ancestral home, and a key part of identity; yet Australia was also home, and they were Australian as well:

> '[Estonia is] a different type of home. That's where my relatives are. [Australia] is where I know how the society operates and the social and political and legal and health systems … I feel as though I've been allowed to become Estonian again, but it's a different kind of home for me. It's like I've got two homes.' [Kristiina]

Visiting Estonia sometimes even triggered new ways of thinking about being Australian. While enjoying their travels, the many differences with life in Australia made some respondents conscious that they were well established in Australia, behaved more like Australians than Estonians, and that Australia was their true home:

> 'Well I'm really Australian, and I identify as Australian here, except in some contexts … [Sometimes] I might feel some of my Estonian things sort of bubbling up, or I might talk about it, and so I think it's a dynamic thing … I'm Aussie mate. Yeah I was born there [Estonia], blah blah, that's it.' [Priit]

As such, notions of home and belonging are multiple, can overlap or be incomplete, and vary between people. Migrants can anchor themselves to multiple geographic 'centres' at the same time, with the places of birth and residence both taking on core significance for their identities (Weingrod and Lei, 2006). Visits to Estonia reinforced some respondents' ethnic identities and there was a sense of a homecoming, whereas others felt looser attachments to the homeland and came to identify more with Australia. This seemed in many cases to depend on individuals' own perspectives and life experiences, and was typically unrelated to their upbringing in Australia or their parents' involvement in Estonian community activities. Nevertheless, those who had been able to visit more frequently, and who had visited earlier on, tended to feel a stronger sense of attachment to Estonia. Many respondents also felt they were simultaneously Estonian and Australian. Both countries were 'home', but in different ways. Australia was the home of everyday life, work and immediate family, whereas Estonia was an identity, a cultural or even spiritual home. Home is where one grows up or lives, forms memories, and develops attachments to that place. Yet for migrants living abroad, a distant homeland can also be considered a home, one around which many stories and cultural activities are based. Estonia was discursively constructed by respondents in ways that made it familiar and special to them, a cultural homeland rather than a literal home or house. Estonia is also the *kodumaa*, the spiritual homeland, even when it is not the sole component of identity.

Conclusion

This chapter has examined visits to the homeland, later in life, by Estonian child migrants in Australia. Having long felt a desire to go there, many have been able to do so only in the 1990s and 2000s, generally aged in their fifties or older. While their experiences were sometimes unexpected, over time many have made repeated visits. These visits have allowed them to engage with their emotions for the homeland and 'myths of return' in the diaspora, in a way that allows both individualised encounters with Estonia and personal connections to be formed while still maintaining their everyday lives in Australia. In essence, attempts by some Estonian migrants to Australia during the post-war era to maintain unchanging and essentialised cultural practices have given way to more flexible and individual engagements with the homeland, in particular by these migrants' children. Visits are a key part of these engagements – a way of maintaining a sense of attachment to two places, Estonia and Australia.

Policy developments in both Estonia and Australia have shaped these migrants' experiences. Government policy has had a profound influence on almost all aspects of their migration experiences – including their settlement in post-war Australia, the ability to communicate with relatives and others in Estonia, and even (in most cases) the very reason their families emigrated from Estonia. Over time, many government policies that restricted their mobility and engagement with the homeland have been relaxed, especially since the fall of the Soviet Union and Estonia's regaining of independence. More recent reforms in Estonia and Australia have also played a role, allowing these migrants to live in Australia while developing new connections to their homeland and being able to safely travel there. In particular, increased economic openness and the relaxation of visa regimes have combined with cheaper travel and improving telecommunications technology to enable transnational links to establish roots and grow (which are further facilitated by Estonia's membership of the European Union and willingness to let emigrants and their children claim passports).

Policy changes that allow greater mobility and connection have given respondents in this study advantages that many other migrants do not enjoy (for example, due to visa regimes (King and Vullnetari, 2006)). Differences in social support and welfare policy, compounded by the difficulty of transferring pensions or financial assets between the two countries, remain features of policy that mitigate against long term residence in their homeland, and are part of the reason why many respondents have chosen not to move back permanently to Estonia.

Acknowledgements

I thank everyone that participated in this research and shared their experiences with me. I am indebted to the volunteers at the Estonian Archives in Australia, and in particular Maie Barrow, for their enthusiasm and extraordinary helpfulness.

References

Australian Bureau of Statistics (ABS) (2007) *2006 Census of Population and Housing*, Canberra, Australia: Australian Bureau of Statistics.

Baldassar, L. (2001) *Visits Home: migration experiences between Italy and Australia*, Melbourne: Melbourne University Press.

Basch, L., Glick Schiller, N. and Szanton Blanc, C. (1994) *Nations Unbound: transnational projects, postcolonial predicaments and deterritorialised nation-states*, Langhorne, PA: Gordon and Breach.

Basu, P. (2007) *Highland Homecomings: genealogy and heritage tourism in the Scottish diaspora*, Abingdon: Routledge.

Brah, A. (1996) *Cartographies of Diaspora: contesting identities*, London: Routledge.

Carter, S. (2004) 'Mobilising *Hrvatsko*: tourism and politics in the Croatian diaspora', in T. Coles and D.J. Timothy (eds) *Tourism, Diasporas and Space*, London: Routledge, pp 188–201.

Christou, A. and King, R. (2010) 'Imagining "home": diasporic landscapes of the Greek-German second generation', *Geoforum*, 41:638–646.

Cohen, R. (1997) *Global Diasporas: an introduction*, London: Routledge.

Coles, T. and Timothy, D.J. (eds) (2004) *Tourism, Diasporas and Space*, London: Routledge.

Duval, D.T. (2003) 'When hosts become guests: return visits and diasporic identities in a Commonwealth Eastern Caribbean community', *Current Issues in Tourism*, 6(4): 267–308.

Kelly, M.E. (2000) 'Ethnic pilgrimages: people of Lithuanian descent in Lithuania', *Sociological Spectrum*, 20:65–91.

King, R. and Vullnetari, J. (2006) 'Orphan pensioners and migrating grandparents: the impact of mass migration on older people in rural Albania', *Ageing & Society*, 26:783–816.

Lomsky-Feder, E. and Rapoport, T. (2000) 'Visit, separation, and deconstructing nostalgia: Russian students travel to their old home', *Journal of Contemporary Ethnography*, 29(1):32–57.

Oxfeld, E. (2004) 'Chinese villagers and the moral dilemmas of return visits', in L.D. Long and E. Oxfeld (eds) *Coming Home: refugees, migrants, and those who stayed behind*, Philadelphia, PA: University of Pennsylvania Press, pp 90–103.

Pehk, T. (2007) 'The story of Estonian Passport: The attitudes of the Estonian diaspora in Australia towards Estonia', unpublished Master's thesis, Department of Anthropology, Macquarie University, Sydney.

Ruting, B. (2012) '"Like touching with your roots": Migrants' children visiting the ancestral homeland', *Australian Geographer*, 43(1):17–33.

Safran, W. (1991) 'Diasporas in modern societies: myths of homeland and return', *Diaspora*, 1(1):83–99.

Salasoo, I. (1986) 'The Estonians in Australia', in M. Cigler (ed) *The Baltic Peoples in Australia*, Melbourne: Australasian Educa Press, pp109–165.

Skrbiš, Z. (1999) *Long-distance Nationalism: diasporas, homelands and identities*, Brookfield, VT: Ashgate Publishing Company.

Smith, G. and Jackson, P. (1999) 'Narrating the nation: The "imagined community" of Ukrainians in Bradford', *Journal of Historical Geography*, 25(3):367–387.

Stephenson, M.L. (2002) 'Travelling to the ancestral homelands: the aspirations and experiences of a UK Caribbean community', *Current Issues in Tourism*, 5(5):378–425.

Tammaru, T., Kumer-Haukanõmm, K. and Anniste, K. (2010) 'The formation and development of the Estonian diaspora', *Journal of Ethnic and Migration Studies*, 36(7):1157–1174.

Weingrod, A. and Lei, A. (2006) 'Paradoxes of homecoming: the Jews and their diasporas', *Anthropological Quarterly*, 79(4):691–716.

NINE

Ageing in the ancestral homeland: ethno-biographical reflections on return migration in later life

Anastasia Christou

Introduction: researching age and migration in the Greek diaspora in Denmark

This chapter is based on a wider research project exploring first and second generation Greek-Danes and their experiences of migration, identity, gender, home and belonging in Denmark and Greece. The study used a multi-method approach based on qualitative, ethnographic, life history, narrative and biographical methodologies. During participant life story narrations and focus group discussions, experiences, feelings, thoughts, reflections and personal information were shared and recorded. From 2004 to 2005 a total of 40 participants contributed to the study[1]; the 16 participants aged between 50 and 85 are the focus of this chapter.

In this chapter I have chosen to follow an eclectic and synthetic approach to narrative that takes into methodological consideration dimensions of emotionality emerging during the interactive research process. I view the process of narrative analysis as being intertwined with both the emotional experience of storytelling as well as in response to the sociocultural context of the themes under discussion, with participants as storytellers. Similarly, Gubrium and Holstein call for a perspective that takes into account 'the practical dimensions of narrativity ... that call for a form of analysis and related research procedure that take us outside of stories and their veridical relationship to storytellers and experience' (2009:22). They call this approach 'narrative ethnography' and point out that while the word *ethnography* has become almost meaningless because it is currently used to mean so many things, Gubrium and Holstein use it in relation to narrative specifically to connote 'a method of procedure and analysis involving the close scrutiny of circumstances, their actors and actions in the process of formulating and communicating accounts'.

It has been argued (Riessman, 1993) that storytelling, while having originated from ancient Greek myths, has been perceived as a fundamental way to interpret experiential meanings, but most importantly, life stories are very often saturated by emotion and constructed subjectively as portrayals of lives that illuminate certain angles of such lives by the experience of re-telling and reflection. My use of narrative analysis focuses on the emotional and embodied ways through which my participants' stories interpret their diasporic worlds, not as 'factual-truthful' accounts but as *phenomenological-interactionist* constructions of sociocultural worlds. These 'ethnobiographies'[2] are storied life accounts, that is, they are in the form of personal stories in a narrative account.

This chapter endeavours to present the embodied and emotionalised trajectory of a relatively unnoticed group of migrants who in many ways have become well 'integrated' into the Danish society but who, several decades later, still struggle with issues of belonging and return to their ancestral homeland as exacerbated by the ageing process. This disrupted, emotionalised and embodied experience of be/longing is illustrated by the fragments of memory, place, time and experience of mobility of the participants, that is, their narratives of temporal and spatial diasporic encounters. In the following sections I provide excerpts from narrative accounts of performative engagement and emotional experiences of ageing and migrancy, in order to illustrate how these shape diasporic be/longing and identification in later life.

The approach I take in this chapter is to focus on return migration not solely as a physical act of relocating bodies and lives to a physical territory but as a complex process of decision-making which is never a one-off act, but, rather, incorporates stages, experiences, thoughts and feelings. Such stages inform and shape the very act of relocation which may happen, although permanency of return may still remain uncertain. Therefore, this chapter, through examination of both pre-return and post-return processes, aims to highlight the agency potential of migrants involved in a variety of forms of mobility. This chapter reflects on transcultural complexities that arise during attempts at return migrating in older age and the possibility that such a return may be ultimately unsustainable and as a result may deprive the ancestral homeland of the contribution of social and economic remittances upon return; this should be of interest, if not concern, to governments and policy makers.

This chapter draws from a larger research project and within the larger project (Christou, 2008) narrative evidence from a smaller sample of participants aged over 50 (Table 9.1) frames the analysis.

Portraying Greek-Danish diasporic, emotional and ageing lives

My study of the Greek diaspora in Denmark was the first ethnography of this population to be conducted, and shows how ageing (oral) histories provide rich, remarkable insights (Andrews et al, 2006). This angle of the study also compliments the emerging literature on transnational care giving and encompasses issues such as the mobility of care, the migrancy of ageing and the social capital of older migrants, as well as the historical and social geographies of gerontology and geographies of ageing (see, for example, King et al, 2000; Andrews et al, 2006; Warnes and Williams, 2006; Baldassar, 2007; Gray, 2009).

Migration studies can benefit enormously from research that investigates the motivations of why those in later life chose to migrate and how those reasons shape the actual phenomenon of return migration in old age. However, in addition to the pragmatic reasons that make migration in later life either a choice or a necessity, there are layers of psychosocial and cultural effects that need to be addressed, as these not only shape the experience but also migrants' identities and interactions, as Leavey and Eliacin discuss in Chapter Ten. Affective dimensions of migration clearly need to be incorporated into qualitative/oral history research of the narrative accounts of older people who are making conscious decisions about return to their ancestral homeland.

My sample of first generation older Greek migrants to Denmark (see Table 9.1) were participants in the wider phenomenon of European labour migration in the 1960s, and had, for the most part, planned to work very hard to earn money in order to improve their livelihoods and to provide more promising futures to their children. All participants were born in Greece, except for one who was born on the island of Imvros, Turkey; pseudonyms have replaced actual names.

While working hard, these participants continued to nurture a passionate desire to return to their homeland within a few years of migration, and to safeguard the cultural and religious values of the family. Of course, as strategic and well-organised as this type of plan may have been, it did not always come to fruition or fully materialise. One reason was that the second generation in many instances had no

Table 9.1: Greek migrants in Denmark (first generation)

Participant profile

	Pseudonym	Gender	Age	Year of emigration
1	Alexander	M	50	1965
2	Lucia	F	54	1969
3	Marcella	F	64	1960
4	Victor	M	62	1967
5	Lucas	M	65	1964
6	Matthew	M	70	1967
7	Dimitris	M	65	1964
8	Elizabeth	F	53	1969
9	Thecla	F	85	1960
10	Dimos	M	62	1964
11	Vasilis	M	64	1961
12	Zarchary	M	50	1974
13	Argyris	M	65	1964
14	Jason	M	55	1989
15	Diogenis	M	62	1969
16	Stratos	M	55	1975

intention of relocation to Greece, or, when they did, soon wished to return to Denmark, having experienced deep disappointment and disillusionment in the ancestral homeland (King and Christou, 2011). This 'myth or dream' of return for some has been a point of obsessive fixation in their life narrative. In such a context of distress as well as anticipation, Dimitris below describes the deeply emotional journey that migration entails when thinking about the return to the homeland:

> 'I live, breathe, sleep and wake up every single day with the dream of return. I am deeply nostalgic about going back to my homeland. Yes, I do have my children here but I also have a very nice house in Greece, detached, two-storey house, fully furnished, and I want to settle there and to find my peace and tranquility. I want to rest. I want to stop hurting, this is painful, being away it is devastating. I would love to go back and I need to be in my homeland because I suffer and long for it.'

Dimitris presents a rather dramatic daily challenge of having to live abroad with the mania of a mythologised plan of ancestral homeland return, which is intensely emotional and overwhelmingly sensory, reinforced by having built a house in the homeland to serve his pragmatic need of enjoying his retirement years in Greece. However, the reality of financial constraints is in some other cases the reason why relocation to the ancestral homeland has not happened. This, combined with the reluctance of children, born and raised in Denmark, to move to what is to them an unknown and difficult country in which to settle (especially when in some cases they do not speak Greek at all), seals the parents' decision to remain in Denmark. Decision making is further complicated in the case of 'mixed' families, where one of the parents is a Dane and the other a Greek. Argyris, a 65-year-old retired carpenter who is married to a Danish woman and is very active in the Greek migrants association in Copenhagen, explained the reasoning and processes that may take place when such factors converge:

> 'Well, the majority of course of those who returned to Greece had their families follow them, they built houses and there were very many who returned in their old age, that was what was expected, returning back to Greece ... of those who returned both spouses were Greek, those were the families that returned rather than the mixed ones. I was also contemplating to return but time went by and the kids went to school, one after the other and now that we, my wife and I are moving into retirement, well, we are now thinking about it, rather to split the time half the year in Denmark and half in Greece, because you cannot abandon the kids. But there is also another problem. Those of us living in Denmark have an additional problem because we receive a segmented pension, which means that you get an amount and then you get another added amount if you have a low income and no capital investments etc., but if they were to move to Greece, then they would lose most of this amount and then they wouldn't have enough to make ends meet.'

Although Argyris in this detailed narrative is very clear about the financial reasons why return migration to the ancestral homeland, in the retirement stage of Greek migrants' lives, may not be the optimal choice, there is an implicit *desire* to return. Of course, return migration is never a simple decision but rather a complex issue as well as a multidimensional mobility phenomenon; return is not only shaped by economic considerations but is perceived by migrants as a moral and cultural act which is often exacerbated by migrants' negative or traumatic experiences within the host community, and may develop as a way to protect the ethnic purity of the family in preserving an authentically collective sense of self based on ancestry and history (Christou, 2006a). Indeed, when I asked Argyris to exclude the financial constraints in Greece and to let me know what are the most important motivations that he considered central for relocation to Greece in later life, this is what he had to say:

> 'Well, most of us who left Greece, we were raised and grew up with very strong Greek values and traditions, and as much as we may have integrated in Denmark, deep inside we remain Greeks. My children have a different mentality, they like going to Greece on vacation and on holiday visits, but once they encounter difficulties with either employment, medical care, bureaucracy, etc., all these issues make them want to hold back. They experience, in a sense, a large degree of insecurity in Greece, while in Denmark not at all, and to a large extent they are correct because the situation in Greece is getting worse. Every year it gets worse and worse … our homeland hurts us and has betrayed us [and] tells us to go and find on our own, whatever doctors we need and social welfare, which has of course improved but still it is in dire need of modernisation and democratisation. Greeks love Greece but Greece does not love Greeks and I see this every time I visit and I experience discrimination and harassment because they know that I live in Denmark and they can see the Danish license plates on my car and I get fines for absolutely no reason. And for us who belong to the working class, we feel even more excluded, I live through this and I see all the negative things and the nepotism, corruption and discrimination that exists in Greece. And, this saddens me. But, we continue to return …'

From Argyris's extract, we realise that the idea and the experience of return migration to Greece in later life involves a series of stark realisations and compromises. These have to do mostly with the lack of services and benefits, as regards medical health care needs, but also everyday life obstacles that entail traumatic experiences of discrimination, harassment, nepotism and corruption in interactions with the public sector and bureaucracy. While these issues of disillusionment, disappointment and despair, upon relocation to the ancestral homeland, are not new and have been discussed elsewhere (Christou, 2006a; Christou and King, 2006), previous research mainly focused on the younger cohorts of second generation returnees, while attention is paid here to those returning in later life.

Similar experiences of disillusionment are shared by those participants of the first generation, who have return migrated in the context of later life, and it is interesting to reflect on how, over time, socialisation or 'assimilation' processes in the host society shape life choices and perceptions. It is also useful to highlight the importance to older returnees of immersing oneself in an 'everyday life of Greekness' in the homeland, which further illustrates how significant such feelings, experiences and acts of homing and belonging are to those involved in such transitions, such as Alexander. Alexander has relocated to Greece and now permanently lives in Athens. However, in order to reconnect further with his ancestral roots he is also contemplating to further relocate to his family village which signifies the place of ancestral origin:

> 'Whether I am here in Athens or the village my roots are here, they are in Greece. … And …every time I go there to the village, a lot of people know me. I get along with everybody and that is nice … But the roots obviously that is the reason. I'm going to the village because that is my village, I wouldn't go to any other village anywhere else. I think I am doing that for that reason, because I wouldn't go to any other village and set up home there and try to become part of this new community. My father's family, my mom' family, we go back generations there, so the cemetery is full of all my ancestors. So there is a sense of connection in terms of family. Yes, my ancestors are there in the cemetery so, yes, that's why I want to go back and live there in the village.'

Visiting the cemetery in the ancestral homeland, in order to reconnect 'roots with routes', is a clear indication of Alexander's need to subsequently relocate from the capital of Athens to the family village. This embodied act of additional internal migration is stimulated by the emotionalities of 'setting up home' and 'trying to become part of the village community'. Further discussion of the importance, to some older people, of return to cities and villages with ancestral links, rather than to the 'home' country, is provided by Blunt and colleagues in Chapter Seven of this volume.

While there has been in the last decade an emergence of literature on 'emotional geographies' (Anderson and Smith , 2001; Bondi, 2005; Davidson et al, 2005) my use of 'emotionalities' here refers to both the ruptures and affective liminalities in everyday social life that participants experience (frequently denoting an emotional boundary zone between ways of constructing self and community) as well as the reflexivity that underpins social research and often is embedded in the research process. Such emotionalities surface through and during the research encounter, the fieldwork experience and become textual as the data collected is 'translated' into this very chapter output. The data arising provides a myriad of complex issues and obstacles that may transform the mythologised sense of the ideal homecoming into an act of exile, if returnees experience alienation in their homeland. These issues will be explored further in the next section of this chapter, on modern 'myths' and 'labyrinths' in the homeland.

The enigma of homecoming: cultural myth and labyrinth in the homeland

Thecla, an 85-year-old first-generation Greek migrant who has spent more than half of her life in Denmark, reflected on several recent stays in Greece and some of the most outstanding changes she had noticed in her homeland:

> 'They have changed, yes indeed, and of course you will tell me you are older and you remember things differently, but they have changed a great deal. There is no respect, which used to be ample ... And the amount of divorce? Don't even mention it, because I have many examples from my own family in Greece. And, I see how many migrants are now living in Greece and they are blamed for being criminals, but Greeks commit a whole bunch of crimes too and I hear about them on television, but, yes, there is a lot of crime there now.'

In this brief extract from her narrative, Thecla manages to capture the core social and cultural issues where change has been observed in Greece. She speaks of a kind of disintegration of family values and the family as the nuclear cell of Greek society and the glue that holds everything together, but also of recent population movement changes with immigration and the media portrayal of the criminalisation of migrants. Although aged eighty-five, and following a series of medical conditions and falls after being recently mugged, Thecla is a very active and energetic person. When she manages to save money from her pension, which is her sole source of income, Thecla still travels to Greece to visit family and her elderly sister but finds it difficult to decide to return permanently to her ancestral homeland. A personal and core issue for Thecla is the fact that she often goes to the cemetery in Copenhagen where her younger son is buried, and she also spends a lot of time with her other son and her grand and great grandchildren who, as third and fourth generations, only speak (and feel) Danish. The 'Danish' family has no intention of moving to Greece and this, along with her other concerns about the vast changes taking place in Greece, makes Thecla's decision not to return rather definitive.

As far as the widespread degree of disillusionment with the ancestral homeland is concerned, this has also been documented in research conducted with other Greek diaspora groups who return migrated to Greece, from Germany and the United States. Virtually all of the returnees narrated lengthy stories of the objective difficulties of the living conditions in Greece, where corruption, rudeness, chaos and clientelism frustrate all aspects of social and economic life, repeatedly contrasted with the perceived efficiency, order, politeness and meritocracy of life in Germany and the United States (Christou and King, 2011).

Participant narratives were saturated by immense negativity reflective of the lived and experienced accounts of the complexities eloquently described. One can infer that if those participants were re-interviewed at the present time, when the Greek socioeconomic crisis is at the forefront of the European and American international political agenda, as well as the subject of daily strikes and clashes on the streets of Athens and other major urban centres, their degree of disappointment and frustration would be additionally exacerbated. Hence, not only do such obstacles as described above shape the actual return experience, or hinder the possible decision to return, they may also cause counter-migration, if living the ancestral homeland dream actually becomes a nightmare (Christou, 2006b].

Tensions, then, may emerge during diasporic journeys to the homeland, revealing both spatial belongingness and cultural (dis)location (Christou, 2003b). In the age of multiple mobilities, transnational and transcultural relations, people today are increasingly living lives across, between, betwixt, beyond and within national and cultural boundaries. It is by no means a recent realisation that the human geography of a migrant life spans multiple spaces (geographical, social, cultural, political, economic), often producing a mode of living which is neither reflective of their home nor of their host 'surroundings', resulting in concepts such as 'hybridisation'[3]. As movement and the mobility of cultural spaces produce intercultural (dis)location, fluidity and hybridity are viewed as the hallmarks of post-modernity (Christou, 2003a). Such arguments make it particularly intriguing when we talk about the struggle to maintain cultural worlds frozen in time and space and then transported to a changed, hyper-modernised homeland. On the other hand, it is also interesting to note that first generation images of the home country can create an idealised portrait that may not correspond to reality. This was not the case with Vasilis, a 64-year-old first-generation man who migrated to Denmark in 1961. He emphasised pragmatic concerns:

> 'Now that I am approaching retirement at 64 I didn't need to do anything, the state got in touch with me and they notified me that from that particular date onwards I will be receiving my pension. They sent me all the paperwork in advance; they told me what exactly to fill in and when to send them back in order to receive my benefits. I completed the paperwork and I sent it back and that is the end of it … In Greece you need numerous certificates, paperwork, you need this and that. In other words the state here is a lot more organised than Greece, a lot more organised.'

For Vasilis, like Thecla, the fact that children and grandchildren will continue to permanently reside in Denmark means that planned return migration will be partial, and he is planning to spend roughly six months in each country. Given that Vasilis is in good health, coupled with his reasonably good pension and the fact that he has paid off his mortgage in Denmark, while in Greece he has inherited a family cottage in the village where he was born and raised, he doesn't have any immediate logistical constraints in implementing his plan of return. Furthermore, the fact that Vasilis potentially will not have to have any dealings with Greek bureaucracy and red tape is an added reason why he can expect to enjoy a smooth everyday life experience retiring in Greece. On the contrary, those returnees who have to cope with the complexities of things that should be simple, such as processing one's pension application, as described above by Vasilis, may find it overwhelmingly intimidating and daunting to consider living in a country where virtually everything becomes a source of consistent frustration.

Elsewhere (Christou, 2006a; 2006b; Christou and King, 2006) I have discussed at length how Greece is received and experienced by diasporic (Greek) returnees, and the trauma they have suffered upon return. Although those traumatic themes are more or less similar in content and description, with disillusionment stemming from one or more of the experiences articulated in the above extracts, nostalgic feelings about relocation in later life are regular and intense. This is usually reiterated with the phrase: *"that's where I want to die"*. The ageing return resembles a mythical return of a similar kind as Odysseus' journey home to Ithaca, the definitive epic 'return home', where obstacles on the way may challenge but ultimately underline how meaningful the actual relocation becomes.

Either in epic historical terms, or everyday life parameters narrated in participant accounts in my research, culture indeed becomes the signifying force that shapes the return into a later life project. In most cases an additional argument strengthens the decision to return to the ancestral homeland: *"I don't want to be buried in a foreign land. I don't want to leave my bones in that frozen, inhospitable soil."* These are two frequent wishes expressed mostly by first generationers but often transmitted as a cultural legacy to the second generation. This is the territoriality of the nation, in the literal form of the fragility of the actual soil and transplanting of the migrant body (even upon death) through a grounding onto the ancestral land by the very act of relocation.

Yet, as such accounts have expressed, the return experience often reveals a strong degree of 'cultural shock', even for those born and raised in Greece, as migrants have become accustomed to the host country's processes of efficiency and organisation, which renders the return rather challenging in respect of adjustment and re-settlement. It remains to be seen how the current social and economic crises in Greece will impact on future return migration there in later life. Furthermore, additional research is required to understand how transnational care will be shaped in the case of diasporic responsibilities to elderly relatives, and if such relations will have an effect on how belonging unfolds in migrant lives.

Conclusion: reflections on ageing, home and belonging

It has been noted by Percival in Chapter One that studies of return migration rarely take account of people's lives at a micro level. Importantly, a focus on the emotionalities of ageing in relation to return migration, home and belonging, is also an under researched theme. This chapter has presented narratives of ageing migrants so as to explore how return deliberations and decisions have been shaped by notions of home and belonging and also how these are situated within more pragmatic aspects of everyday life in the ancestral homeland.

From extensive conversations with participants, it appears that both pragmatic and emotional factors are equally important as regards the thought processes of older potential return migrants. Given the qualitative context of this research, the extent and degree of impact of each of those categories is impossible to 'weight'. However, as return migration to the ancestral homeland involves to a very large and pertinent extent major health and social welfare implications for those older participants, as highlighted by informant narrative extracts, the fact that Greece is currently undergoing a major economic crisis and social welfare restructuring process may significantly constrain decisions to return now or in the near future.

In addition to emotional aspects, Leavey and Eliacin, in Chapter Ten, and Barrett and Mosca (2012) assert that migration and return migration may be accompanied by an increased risk of psychological health disorders, an issue that is also insufficiently explored but one that may help explain patterns of mobility. For example, the 'dual orientation' and 'bifocality' (Vertovec, 2004), or 'dual consciousness' (Agnew, 2005), of transnational migrants is one that entails the complexity of 'here and there', 'home and host' experiences, and thereby challenges any possibility of a static relationship with the ancestral homeland. For my participants, transformations of the homeland during the years of their absence form a matrix of temporal, social and spatial dimensions of change, which can result in a degree of 'psychic cost' for those who return. The constellation of such factors requires attention by governments and policy makers as the impact of such 'psychic costs' may have consequences across societies and institutions.

Wright (2012) focuses on the dynamic interplay between material, perceptual and relational dimensions of human wellbeing, which has benefits for a more holistic analysis of transnational migration. In this chapter I have tried to unpack the paradox of considering and implementing return migration plans in later life as regards Greek migrants to Denmark relocating back to their ancestral homeland. To encapsulate this paradox into a cost-benefit analysis is to ignore the complexity of human relations.

Material benefits and drawbacks may enter the decision making process but there are more intense and in-depth relational parameters that enhance the attractiveness of return migration and may be correlated with self-esteem, social status and wellbeing. At the same time, an increase in levels of anxiety and the pressure of a possible deterioration of family relations when children, grandchildren and possibly spouses do not wish to return may all generate additional layers of complication that accentuate the oftentimes unbearable and irreconcilable decision to return to the homeland. It may be useful, therefore, to further investigate the issue of moral commitment to kin and country as a signifier of a code of ethics of the diaspora, very much an additional social and cultural force that needs to be taken into consideration when we examine return migration in later life.

Return in later life may be an expression of the emotional need to belong but older migrants' experience may also be conditioned by the myriad of practical difficulties that returnees face in the ancestral homeland, especially when contrasted with the comparative advantages of better and more efficient medical provision, benefit packages and social welfare in the host country. Although return in later life is an exciting social and research phenomenon, it nevertheless is also a multi-dimensional one, and requires further attention and examination, particularly in an era of global social transformations. Furthermore, the complexities involved with increases in levels of translocal and transnational interconnections need to be analysed so that we better understand social relations in the societies we study.

References

Agnew, V. (2005) 'Introduction' in V. Agnew (ed) *Diaspora, Memory, and Identity: A Search for Home*, Toronto: University of Toronto Press, pp 3–21.

Anderson, K. and Smith, S. (2001) 'Emotional geographies', *Transactions of the Institute of British Geographers*, 26:7–10.

Andrews, G.J., Kearns, R.A., Kontos, P. and Wilson, V. (2006) '"Their finest hour": older people, oral histories, and the historical geography of social life', *Social and Cultural Geography*, 7(2):153–177.

Baldassar, L. (2007) 'Transnational families and aged care: the mobility of care and the migrancy of ageing', *Journal of Ethnic and Migration Studies*, 33(2):275–297.

Barrett, A. and Mosca, I. (2012) 'Social Isolation, Loneliness and Return Migration: Evidence from Older Irish Adults', *IZA Discussion Paper No. 6331*.

Bondi, L. (2005) 'Making connections and thinking through emotions: between geography and psychotherapy', *Transactions of the Institute of British Geographers*, 30:433–448.

Christou, A. (2003a) '(Re)collecting memories, (Re)constructing identities and (Re)creating national landscapes: spatial belongingness, cultural (dis)location and the search for home in narratives of diasporic journeys', *International Journal of the Humanities*, 1:1–16.

Christou, A. (2003b) 'Persisting identities: locating the self and theorizing the Nation', *Berkeley Journal of Sociology: A Critical Review*, Special issue: Nationalisms: Negotiating Communities, Boundaries, and Identities, 47:115–134.

Christou, A. (2006a) *Narratives of Place, Culture and Identity: second-generation Greek-Americans return 'home'*, Amsterdam: Amsterdam University Press.

Christou, A. (2006b) 'American dreams and European nightmares: experiences and polemics of second-generation Greek-American returning migrants', *Journal of Ethnic and Migration Studies*, 32(5):831–845.

Christou, A. and King, R. (2006) 'Migrants encounter migrants in the city: the changing context of 'Home' for second-generation Greek-American return migrants', *International Journal of Urban and Regional Research*, 30(4):816–835.

Christou, A. (2008) 'Spaces of Europe – places of homeland: Greek-Danish diaspora life in narratives of home and return', *International Journal on Multicultural Societies*, 10(2):194–207.

Christou, A. (2009a) 'No place is (like) home: mobilities, memories and metamorphoses of Greek migrants in Denmark', in D. Tziovas (ed) *Diaspora and Exile: Changes in Greek Society, Politics and Culture since 1700*, Aldershot: Ashgate Publishers, pp 83–95.

Christou, A. (2009b) 'Telling diaspora stories: theoretical and methodological reflections on narratives of migrancy and belongingness in the second generation', *Migration Letters*, 6(2):143–153.

Christou, A. and King, R. (2011) 'Gendering diasporic mobilities and emotionalities in Greek-German narratives of home, belonging and return', *Journal of Mediterranean Studies*, 20(2):283–315.

Davidson, J., Bondi, L. and Smith M. (eds) (2005) *Emotional Geographies*, Aldershot: Ashgate.

Gray, A. (2009) 'The social capital of older people', *Ageing and Society*, 29:5–31.

Gubrium, J.F. and Holstein, J.A. (2009) *Analyzing Narrative Reality*, Thousand Oaks, CA: Sage.

Hutnyk, J. (2005) 'Hybridity', *Ethnic and Racial Studies*, 28(1):79–102.

King, R., Warnes, A. and Williams, A.M. (2000) *Sunset Lives: British Retirement Migration to the Mediterranean*. Oxford: Berg.

King, R. and Christou, A. (2011) 'Of counter-diaspora and reverse transnationalism: return mobilities to and from the ancestral homeland', *Mobilities*, 6(4): 451–466.

Long, L. and Oxfeld, E. (2004) *Coming Home: refugees, migrants and those who stayed behind*, Philadelphia, PA: University of Pennsylvania Press.

Riessman, C.K. (1993) *Narrative Analysis: qualitative research methods*, Newbury Park, CA: Sage, Series No. 30.

Vertovec, S. (2004) 'Migrant transnationalism and modes of transformation', *International Migration Review*, 38(3):970–1001.

Warnes, A.M. and Williams, A. (2006) 'Older migrants in Europe: a new focus for migration studies', *Journal of Ethnic and Migration Studies*, 32(8):1257–1281.

Wright, K. (2012) 'Constructing human wellbeing across spatial boundaries: negotiating meanings in transnational migration', *Global Networks*, 12(4):467–484.

TEN

'The past is a foreign country': vulnerability to mental illness among return migrants

Gerard Leavey and Johanne Eliacin

Introduction

A recent report by the United Nations Development Programme (2009) provided an estimate of 740 million internal migrations and 214 million international migrations worldwide. Significantly, most international migrants moved from one developing country to another or between developed countries, just over a third moved from a developing to a developed country (OECD, 2009). The high level of involuntary migrations caused by global warming and natural disasters, armed conflicts, political tension, deportation and illegal human trafficking are not expected to diminish. With such a high level of geographic mobility the need to record and explore the changes that occur as a result of migration is essential as migration can affect the economic, health and social sectors in both the host and sending nations (Katseli et al, 2006; OECD, 2009).

Migration always involves a cost to the individual migrant, his or her family, their community and the wider society (Ratha et al, 2011: Silver, 2011). Thus, the act of voluntary migration, regardless of motivation and ultimate outcome, demands a choice; certainly between alternative places but often between communities and life trajectories. With choice comes loss. While migration tends to improve the economic standing of an individual, compared to what might have been expected in their home country, the cost to the migrant's sense of wellbeing appears considerable.

One of the most notable costs of migration on individual migrants and their families is the possibility, for some, of deteriorating mental health. Since Ødegaard's study of schizophrenia among migrants to the US (Ødegaard, 1932), the relationship between migration and mental illness has attracted considerable attention from psychiatry and the social sciences. Explanations for the excess rates of mental disorder among migrant populations range from the biological and cultural to environmental, race and class. Further, while problems related to identity and belonging have been theoretically explored with regard to migrant stress, empirical examination is lacking.

Within such theoretical perspectives, researchers have explored the concept of *the myth of return* among various migrant populations, that is, the failed ambition of returning to homeland and the existential anxieties and/or the psychological distress provoked by this realisation (Al-Rasheed, 1994; Leavey et al, 2004; Sinatti, 2011). However, less explored still is the psychological wellbeing of those people who do return, usually in middle to later life stages. Once again, this requires choice and loss, a resettlement in what tends to be an idealised community and place, an imagined connection with community long since transformed.

With the growing number of transnational families, and increasing movement of individuals back and forth between countries, researchers are re-conceptualising the immigration process from a simple linear trajectory that ends with migration and integration in the host country, to a more fluid, and cyclical journey that takes into account the experiences of those who return home after migrating abroad for several years. As the subject of return migration and mental illness remains largely neglected within the academic community, recent trends in migration studies indicate that significant social and psychological challenges are associated with the crossing of cultural bridges and transition to one's home country after a long sojourn abroad (Szkudlarek, 2010; Davies et al, 2011; Barrett and Mosca, 2013).

In this chapter, the authors review some of the central themes that have emerged thus far from the literature on return migration in later life and outline areas for future research. This is not a meta-analysis of the literature nor a complete review of the literature on re-entry of older immigrants, as research studies on return migration in later life are scarce and those existing studies vary significantly in terms of focus and methodology, spanning individual auto-biography, case studies and qualitative studies[1]. Despite the shortcomings of available literature, a review of some of the main themes and trends in existing studies will provide valuable insights into this emergent field of study as well as the features, experiences, and challenges associated with return migration.

We begin by arguing that any understanding of the mental health impacts of return migration is only possible through first apprehending the complex risk factors between migration and mental illness and conversely, the resilience and salutogenic factors that underpin successful transition and settlement. However, we feel it is also important to attempt to clear up the often very slippery definition of migrant status and the concept of voluntariness in migration, not least because the terminology has become profoundly marked by political and ideological concerns but also has relevance to vulnerability to psychological distress. Thus, drawing on research of the migration experiences and mental health of the Irish in Britain, we explore the risk factors, pre and post migration, that seem to be of significance to the determinants of wellbeing, or otherwise, of return migrants. We finish with an outline of key theories of return migration and how they might relate to psychological wellbeing.

The mental health of migrant communities

There has been a growing interest in the mental health, or more truthfully, mental illness among migrants since Ødegaard, a Norwegian psychiatrist, noted a higher incidence of schizophrenia among migrants, which he suggested could be explained by the selective migration of people who were genetically predisposed to develop the disorder (Ødegaard, 1932). His analysis of the biographies of Norwegian immigrants who had developed schizophrenia, but who also had a history of poor social adaptation in their home country, convinced Ødegaard that they would have developed mental illness had they not migrated.

Since these early studies the issue of migration and mental illness has attracted substantial research, comment and debate, the findings and conclusions often contradictory and contentious. The stakes are considerable; the debate is not simply an academic matter but, rather, its component issues have been incorporated into wider, often politicised theories about migration, ethnicity, genetics, citizenship, culture and racism. Central to research on this subject are questions such as: Do migrants bring their mental health problems with them or does the migrant experience provoke illness? Is some form of suffering inevitably attached to the migrant experience? Who or what is responsible for the suffering of the migrant?

Let us consider the question of the elevated risk of schizophrenia among African-Caribbeans in the UK, estimated to be four to sixteen times higher than their white counterparts. The rates of the illness are even greater among second and third generations African-Caribbeans (Harrison et al, 1988, 1990, 1997, 2001; Bhugra et al, 2000; Fearon et al, 2006; Morgan et al, 2006; Fearon and Morgan, 2006). Various hypotheses have been raised, though not fully tested, in relation to the evidence of an excess of psychoses among this population. Thus, various academics have suggested a greater genetic vulnerability, the psychological legacy of slavery, maladaptive family systems, acculturation difficulties, racism and discrimination, marijuana use, social class, social capital, cultural presentation of distress and misdiagnosis (Littlewood and Lipsedge, 1988, 1989; McKenzie and Bhui, 2007). Each of these explanations is freighted with moral anxiety and risk and each poses a sub-text of faultiness at the level of structure or agency, in biology, lifestyle, culture, social economy or medicine (Warfa et al, 2007). What is also at stake on the basis of such questions and explanations are the policy choices and consequences, the resource allocation and interventions for migrant communities that flow from the evidence base.

There are two particular discourses, crudely implicit in these debates, on the relationship between migration and mental illness that have significance for our understanding of return migration. The first relates to an often oversimplified theorising of the drivers and individual motivation for migration and the conceptual distinctions between refugee and migrants hinging on the voluntariness, or otherwise, of the migration act. The second, interrelated, discourse relates to the split between the psychological life and wellbeing of the migrant before and after the migration event. That is, the migrant's susceptibility to mental disorder is crudely dichotomised into destabilising pre or post-migration factors.

In the following sections we try to show that while the empirical evidence on migration and mental illness has provided some understanding of the risk factors associated with various categories of migrant, too often the measurement of migrant status, motivation, intention and experience is either missing or lacks sufficient sophistication. Through ascertaining the complexity of these factors, we can shed some light as to why some migrants want to return home and why some might experience a mental illness when they do.

We aim to explore these ideas further and with particular reference to the high rates of mental illness among Irish migrants in Britain. This case illustrates how a compendium of factors – structural inequalities, social adversity, identity and cultural determinants, life events and peer pressure – all impinge on the concepts of choice and freedom in migration. The research that we draw from also shows that events over the lifecourse influence and determine migration and settlement behaviour. It follows then that these will have a determining effect on the desire to return home and the mental health of the individual following return.

The case of Irish migration and mental illness

Evidence gathered over several decades showed that Irish migrants, historically the biggest migrant group in Britain, not only experienced the highest mortality rates for all major disease categories but were also more likely to experience common mental disorders and commit suicide, relative to the indigenous white community and any other minority ethnic group (Raftery et al, 1990; Balarajan, 1995; Weich et al, 2004). Commentators make the point that the Irish are the only migrant group to Britain whose health deteriorates after arrival, instead of converging with the health profile of the host population (Harding and Balarajan, 1996).

At first sight, it is not clear why this should be so. The Irish, also relative to other migrant groups, appear to have some distinct advantages. In their relationship with the host country they have a shared language and considerable cultural commonalities, a familiarity produced by a long history of migration, contact and settlement. Moreover, as a white ethnic group, they might be expected to have an enhanced opportunity to assimilate with the host population and avoid much of the racism and discrimination faced by black minority ethnic communities. Importantly, a longstanding political agreement between Ireland and Great Britain and a close proximity permitted an ease of access not available to many groups. However, set against these advantages there are a number of undermining factors. These include a long history of colonial conflict and an entrenched anti-Irish racism in Britain that was reinvigorated in the late 20th century in the context of Irish republican political violence (Greenslade, 1991; Leavey, 2001) and arguably had an impact on the wellbeing of this migrant community.

Identity and strategies of belonging

The internalisation of a positive and integrated sense of identity is key to an individual's self-esteem and the capacity to develop relationships directed towards growth and wellbeing (Phinney, 1991). This is true for all individuals but arguably more compromised among migrants. Borrowing from Antonovsky's perceptions of American Jewry as unable to construct an 'authentic' ethnic identity (Antonovsky, 1963), Kelleher and others suggested that the particular experience of the Irish as a previously colonised people living in Britain similarly found an environment in which a positive ethnic identity failed to be developed and celebrated (Kelleher and Hillier, 1996; Leavey, 1999; Kelleher and Cahill, 2004). Thus, it was argued that the adversities experienced by the Irish in Britain and their 'invisibility' as an ethnic group left the community not only vulnerable to mental distress but lacking political redress (Hickman and Walter, 1997).

The concept of a fragile ethnic identity and its linkage with mental illness has received negligible attention from researchers. However, there is some empirical evidence of a causal linkage. For instance, Veiling and colleagues in the Netherlands using a case control study sought to understand the relationship between social adversity and psychotic illness among migrant communities and the mediating effects of ethnic group identity (Veiling et al, 2008). Thus, a positive identification with one's own ethnic group appears to buffer negative consequences of racial discrimination and is a strong predictor of mental health in first- and second-generation immigrants.

This kind of identification within one's own ethnic community may protect the individual against perceptions of exclusion. Similarly, absence of strong identification to one's ethnic group may put the individual at greater risk of emotional distress (Halpern, 1993). Such findings chime with Berry's theory about immigration adjustment (1997, 2001) in which the migrant is considered to opt for one of four strategies of acculturation: *assimilation* (the migrant has no wish to maintain their cultural heritage and instead chooses immersion in the new cultural milieu and identity); *integration* (she/he fully intends the maintenance of their own cultural identity/heritage while mixing with a new culture); *separation* (she/he maintains cultural identity but rejects social contact with the host nation culture; *marginalisation* (she/he rejects their cultural identity/heritage and also rejects social contact with host nation culture).

Integration appears to offer the most advantages for migrants as long as the cultural distance is low and the host nation is receptive to other cultures; a strategy that may result in the emergence of a new cultural identity and offering opportunities for growth and development (Berry, 1997, 2001). In many cases the acculturative process results in a dual cultural identity being formed which may be problematic if the emerging identity is incompatible with the previous cultural identity. Separation and marginalisation appear to be the least effective acculturation strategies as they often lead to the isolation and alienation of the migrant (Berry, 1997). However, the causal relationship is not clear in that people suffering from mental illness are more likely to be marginalised and isolated due to the illness and the associated stigma (experienced and anticipated by the individual). Moreover, as we discuss below, marginalisation and the ability to avoid it is determined by the abilities and competencies of the individual, to negotiate social boundaries that are encountered at home or abroad and which also determine ease of settlement or return.

Cultural capital

While the term 'strategy' as used by Berry and others suggests a high degree of agency and predetermination, the categorical behaviours are in fact the outworking of various other psychosocial and economic determinants. Bourdieu's concept of habitus has explanatory value here (Bourdieu, 1977, 1985). Thus, migrants, even from the same region and however culturally close to one another, do not set out from the same social position and with the same worldviews; different individuals from various social backgrounds bring with them not only different financial backing but differential levels of cultural capital that can be employed in the new environment – language skills, for instance, and transferable knowledge and educational skills that are marketable in a new environment.

Professional skills and training may open up employment as well as social possibilities. There are also tastes and cultural dispositions that permit access to particular fields and groups that are similarly inclined; individuals from quite different national and ethnic groups, with cosmopolitan tastes, can find more affinity with each other than with other people from their homeland. Allowing for the possibility of hybrid identities, Hall (1992) maintains that such individuals may be able to manage and negotiate the various aspects of identity and self in a relatively sophisticated way.

However, people from somewhat educationally and culturally restricted backgrounds are likely to be found in similarly constrained and constraining employment fields and lifestyles (Bourdieu, 2010). For example, rural to urban migration may pose greater acculturation difficulties than for those migrating from urban to urban areas, exacerbating the sense of dislocation and diminished competence. In consequence, such opportunities and limitations as encountered by the migrant may well determine health behaviour and outcomes that arise from the 'structuring structures' pre and post migration.

Moreover, as we describe in the following sections, the social, political and economic contexts of home and host countries are often fluid, sometimes rapidly so. These changing societies and their relationships have considerable influence on the profiles of migrant cohorts and the wellbeing of the individuals. However, these relationships are forged not just by political circumstances – a history of colonialism for example – but also quite simply by distance.

Proximity and unplanned migration

Research on Irish migrants and mental illness also reveals a range of factors that suggest something about the complexity of the determinants of migration and their relationship with mental illness. Leavey's study (2001) for example hypothesised that it was Ireland's proximity to Britain that resulted, paradoxically, in the psychological distress of its migrants. It facilitated a type of migration that made relatively few demands on the intending migrant, particularly in terms of the level of planning and preparation that migration from further distances required. This type of spontaneous migration to England was perceived as permitting a degree of hazardous complacency about the ease of return should the migration fail. In this model, individuals lacking a strategy for settlement or return would drift without any social anchorage, becoming marginalised in the host country but decreasingly likely or able to return to Ireland. The psychosocial factors associated with this scenario indicate a poor outcome for health and wellbeing.

In support of the proximity hypothesis a follow-up study using in-depth interviews with older Irish migrants provided a picture of these single men (Leavey et al, 2004). Generally in poor health, they recounted narratives of drift and dislocation, leaving them with profound social isolation and diminishing contact within the Irish community in the UK and little or no contact with Ireland. Commonly possessing powerfully negative memories of Ireland or at the very least an ambiguity, these migrants nevertheless articulated a longing to return. The authors suggested that migrants who tended to be positive about growing old in England (a) held clearer plans at migration; (b) were less ambivalent about remaining in England; (c) maintained frequent contact with Ireland; and (d) were secure in their identity. Additionally, important differences related to work and settlements were observed between men and women.

The findings of a case-control study confirmed these hypotheses, but only partially (Leavey et al, 2007). Thus, the association between unplanned migration and current depression was stronger among younger male participants. Unlike their male counterparts, the women had more unanticipated protective factors. Other research suggests that Irish women considered the prospect of migration more distressing than their male counterparts and it may be that male risk-taking contributes to poor planning (Carlsen and Nilsen, 1995). Among women, a poorly planned migration may have been more closely, and temporarily, associated with escape but not as a continued or general pattern of behaviour. Moreover, younger men and women who migrated from the

1960s onwards tended to have more unplanned migration than older migrants. This may be explained by the increased access to travel that opened up in the latter part of the 20th century. Leavey and colleagues' findings also suggest that positive post-migration influences such as adequate social support can be protective against depression (Leavey et al, 2007).

The same researchers used in-depth interviews with 40 men and women who participated in the case-control study to explore the participants' explanations for migration and, for some, their experience of depression. Not surprisingly, the moribund economy in Ireland and the desire for employment are offered as primary reasons by many migrants, both men and women. However, the narratives reveal important distinctions in motivation influenced by social context and the differing personal lives and life-events of men and women. The narratives of older participants, that is, those who migrated prior to the 1970s, were commonly suffused with painful memories of growing up in Ireland. Typically, this older cohort held unskilled, low-paid occupations or were agricultural labourers and among rural migrants in particular, life was described as stultifying and miserable. Several participants recounted the systematic abuse, sexual and physical, they suffered in the boarding and industrial schools run by priests and nuns. Related to both their reasons for leaving Ireland and their later episodes of mental illness, these experiences created 'enduring problems of blighted education and job opportunities, low-self esteem and difficulties with authority figures throughout their adult lives' (Leavey et al, 2007).

The narratives of such migrants also reveal considerable gender differences, particularly with regard to motivation, employment networks and opportunities, lifestyle behaviours and settlement (Ryan, 2003; Leavey et al, 2004). Additionally, these studies highlight the crucial importance of (a) maintaining family connections with those left behind in Ireland and (b) building a new and positive family life in England. The authors also differentiate between 'adventurers' and 'escapees' which, as the terms suggest, contain quite distinct types of vulnerability, motivations for migration and preparation for settlement and return. Within these categories, too, one observes a wide range of motivations or, at least, aspects of motivation, conscious and unconscious, such as envy associated with a perception of the successful migrant and the fear of being abandoned. For some, migration was regarded as a rite of passage, a culturally expected approach to personal economic independence as well as sexual maturity and quest for a different, individuated identity. As noted previously, difficult experiences and poor family relationships in Ireland tended to have long standing effects on their lifestyles, mental health and their ability and desire to return 'home'. In the next section, we examine some of the literature on return migration and the related psychosocial difficulties.

Going back home, reintegration, and its challenges

Theorising return migration

In his landmark article, reviewing major findings and breakthroughs in the field of return migration, Gmelch (1980) lamented that despite slow, but continuous growth of publications on the subject, there is a lack of comparison across the studies and an absence of theories that connect them. In an effort to theorise the field of return migration, researchers have undertaken a range of studies in order to understand and map out the process of return migration. Many of these theories have sought to explain why immigrants return and the characteristics of those who choose to return. The 'disappointment' theory, for example, purports that immigrants return home because they have failed to achieve their goals for migration (Herzog and Schottman, 1982). Other theories include the circular migration theory; the target income theory; the social network theory, and the modernisation theory and we will briefly describe these.

Circular migration theory refers to repetitive, short-term migration abroad without any declared intention for a long-lasting residence in either the home or host country (Zelinskil, 1971; Massey et al, 1994). Much has been written about the circular nature of immigration among migrant workers, especially Mexican immigrants in the US. (Reyes, 1997). The social network theory views immigration as a dynamic process that is based on more than just economic pursuits. It asserts that immigration, despite one's initial reasons for relocating abroad, affects multiple spheres of a person's life and social world, including social structures and interpersonal relationships (Massey, 1990). Within this framework, the development and maturation of social networks may influence whether migrants stay, extend their sojourn abroad or decide to return to their home countries (Greenwood, 1969; Mines and Massey, 1985; Taylor, 1986).

In his critique of modernisation theory, Kearney (1986) suggests that 'Migrants were seen as progressive types who would have a positive impact on development by bringing back to their home communities innovations and knowledge that would break down traditionalism. The main unit of analysis is the individual migrant, who because of critical factors such as age, gender, marital status, personality or economic status 'decides' to migrate. However, the overly positive assumptions of modernisation theory, as Kearney suggests, began to crumble as research explored the patterns and impacts of 'return migration' most commonly found in post-war European states, whereby the migrant workers live temporarily in the host country for several years and then return home, having accrued savings and 'other less tangible effects of their sojourn'[2]. While the target income theory suggests that return migration has a positive collateral effect in the form of economic and cultural capital, with savings and skills reinvested for development, the evidence suggests that any capital brought back was invariably used for immediate, survival purposes rather than for investment in infrastructure (King, 1979; Rhoades, 1980).

Focusing more on the psychological distress of return, Gullahorn and Gullahorn (1963) suggest in the W-curve model that returning migrants are likely to experience periods of culture shock, followed by acculturation or adjustment to their home countries, thus a similar, but mirrored process to the experiences of migrants relocating for the first time to a foreign, host country. Returnees re-experience similar affective, cognitive, and social cultural adjustments in their home countries. The theory was one of the first to raise the possibility that, for many returnees, going home can be as traumatic as their first experience of immigration and that it often involves a period of disillusion, re-adjustment, and re-acculturation.

While the W-curve model takes into account the acculturative stress and reintegration challenges involved in the process of return migration, it has been criticised for framing return migration as having a final end point. Thus, other commentators have argued that return migration is much more fluid and cyclical, and that return migration, even during late life or after retirement, does not end with the final trip to home (Sussman, 2000; Ley and Kobayashi, 2005); in this era of transnational movement, return migration does not signal the closure and completion of the immigration narrative (a theme elaborated on in other chapters in this collection). Rather, return migration is often strategic at different stages of life and entails multiple transitions, travels back and forth, negotiation moments, and ongoing identity development (Sussman, 2000; Ley and Kobayashi, 2005).

Although there is not substantive research on the mental health of older returnees, the existing literature suggests that return migrants risk experiences of grief and other psychological distress (Ahktar, 1999; Leavey et al, 2007; Tannenbaum, 2007). In the following section we draw from the literature on migration and return migration to outline themes and factors that influence the acculturation and reintegration experience of return immigrants, and how these affect emotional wellbeing.

Acculturation and reintegration

Acculturation has been a central focus in both migration and return migration studies. It remains a complex factor in predicting how well migrants adjust and excel in the host countries and upon return, at home. Acculturation in the host country is also an impactful factor on returnees' adjustment and success at home.

Some researchers have noted a positive association between overseas adjustment and the remigration process (Cui and Awa, 1992), suggesting that individuals who are able to integrate in the host countries are easily adaptable and are open to new cultural experiences and social changes. Consequently, such returnees will also fare well in re-adjusting to their home culture. Others are less convinced, claiming that acculturation and integration upon return is qualitatively different and more difficult than the initial stage of adjustment during migration, mainly due to high expectations that re-immigrants often have of their home and the transformations that many immigrants undergo while abroad (Howard, 1980; Adler, 1981; Suda, 1999; Szkudlarek, 2010). Thus, upon return, many migrants are confronted with the realisation that they as individuals as well as their home environment have changed substantially during their period of migration abroad.

Indeed, as Szkudlarek (2010) noted in her review of the re-entry literature, many immigrants rarely anticipate adjustment difficulties upon returning home, which often create feelings of isolation and marginalisation. They also underestimate the impact of their immigration experiences on their worldviews, their attitudes, behaviours, and values. They are unaware of how these changes would impact the dynamics of their social interactions at home and their day to day experiences (Martin, 1984; Arrowolo, 2000; Sussman, 2000). For example, some returnees face the challenges of meeting relatives' financial expectations, difficulties in making friends, role-reversals, managing traditional gender roles, and varied cultural and bureaucratic aspects of their homelands (Cox, 2004; Potter, 2005; Boccagni, 2011).

The acculturation and reintegration process for return migrants shares similar characteristics and parallel processes to the initial stages of immigration. Upon re-entry to their home countries, returnees share many characteristics that identify them as 'others' and that isolate them to varied degrees to the margins of their societies. Return migration also involves sociocultural adjustments and multiple losses that may include the loss of social roles and status, significant attachments to people and culture, loss of familiarity, loss of ways of life, and one's sense of identity (Akhtar, 1999; Tannenbaum, 2007).

This adjustment period often demands a rethinking of one's sense of self and identity, reshaping of one's social networks, and renegotiation of one's roles and positionality in a given sociopolitical and cultural context. Such process is often accompanied by feelings of emotional distress, anxiety, anger, depression, melancholia, emptiness, and longing for contact with one's previous world (Alsop, 2002). For instance, Sahin (1990) observed that the adjustment period for repatriated sojourners and former expatriates may cause significant distress comparable to bereavement and that may reach clinical levels (see also Eisenbruch, 1991).

Moreover, the hardship of the immigration process is also likely to take a toll on returnees' health (Ho, 2003; Fong, 2008) with some epidemiological evidence suggesting that longer sojourn or residence in the host country is associated with poorer physical and mental health upon return in the home countries (Breslau et al, 2007; Davies et al, 2011; Ullmann et al, 2011). Working age returnees also struggle at times with difficulties finding employment, and some with reintegration in their local communities and cultures. Others have difficulty finding a peer network of individuals with similar migrant experiences and this may increase the risks of depression and other emotional health problems (Neto, 2012).

Language

After long sojourn abroad, some immigrants lose competency in their native tongue as they become more fluent in the language of their host country. Upon return, they often have an accent that sets them apart from the locals or that suggests that they have spent time abroad. Their newly acquired accent may serve as both a tool for social status enhancement and/or as a mechanism for marginalisation. As with migration abroad and the process of navigating language barriers, return migrations sometimes entail a similar process. For example, researchers such as Phillips and Potter (2005) noted the 'power of the English accent' as powerful brokering tool in the Caribbean for returnees. Potter (2005) also theorised that the dynamics of return immigration play out and reinforce racial barriers and English hegemony in the Caribbean and that a returnees' foreign accent also functions as an indicator of one's otherness and isolates returnees from their local communities.

Gender

Few studies have investigated the impact of gender on the experience of return migrants, specifically those who return home willingly in later life (Pedrazza, 1991; Pessar and Mayler, 2001; Pratt and Yeoh, 2003; Phillips and Potter, 2005), although this is an issue attracting increasing attention, as evidenced by chapters in this present collection. As regards Irish migrant research studies, the evidence that exists suggests that men and women experience re-entry or return migration differently (Rohrlich and Martin, 1991) and that gender may be the most influential factor in predicting return migration problems. Brabant et al (1990) for example, noted that women were more likely to report problems with family and daily life upon their return (Gama and Pedersen, 1977; Cox, 2004). Phillips and Potter (2006) noted similar adjustment difficulties for their participants who encountered role reversals and different gender expectations in their home countries. The female participants in the study, who were mostly second-generation British-born Caribbeans of middle class background, expressed the view that their female roles have been circumscribed to the home and family life, and that their independence has been markedly constrained by local moral codes of respectability and shame that implies modesty, restraint, obedience, and discretion.

Conclusion

The myth of return was coined by Anwar in relation to Bangladeshi/Pakistani migrants in Bradford, most of whom had arrived in Britain to take up work within the already declining cotton industry (Anwar, 1979). It was observed by mental health professionals working in the area that these men[3] had a tendency to depression in later life. Rack (1982) attributed their mental health problems to their failure to achieve the aspirations they held on arrival, that is, to work hard and to save money for a return migration to Pakistan. It was argued that the myth of return allowed migrants to consider their hardships as transient, something to be endured while holding on to the belief in a future reward in the homeland. However, the psychological problems begin to arise for these men as they age, emerging from the growing recognition that the earlier dreams of returning home will never be realised; instead, they will remain in the host country to see out their days in proximity to their children and grandchildren. Subsequent research has examined the myth of return in other migrant contexts

(Al-Rasheed, 1994; Zetter, 1999; Leavey et al, 2004; Bolognani, 2007; Boccagni, 2011).

A theme that emerges within most of these studies is that of the liminal nature of migration and the migrant's life, the sense of being left midstream between places. For most, it is an uncomfortable position that requires resolution of some sort. In her autobiographic article about her return to Iran after migrating to the United States for four decades, Razavi-Newman described her experience as a returnee as follows: 'I will not belong to one land, nor be able to let go of another' (2008:58). Razavi-Newman argues that for the immigrant, it is indeed a 'fact of life' to live in between two cultures. She maintains that like herself, most migrants 'could never fully integrate or sever connections with the host or their home country.'

Many returnees like Razavi-Newman had hoped that returning home would resolve the liminal existence, marginalised in both cultural spaces, but for many returnees the imagined home no longer exists, if in fact it ever did. However, as noted above many migrants are able to negotiate the sense of liminality, building positive social capital in both places. The capacity to do so is likely to be based on the desire to do so and the social dexterity of individuals. The ease and speed of modern travel and communication make this more possible. While the presence of supportive networks on return is clearly protective, the avoidance of some degree of psychological discomfort, if not distress, is still likely.

Substituting the words 'home' and 'family' for terms such as 'country', 'society' or 'community' helps dissolve some of the abstraction associated with migration, permitting a sharper focus on the psychosocial challenges that face people as they attempt resettlement. While structural and often interrelated determinants – economic, political and cultural – are always significant in determining the 'social gradient' of morbidity (Wilkinson, 1996), behind these facts lie differences in personality and personal experience: the people who embrace or fear change; the adventurers; and the escapees.

In this chapter we have attempted to show that for many migrants, the degree of agency and control over the migration pathway may be slight, influenced by a range of factors that diminish the chances of positive settlement or re-settlement. Even when such factors are absent there remains the commonplace difficulties of interpersonal relationships in which the dynamics of power and insecurity, superiority and envy, betrayal and abandonment, get played out between those left behind and those who leave and later return.

To conclude, the phenomena that drive human migration are unlikely to disappear. The financial crises within Western states in the early 21st century and the perennial material shortages elsewhere guarantee the redistribution of people rather than wealth. While history suggests a large proportion of such people are destined to remain and settle in their new homelands, others will be compelled for diverse reasons, and often many years elapsing, to return.

As the literature, and our own reading of it suggests, return is seldom psychologically and socially comfortable. The altered realities of the once-familiar can also be disorienting and alienating, perhaps doubly so because of the felt rejection and betrayal by the 'returned to'. Also, the psychosocial difficulties that so often prompt escape or adventure for so many migrants are never easily healed or wholly abandoned; these tend to remain. Added to this are the losses that accompany old age; attrition likely to be exacerbated by migration.

However, while it seems reasonable then to argue that the health and social care needs of return migrants require early recognition and intervention, the opportunities for doing so are few. Unfortunately, this problem, particularly in the UK and other European countries, is compounded by the absence of an evidence base in this area. Moreover, as we have suggested above, research on migration and especially our conceptualisation of agency and structure in migration is hampered by a limited theorisation. Thus, without a more nuanced understanding of push and pull factors as they relate to personal motivation, the epidemiology of mental illness and migration will continue to be unclear.

References

Adler, N. (1981) 'Re-entry: managing cross-cultural transitions', *Group and Organizational Studies*, 6:341–356.

Akhtar, S. (1999) 'The immigrant, the exile, and the experience of nostalgia', *Journal of Applied Psychoanalytic Studies*, 1:123–130.

Al-Rasheed, M. (1994) 'The myth of return: Iraqi Arab and Assyrian refugees in London', *Journal of Refugee Studies*, 7:199–219.

Alsop, C.K. (2002) 'Home and away: self-reflexive auto/ethnography', *Qualitative Social Research [Online Journal]* Available at: www.qualitative-research.net/fqs/fqs-eng.htm

Antonovsky, A. (1963) 'Like everyone else, only more so; identity, anxiety and the Jew', in A. Vidich and M. White (eds) *Identity and Anxiety*, Glencoe, IL: Free Press.

Anwar, M. (1979) *The Myth of Return: Pakistanis in Britain*, London: Heinemman.

Arrowolo, O.O. (2000) 'Return migration and the problem of reintegration', *International Migration*, 38:59–82.

Balarajan, R. (1995) 'Ethnicity and variations in the nation's health', *Health Trends*, 27:114–119.

Barrett, A. and Mosca, I. (2013) 'The Psychic Costs of Migration: Evidence from Irish Return Migrants. The Irish Longitudinal Study on Ageing', *Journal of Population Economics*, 26(2):483-506.

Berry, J.W. (1997) 'Immigration, acculturation and adaptation', *Applied Psychology: An International Review*, 21:491–511.

Berry, J.W. (2001) 'A psychology of immigration', *Journal of Social Issues*, 57(3):615-631.

Bhugra, D., Hilwing, M., Mallett, R., Corridan, B., Leff, J., Nehall, J. and Rudge, S. (2000) 'Factors in the onset of schizophrenia: a comparison between London and Trinidad samples', *Acta Psychiatrica Scandinavica*, 101:35–141.

Boccagni, P. (2011) 'The framing of return from above and below in Ecuadorian migration: a project, a myth, or a political device?' *Global Neworks*, 11(4):1–20.

Bolognani, M. (2007) 'The myth of return: dismissal, survival or revival? A Bradford example of transnationalism as a political instrument', *Journal of Ethnic and Migration Studies*, 33: 59-76.

Bourdieu, P. (1977) *Outline of a Theory of Practice*, Cambridge: Cambridge University Press.

Bourdieu, P. (1985) 'The forms of social capital', in J.G. Richardson (ed) *The Handbook of Theory and Research for the Sociology of Education*, New York: Greenwood.

Bourdieu, P. (2010) *Distinction: a social critique of the judgement of taste*, Abingdon: Routledge.

Brabant, S., Palmer, C.E. and Gramling, R. (1990) 'Returning home: an empirical investigation of cross-cultural re-entry', *International Journal of Intercultural Relations*, 14:387–404.

Breslau, J., Aguilar-Gaziola, S., Borges, G., Castilla, R.C., Puete, K., Kendler, S., Medina-Mora, M.E., Su, M. and Kessler, R.C. (2007) 'Mental disorders among English-speaking Mexican immigrants to the U.S. compared to a national sample of Mexicans', *Psychiatry Research*, 151:115–122.

Carlsen, H.M. and Nilsen, E.L. (1995) 'Ireland, gender, psychological health and attitudes towards emigration', *Psychological Reports*, 76:179–186.

Cox, B.J. (2004) 'The role of communication, technology, and cultural identity in repatriation adjustment', *International Journal of Intercultural Relations*, 28:201–219.

Cui, G. and Awa, N.E. (1992) 'Measuring intercultural effectiveness: an integrative approach', *International Journal of Intercultural Relations*, 16:311–328.

Davies, A.A., Borland, R.M., Blake, C. and West, H.E. (2011) 'The dynamics of health return migration', *Plos Medicine*, 8:1–4.

Eisenbruch, M. (1991) 'From post-traumatic stress disorder to cultural bereavement: diagnosis of Southeast Asian refugees', *Social Science & Medicine*, 33:673–680.

Fearon, P. and Morgan, C. (2006) 'Environmental factors in schizophrenia: the role of migrant studies', *Schizophrenia Bulletin*, 32(3):405–408.

Fearon, P., Kirkbride, J.B., Morgan, C., Dazzan, P., Morgan, K., Lloyd, T., Hutchinson, G., Tarrant, J., Fung, W.L., Holloway, J., Mallett, R., Harrison, G., Leff, J., Jones, P.B. and Murray, R.M. (2006) 'Incidence of schizophrenia and other psychoses in ethnic minority groups: results from the MRC AESOP Study', *Psychological Medicine*, 36(11):1541–1550.

Fong, V. (2008) 'The other side of the healthy immigrant paradox: Chinese sojourners in Ireland and Britain who return to China due to personal and familial health crises', *Culture, Medicine, and Psychiatry*, 32:627–641.

Gama, E. and Pedersen, P. (1977) 'Readjustment problems of Brazilian returnees from graduate study in the United States', *International Journal of Intercultural Relations*, 1:45–49.

Gmelch, G. (1980) 'Return migration', *Annual Review of Anthropology*, 9(1):135-159.

Greenslade, L. (1991) 'White skins, white masks; psychological distress among the Irish in Britain', in P. O'Sullivan (ed) *The Irish in the New Communities Vol.2*, Leicester: Leicester University Press.

Greenwood, M.J. (1969) 'An Analysis of the Determinants of Geographic Labor Mobility in the United States', *The Review of Economics and Statistics*, 51(2):189-194.

Gullahorn, J.T. and Gullahorn, J.E. (1963) 'An extension of the U-Curve Hypothesis', *Journal of Social Issues*, 19:33–47.

Hall, S. (1992) 'New ethnicities', in J. Donald and A. Rattansi (eds) *Race, Culture and Difference*, London: Sage.

Halpern, D. (1993) 'Minorities and mental health', *Social Science and Medicine*, 36:597–607.

Harding, S. and Balarajan, R. (1996) 'Patterns of mortality in second generation Irish living in England and Wales: longitudinal study', *British Medical Journal*, 312:1389–1392.

Harrison, G., Owens, D. and Holton, A. (1988) 'A prospective study of severe mental disorder in Afro-Caribbean patients', *Psychological Medicine*, 18:643–657.

Harrison, G., Gunnell, D., Glazebrook, C., Page, K. and Kwiencinski, R. (2001) 'Association between schizophrenia and social inequality at birth: case-control study', *British Journal of Psychiatry*, 179:346–350.

Harrison, G., Glazebrook, C., Brewin, J., Cantwell, R., Dalkin, T., Fox, R., Jones, P. and Medley, I. (1997) 'Increased incidence of psychotic disorders in migrants from the Caribbean to the United Kingdom', *Psychological Medicine*, 27(4):799–806.

Harrison, G. (1990) 'Searching for the causes of schizophrenia: the role of migrant studies', *Schizophrenia Bulletin*, 16(4):663–671.

Harrison, G., Owens, D., Holton, A., Neilson, D. and Boot, D. (1988) 'A prospective study of severe mental disorder in Afro-Caribbean patients', *Psychological Medicine*, 18:644–657.

Hartley, L.P. (2004) *The Go-Between*, London: Penguin Classics.

Herzog, H. and Schottman, A.M. (1982) 'Migration Information, Job Search and the Remigration Decision', *Southern Economic Journal*, 50 (1):43–56.

Hickman, M.J. and Walter, B. (1997) *Discrimination and the Irish Community in Britain*, London: Commission for Racial Equality.

Ho, M.J. (2003) 'Migratory journeys and tuberculosis risk', *Medical Anthropology Quarterly*, 17:442–458.

Howard, C.G. (1980) 'The returning overseas executive: culture shock in reverse', *Human Resource Management*, 13:22–26.

Katseli, L.T., Lucas, R.E.B. and Xenogiani, T. (2006) OCED Development Centre, Working Paper 250, Research programme on: Economic and Social Effects of Migration on Sending Countries, Available at: www.oecd.org/dataoecd/24/54/37053726.pdf

Kearney, M. (1986) 'From the invisible hand to visible feet: anthropological studies of migration and development', *Annual Review of Anthropology*, 15:331–361.

Kelleher, D. and Cahill, G. (2004) 'The Irish in London; identity and health', in D. Kelleher and G. Leavey (eds) *Identity and Health*, London: Routledge.

Kelleher, D. and Hillier, S. (1996) 'The health of the Irish in England', in D. Kelleher and S. Hillier (eds) *Researching Cultural Differences in Health*, London: Routledge.

King, R.M.S. (1979) 'Return migration: A review of some case studies from Southern Europe', *Mediterranean Studies*, 1:30.

Leavey, G. (1999) 'Suicide and Irish migrants in Britain: identity and integration', *International Review of Psychiatry*, 11:168–172.

Leavey, G. (2001) 'Too close for comfort: mental illness and the Irish in Britain', in D. Bhugra and R. Littlewood (eds) *Colonialism and Psychiatry*, New Delhi: Oxford University Press.

Leavey, G., Rozmovits, L., Ryan, L. and King, M. (2007) 'Explanations of depression among Irish Migrants in Britain', *Social Science & Medicine*, 65:231–244.

Leavey, G., Sembhi, S. and Livingston, G. (2004) 'Older irish migrants living in London: identity, loss and return', *Journal of Ethnic and Migration Studies*, 30:763–779.

Ley, D. and Kobayashi, A. (2005) 'Back to Hong Kong: return migration or transnational sojourn?' *Global Networks*, 5:111–127.

Lindstrom, D.P. (1996) 'Economic opportunity in Mexico and return migration from the United States', *Demography*, 33:357–374.

Littlewood, R. and Lipsedge, M. (1988) 'Psychiatric illness among British Afro-Caribbeans', *British Medical Journal*, 296:950–951.

Littlewood, R. and Lipsedge, M. (1989) *Aliens and Alienists*, London: Unwin Hyman.

Martin, J.N. (1984) 'The intercultural re-entry: conceptualization and directions for future research', *International Journal of Intercultural Relations*, 8:115–134.

Massey, D.S. (1990) 'Social Structure, Household Strategies, and the Cumulative Causation of Migration', *Population Index*, 56(1):3-26.

Massey, D.S., Arango, J., Hugo, G., Kouaouci, A., Pellegrino, A. and Taylor, J.E. (1994) 'An evaluation of international migration theory: the North American case', *Population and Development Review*, 20:699–751.

Mckenzie, K. and Bhui, K. (2007) 'Institutional racism in psychiatry', *Psychiatric Bulletin*, 31:397.

Mines, R. and Massey, D.S. (1985) 'Patterns of Migration to the United States from Two Mexican Communities', *Latin American Research Review*, 20(2):104-123.

Morgan, C., Dazzan, P., Morgan, K., Jones, P., Harrison, G., Leff, J., Murray, R. and Fearon, P. (2006) 'First episode psychosis and ethnicity: initial findings from the AESOP study', *World Psychiatry*, 5(1): 40–46.

Neto, F. (2012) 'Mental health among adolescents from returned Portuguese and immigrant families from North America', *North American Journal of Psychology*, 12:265–278.

OECD (2009) OECD Database on Immigrants in OECD Countries. Available at: http://stats.oecd.org/index.aspx?lang=en

Ødegaard, O. (1932) 'Emigration and insanity', *Acta Psychiatrica et Neurologica*, (suppl. 4):1–206.

Pedrazza, S. (1991) 'Women and migration: the social consequences of gender', *Annual Review of Sociology*, 17:303–325.

Pessar, P. and Mayler, S. (2001) 'Gender and transnational migration', *Working Paper 01–06e*, Center for Migration and Development: Princeton University.

Philipps, J. and Potter, R.B. (2006) '"Black skins-white masks": postcolonial reflections on "race", gender, and second generation return migration to the Caribbean', *Singapore Journal of Tropical Geography*, 27:309–325.

Phillips, J. and Potter, R.B. (2005) 'Incorporating "race" and gender into Caribbean return migration: the example of second generation "Bajan-Brits" in R.B. Potter, D. Conway and J. Phillips (eds) *The Experience of Return Migration: Caribbean Perspectives*, Aldershot: Ashgate.

Phinney, J.S. (1991) 'Ethnic identity and self-esteem: a review and integration', *Hispanic Journal of Behavioural Sciences*, 13:193–208.

Potter, R.B. (2005) 'Young, gifted and black: second-generation transnational return migrants to the Caribbean', *Progress in Development Studies*, 5: 213–236.

Pratt, G. and Yeoh, B. (2003) 'Transnational (counter) topographies', *Gender, Place and Culture*, 10:159–166.

Rack, P. (1982) *Race, Culture and Mental Disorder*, London: Tavistock.

Raftery, J., Jones, D. and Rosato, M. (1990) 'The mortality of first and second generation Irish immigrants in the UK', *Social Science & Medicine*, 31:577–584.

Ratha, D., Mohapatra, S. and Scheja, E. (2011) 'Impact of Migration on Economic and Social Development. A Review of Evidence and Emerging Issues', *Policy Resarch Working Paper 5558, The World Bank Development Prospects Group Migration and Remittances Unit & Poverty Reduction and Economic Management Network*. Available at: www-ds.worldbank.org/servlet/WDSContentServer/WDSP/IB/2011/02/07/000158349_20110207093552/Rendered/PDF/WPS5558.pdf

Razavi-Newman, M. (2008) 'I belong', *Psychoanalytic Social Work*, 15:53–59.

Reyes, B.I. (1997) *Dynamics of Immigration: Return Migration to Western Mexico*, San Francisco, CA: Public Policy Institute of California.

Rhoades, R. (1980) 'European cyclical migration and economic development: the case of Southern Spain', in G. Gmelch and W. Zenner (eds) *Urban Life*, New York: St Martins.

Rohrlich, B.F. and Martin, J.N. (1991) 'Host country and reentry adjustment of student sojourners', *International Journal of Intercultural Relations*, 15:163–182.

Ryan, L. (2003) 'Moving spaces and changing places: Irish women's memories of emigration to Britain in the 1930s', *Journal of Ethnic and Migration Studies*, 29:67–82.

Sahin, N.H. (1990) 'Re-entry and the academic and psychological problems of the second generation', *Psychology and Developing Societies*, 2:165–182.

Silver, A. (2011) 'Families Across Borders: The Emotional Impacts of Migration on Origin Families', International Migration, doi: 10.1111/j.1468–2435.2010.00672.x

Sinatti, G. (2011) 'Mobile transmigrants or unsettled returnees? Myth of return and permanent resettlement among Senegalese migrants', *Population Space and Place*, 17:153–166. doi: 10.1002/psp.608

Suda, N. (1999) 'Issues of adjustment abroad and readjustment to their home country of Japanese spouses', *Journal of Intercultural Communication*, 3:75–86.

Sussman, N.M. (2000) 'The dynamic nature of cultural identity throughout cultural transitions: why home is not so sweet', *Personality and Social Psychology Review*, 4:355–373.

Szkudlarek, B. (2010) 'Reentry: a review of the literature', *International Journal of Intercultural Relations*, 34:1–21.

Tannenbaum, M. (2007) 'Back and forth: immigrants' stories of migration and return', *International Migration*, 45:147–178.

Taylor, J. (1986) 'Differential migration, networks, information and risk', in O. Stark (ed) *Research in human capital and development (vol. 4)* Greenwich, CN: JAI Press.

Ullmann, H.S., Goldman, N. and Massey, D.S. (2011) 'Healthier before they migrate, less healthy when they return? The health of returned migrants in Mexico', *Social Science and Medicine*, 7:421–428.

United Nations Development Programme (2009) *Human Development Report 2009*. Available at: http://hdr.undp.org/en/media/HDR_2009_EN_Complete.pdf

Veling, W., Susser, E., van Os, J., Mackenbach, J., Selten, J-P. and Hoek, H. (2008) 'Ethnic density of neighborhoods and incidence of psychotic disorders among immigrants', *American Journal of Psychiatry*, 165:66–73.

Warfa, N., Klein, A., Bhui, K., Leavey, G., Craig, T. and Stansfield, S.A. (2007) 'Khat use and mental illness: A critical review', *Social Science & Medicine*, 65:309–318.

Weich, S., Nazroo, J., Sproston, K., Mcmanus, S. and King, M. (2004) 'Common mental disorders and ethnicity in England: the EMPIRIC study', *Psychological Medicine*, 34:1543–1551.

Wilkinson, R.G. (1996) *Unhealthy Societies: the afflictions of inequality*, London: Routledge.

Zelinsky, W. (1971) 'The hypothesis of the mobility transition', *Geographical Review*, 61: 219–249.

Zetter, R. (1999) 'Reconceptualizing the myth of return: continuity and transition amongst the Greek-Cypriot Refugees of 1974', *Journal of Refugee Studies*, 12(1): 1–22.

ELEVEN

The blues of the ageing *retornados*: narratives on the return to Chile

Erik Olsson

Introduction

The exiled migrant, who after many years is able to return to his or her former homeland, may have ambiguous feelings, related, for instance, to the drama of being forced to leave the homeland and to the dreams and longings accumulated in exile. This may also carry with it a dilemma, given development of social bonds in the host country during their time in exile. This creates a dynamic situation, one that the key-persons in this study, diasporic Chileans in Sweden, are familiar with. Nowadays, return migration is receiving increasing attention in the research literature but theoretically there is still much to explore (King, 2000; Cassarino, 2004), not only 'labour' or 'refugee' migrant circumstances but also how gender, age, class or generational aspects variously shape plans and actions. In this chapter I will contribute to this more comprehensive exploration of the return-migration phenomenon by focusing on age and refugee aspects, while also considering transnational social ties.

Decisions on return migration are shaped by many factors, for example, economic means, social relations and networks, working life, security in the country of origin, and so on. This acknowledges an analysis of return-migration that takes us beyond the individual decisions and plans regarding whether one should stay or leave (Hassanen, 2007; Jansen and Löfving, 2008). As a phenomenon embedded in a complex social reality, return appears more as something like a *project* – which is the notion preferred here – instead of being a once-and-for-all 'event' (Olsson, 2004). With this in mind, I believe that we should avoid seeing return-migration simply as an effect of economic 'failure' or 'success' in terms of 'calculated strategy', which is common in economically oriented migration research (Cassarino, 2004:255–257). On the contrary, we need careful examination of how returnees experience and take action in a social world where 'rational choices', in the economic sense, is not so much the issue – a statement that I believe is well substantiated in the accounts of those returning refugees I have interviewed.

As Leavey and Eliacin highlighted in Chapter Ten, return migration is not a straightforward matter of re-uniting with the society in the country of origin. When travelling back to their country of origin, migrants often experience problems of estrangement and of 'integration' (King et al, 1985; Cassarino, 2004), difficulties that cast return-projects in a different light from a one-way journey to one's roots. In general, return-projects are fluid, reversible and open-ended (Al-Ali and Koser, 2002; Olsson, 2004), evident among those migrants who, after returning, re-migrate from the country of origin to the former host-country. These individuals often become 'transmigrants' (Glick Schiller et al, 1995) ending up in circulation between the host-country and the country of origin. The transnational approach to migration (Glick Schiller et al, 1992, 1995; Vertovec and Cohen, 1999; Al-Ali and Koser, 2002; Wimmer and Glick Schiller, 2002; Bauböck and Faist, 2010) is important to our understanding of the impact on people who have ties to several social contexts.

To return to the country of origin may involve leaving behind a social life developed over years in 'diaspora' and 'exile'. Furthermore, older returnees are likely to have a different project in front of them compared to individuals at a younger age. For example, in later life the potential returnee is probably not expecting to realise a new career in his or her country of origin. This would be unlikely, especially in economically less prosperous countries. On the other hand, living in a welfare state like Sweden allows older people the possibility of receiving a portable pension, which could be a substantial contribution when planning a return. Furthermore, older people's family-situations would also differ in comparison with younger people, since in most cases children will most likely have already moved out to lead independent lives. Also, older age may invoke feelings of insecurity in terms of health and impairment, and planning return to the country of origin may require consideration of a strategy regarding how to get access to support of a different kind.

In this chapter I will discuss the conditions and circumstances shaping return-projects among older Chilean former refugees, with an examination of how returning migrants themselves account for these return-projects and how the encounter with the Chilean society is conceived from the position of a 'returnee'. Accounts are seen as narratives of a trajectory into a future in which not only is the contemporary Chilean society a significant factor but also the social context and society they have left. Therefore, the chapter is an attempt to understand the social complexity involved when returning migrants intend to leave a former diasporic residence and settle into a society which they have long considered to be their 'homeland'.

The study originates from my general interest in return-migration and the social and political implications associated with such projects. The ethnographic field studies underlying the present chapter started in 1993 with field visits to Chile. The empirical material consists of interviews and ethnographic meetings with older returnees, as well as younger returning migrants who, during the course of my field visits from 1993 to 2012, became older. The discussion that follows contributes to our understanding of the return-projects of these older migrants and how they incorporated different social concerns in their accounts of 'return-projects'. Before that, however, some context and history is necessary.

Context: the Chilean diaspora in Sweden and the return to Chile

Chilean migrants in Sweden are an interesting category for a study of return projects among refugees. They were one of the first large refugee groups arriving into Sweden. Being genuinely a refugee diaspora it is one of the few that also generated a significant return movement (Olsson, 2009). The political situation in Chile has maintained its stability after the democratisation of Chile at the end of the 1980s, and the return movement has since been uninterruptedly 'safe'. Significant economic progress in Chile from the mid-1980s has also provided relatively favourable material conditions for a return. This relatively long and stable return option makes the Chilean return migration unique in a Swedish context and allows for an examination of how the views and implementation of return has changed over the years. The Chilean-born population aged over 55 living in Sweden, reached more than 3,000 in 1991 and 20 years later totalled 7,900 (SCB, 1991; SCB, 2011).

Chileans as an immigrant category in Sweden are probably about average in terms of income and labour market performance and yet, although the economic incentives for leaving Sweden are not advantageous, in comparison with refugee groups with similar characteristics (for example, Poles and Iranians), Chileans have nevertheless showed a somewhat higher propensity to return (Klinthäll, 2003). In the wake of the civilian government in Chile, several thousand officially registered their 'emigration' to Chile. The first to leave were those who arrived in the early part of exile (Klinthäll, 2003, 2007).

The number of individuals increased during the first few years after the democratic election in 1989 to figures above 500 individuals each year but decreased to a relatively stable figure of not more than a few hundred individuals per year after 1994. In 2012, the statistics showed that 229 individuals – among them, individuals born in Sweden – registered their emigration to Chile (SCB, 2013). It is well known, however, that people keep a door open to the Swedish society and therefore hesitate to register. At the same time the statistics show an inflow of Chilean migrants to Sweden, which during the first 10 years of 2000s was equal to the immigration during 1970s. These figures, however, include a significant number of 'former' returnees that are re-migrating to Sweden.

Despite Chile's economic progress for more than two decades, return there is, for good reasons, still often depicted by Chileans themselves as an economic hazard. People seem in reality to keep their projects 'open' and perhaps 'postpone' the project until retirement and the 'circumstances being right'. All Swedish citizens and all others who have been working in Sweden receive a pension, which is available even when they live in another country (Pensionsmyndigheten, 2012). Chile is also one of the countries that through an inter-state agreement allows for their pension to be transferred to them. The Chileans who intend to move back to their country of origin could, therefore, at least secure a basic living standard through a Swedish pension.

Also, Swedish immigrant-regulations allow for a new residence permit for those who lived with a permit in Sweden for several years. This means that a prospective returnee could count on a new permit if he or she for some reason would like to return to Sweden. In addition, many Chileans obtained Swedish citizenship and therefore have the option to come back to Sweden, guaranteed and without any bureaucracy. I have noticed (and discuss more fully presently) that some of the migrants maintained their old Chilean nationality and kept the 'informal' option of having a double citizenship, which was officially permitted in 2002.

From exile to post-exile

Political identity was an important self-image for many Chilean exiles for a long time (Hite, 2000). For this reason the history of a Chilean diaspora in Sweden is largely connected with the political tensions in Chile. At the same time, the prospects of returning and reinstalling democracy became important. The activists and organisations institutionalised the idea of return as one major cornerstone of the Chilean's life in exile (Wright and Oñate, 1998). One example was the formation of the *Comite pro retorno a Chile* – a special committee promoting the issue of return (Wright and Oñate, 1998:91–122). Furthermore, the cultural life of exiled Latin American artists and intellectuals contained an important element of 'constant interweaving of space and displacement' (Kaminsky, 1999:49).

In the diasporic life of Chileans, 'homeland' became the main symbol of the struggle for freedom and return was a symbol of 'revenge' against the political oppressors who forced them into exile (Kaminsky, 1999; Hite, 2000; Tollefsen Altamirano, 2000). Return expressed a collective idea that was constantly manifested in the activities of diaspora (Leiva, 1997; Kaminsky, 1999), in many cases to such an extent that it was expressed as more or less a 'duty' to voice a commitment to return when the time arrived. The return became in itself the meaning of exile (Lundberg, 1989).

The majority of the exiles were, in the wake of post-exile, in their middle age and had a regular life in Sweden. It is, however, apparent that many of them in some way experienced a displacement that could be traced to the exile discourse, which to some extent represented Sweden as an undesired parenthesis in their life (Leiva, 1997). Nevertheless, this does not mean that all Chilean migrants in Sweden listened to the diasporic discourse on the need to return. Some of them hesitated since they knew from earlier journeys that it would not be easy. For those with children in school, young family responsibilities was another factor to take into account.

The 'return' to Chile, as a vivid idea alive in the minds of the diaspora, continued in the post-exile period, although Chileans increasingly treated the issue in a less morally demanding way. Instead of being the route for a political pilgrimage, Chile more and more became the symbol of a 'good life' with a friendly and welcoming social atmosphere. I noticed in my interviews with migrants living in Sweden how the image of Chile and the main reasons for a prospective return underwent change. Rather than mentioning the exile and the political mission as a driving force for a return, now people were more 'relaxed' and talked about the climate, how they missed having the family around them as they used to have in Chile, and other aspects of the social atmosphere of life in Chile. The 'family' as well as something like 'life-quality' is replacing the political motives of moving back to Chile (Olsson 2007, forthcoming 2013).

Return projects from Sweden: after implementation

After the removal of the dictatorship, a wave of returning exiles was expected to arrive in Chile. The Chilean civilian regime's efforts to implement a 'return' policy for these returnees was, however, not impressive. The initiatives were limited to a small number of programmes. One example is the establishment of Oficina Nacional de Retorno (National Office for Return) between 1990 and 1994, which in various ways provided social and economic support for 56,000 persons during its four-year existence (Wright and Oñate, 1998). Examples of other initiatives were the validation of degrees and professional certificates from abroad, and exempting goods and belongings from custom duties for the returning exiles (Wright and Oñate, 1998). Returnees could also be offered loans in order, for instance, to invest or establish a business. Statistics show that the majority of the returnees to Chile from Sweden during the first years of the 1990s were those who emigrated to Sweden during the politically intense period of the 1970s and early 1980s (Klinthäll, 2003, 2007). Of these, many were well above 50 and in some cases already retired, although I have no statistical data of the exact numbers.

The return to Chile was, however, becoming a much more complicated affair than just the packing of suitcases and booking of a flight. When the returnees encountered their 'homeland-society', they also encountered a society completely changed, economically and socially. Many of these returnees faced a situation with material problems. At the same time, there was limited public welfare support in coping with them.

Narratives of return

My analysis of exiled Chileans' return projects builds upon the informants' own accounts of their reasons for leaving their Swedish residence, as well as their experiences upon attempting to resettle in Chile. This includes their plans for establishing themselves in the country and their future prospects for staying there or re-migrating to Sweden (or some other place). From these accounts a picture of an individual's representations of their social context is provided, along with the meanings they associate with ideas of return and what consequences it may have for their current situation. The narrative accounts are, however, also a form of social positioning and an important aspect in the formation of a social identity (Somers, 1994; Anthias, 2002; Denzin, 2004). In other words, through an analysis of what people tell us about their 'reality' and how they see themselves within it, we should be able to better understand the complexity of people's ideas and plans, in this case migrants' return projects.

The study of return projects deployed an ethnographic method, which included field visits in Chile during 1993–94, 1999, 2004, 2005 and 2006, with a follow-up in 2012. The first visit was for a period of six months while the later visits were shorter stays between three and five weeks. I have informally met people and collected interviews as in any ethnographic fieldwork study. More precisely, I have recorded more than 100 interviews with men and women who at the time of the interview expressed an intention to stay in Chile. During the course of my fieldwork visits, I have also informally talked to individuals who were either trying to return to Chile or who were 'semi-returnees' with their formal residency in Sweden. I knew a minority of these informants from previous contacts I had in Sweden, prior to them setting their return-project into motion (and in fact, I met a few of them after they returned to Sweden once again). Otherwise, I met informants via social contacts and 'snowball' processes.

Most of the informants from my earlier visits fit into the picture of being former 'exiles' as their move to Sweden was in some way politically related. Only a few of these could be described as former leaders or 'visible activists' within the Chilean 'revolutionary generation' (Hite, 2000). The majority belonged to a less visible category of refugees, but in later visits I have also interviewed a significant number of people who were children and relatives of refugees living in Sweden. Eight informants, three men and five women, were followed for a longer period of time by meeting them in various situations both at their homes in Chile and in public settings. At the time of the first interview, informants were of various ages: 30 were under 30 years of age; 50 were between 35–55 years of age at the time of the interview; and the remaining 21 informants were over 55. Of the latter, four informants were already retired when they returned to Chile.

The distribution of age makes it possible to discern the particular issues of relevance for the older returnees. I interviewed informants who arrived during different time-periods of the 'post-exile' period, which, as will be discussed more fully later, may influence the way informants account for their return. For example, sixteen of the older informants returned during the first five years of post-exile, at a time when the possibility of return was quite recent and public debate about it quite intense, and their experiences differed from other older informants who returned later. Eight of the interviewees were in the middle-age category at our first meeting but during the course of their return-project, and my repeated visits, they became 'seniors'. This also allowed for an examination of how the accounts of return-projects changed over time.

Accounting for the decision

The analysis of the interviews with the returning informants from Sweden demonstrates how the previously discussed contextual features, namely the conditions of diaspora and encounters with the Chilean society, are mirrored in their accounts (Olsson, forthcoming 2013). More specifically, leading themes within their accounts inform us of the reasoning concerning why the informants had left Sweden for Chile, how they conceived of Chilean society and how they managed or did not manage to get by while living there. In order to capture the development over time, I will present my data in relation to 'early' as well as 'late' return, in respect of differences in the accounts for those arriving in Chile in the early 1990s and those in 2005, as well as the differences in views when interviewed several years later. In addition to these themes, the accounts consisted of a number of references to life and social networks in Sweden.

When accounting for their return-projects, the 'decision' often seemed to overlap with the discourse in diaspora, and its changes over time. Hence, the early accounts indicated the self-evident importance of politically motivated return, while later accounts were less politically coloured and more suggestive of sentimental reasoning involving roots and family reunion. Jaime (I have used pseudonyms throughout this chapter), a celebrated writer and cultural personality while he was living in Sweden, is a typical example of the former. After the plebiscite, he immediately started arranging for his return. From 1993, when he was 50, he returned to be a resident in Chile:

> 'When someone is forced to leave his country, not by a free choice, one also wants to get back in some way. Okay, I had already a career in Chile. I was very young when I took up a job as a journalist and I had already a radio program. Well, it was a small radio-station in Valparaìso but I had even won a prize in 1971. ... So you could imagine, they cut off my pathway, my road direction. So I needed to come back to everything of this. Okay, it was romanticised [in exile] but I needed to come back to it, to this prosperous time. ... When the bastard backed off [referring to the dictator Pinochet] there was no question about it, I had to go. If

not [doing this], it would be like confessing that they had won. That would have been impossible for me to accept!'

Jaime is a typical example of harbouring an uncompromising, almost 'programmed', intention of returning (Tollefsen Altamirano, 2000:140), which could be found among the politically committed 'early' returnees. The 'programme' was nurtured by experiences and persecutions from the period of the Pinochet regime and from the emotional consequences when living in the parenthesis that characterised the life of exile. Another example is Ana, who came to Sweden in her fifties, who bears witness to the perceptions many Swedish Chileans have of their situation as exiles:

> 'The first years we always had our suitcases packed by the door. All our furniture was bought for practical reasons but not because we liked it. It all felt borrowed. The first seven, eight years we just waited for Pinochet to fall and for us to return. We later realised that this was impossible as the dictatorship continued.'

In this account, Ana seems to confirm the picture of an ideological force behind the return-project as it was represented during exile. Ana was over 60 when she first returned, Jaime about 50, but the same statements are also found among younger returnees. The older migrants who returned during these years in most cases belonged to the 'political generation' of the seventies. Many of them were, like Ana, waiting for the moment, but there was also a social expectation of individuals to return after the Pinochet government was removed. Return to Chile gave them relief, their waiting was over, their dreams came true – the picture presented in the accounts of Ana and Jaime.

These early accounts often have 'restitution' in sight, and represent a situation where return was something of a no-choice option. The military coup was 'at the base of their biographical event' (Cornejo 2008:345) and a return was the only way to make them 'whole' again. This commitment is also found in several of the 'voices of exile', accounted for by Wright and Oñate (1998) and in the political leaders studied by Hite (2000). For the exiles, the transition from exile to post-exile is filled with an ambiguity. To some extent the exile provided a possibility to distance oneself from the reality in the Chilean society, which was partly taken away from them in post-exile. Kaminsky (1999:129) exemplifies this in the case of 'Mañungo, the returning exile, who has believed that he could make the choice to escape once again, learns that he cannot, any more than those who stayed can make the choice.'

From my field visits in 2005 and 2006, particularly, I received a somewhat changed picture of the return-projects. When giving a retrospective account of their move, the returnees (or semi-returnees) who arrived in recent years, as well as the earlier returnees, seldom described their motives for return in political terms. Instead, sentimental metaphors were used to capture the importance of 'natural [belongingness]', 'family-life' and 'home'. The friendly and welcoming atmosphere they experienced in their homeland was portrayed as typically Chilean.

Closely associated to this is a celebration of a life where family and kin is a central point of reference and where one could enjoy the sweet fruits of a more relaxed life than that in Sweden. Altogether, the changes in the diasporic discourses when exile transformed to post-exile is captured in these narratives. Chile represents a location where they could reunite with their family (Olsson, 2007). A reunion of the family was however more symbolic than a re-union in the physical meaning of the word. Since many have their children, grandchildren, siblings and cousins spread out all over the world – not only in Sweden – they could not solve a 'spatial' separation by a move to Chile. Their moves represent more of a pilgrimage to what is considered to be their 'real' home.

Materiality, roots and family

Certainly, return is not simply a matter of purchasing a ticket, getting the luggage and leaving. All returnees have to give consideration to their private situations, including, of course, the need to negotiate their decision with family members and employers. In the accounts of the returnees, however, these kinds of negotiations were often disregarded. A few of the informants also later confessed that they never discussed the matter of returning until the day came; in one case I noticed that the husband and wife in a returning family had completely different views about the decision. When asking about this the husband admitted that at that time he took it all for granted and never asked his wife about her opinion. The wife, on the other hand, had anxieties over a return, based on some dramatic experiences related to the repercussions in Chile during the dictatorship. The couple simply did not discuss the move and when they finally confronted the issue, the husband had already made the plans and according to him it was too late to change them. Couples' difficulties in sharing information and decision making may not be uncommon among older potential returnees, as indicated by Percival in Chapter Six.

When making the decision to return, the older migrants could be expected to be less dependent on the family situation compared to families having younger children, who often have to plan their move taking into account, for instance, school and the peers of their children. Moreover, these older migrants who expect a Swedish pension upon retirement may have a less complicated decision to make. In Ana's case, she was already close to retirement age at the time of the return. She could return to Chile, together with her husband, quite independently of the negotiations with family members and employers. All of her children lived in different places: Sweden, Spain and Chile. In her case there were less family obligations and even though she was eager to be close to her children and their families, the move to Chile didn't make much of a difference. The same is true for the other retired returnees whom I interviewed. They had similar family situations or were divorced from a partner, which allowed them to make decisions quite independently. In many cases the families of their children stayed in diaspora (not only in Sweden); however, this did not prevent them from seeing their families.

On the contrary, I observed a few cases when the returnee could act as a 'familial centre' for the globally dispersed kin (Olsson, 2007). An example of this is Sonia, who was 61 years old when she returned in 1990. In my research she was an exception, as she never returned to Sweden again. She was materially well off in Chile as she inherited a large house in Santiago, and in combination with her Swedish pension she could afford a relatively high standard of living. In this house she often hosted relatives, and other visitors, like me, coming from different parts of the world on their visits to Chile. For instance, her daughter from Sweden could live together with her for several months while searching for a place of her own in Santiago.

Older returnees are less likely to negotiate their *decision* to return out of concern for children or employers. For these individuals, it is probably also less complicated to make the decision to move since they were less afflicted by the economic concerns involved in return-projects. This does not mean, however, that retired people do not have concerns about return migration and may therefore remain in diaspora due to family and other reasons. For example, I followed a group of older émigrés in Sweden who were all certain about their decision *not* to move back to Chile. The reasons included a desire to stay close to friends, families and relatives in Sweden but, above all, a concern over having access to sufficient welfare services and health treatment since they were facing different impairments (Olsson, 1995).

The authentic home

Most of the returnees I met early in my fieldwork, in 1994 and 1999, also described their return projects as a result of their 'displacement' in the Swedish society. For them, exile in some sense meant a life in a country that was not 'theirs', with a system they didn't understand and with a culture one could not get accustomed to. Many made it clear that they could never become full members of the Swedish nation and society. Instead, sentiments of being an outsider were repeatedly expressed. Andres, who was 62 years old at the time of the interview, described his displacement, which in the end took him to Chile:

> 'I was seriously determined to stay in Sweden; nevertheless, I'm here in Chile. My intention was to integrate in Sweden and for this reason I felt for a while excluded [from the community of Chilean migrants]. I felt excluded and I have to tell that I tried to take any job also; one I had when I was living in Chile [before the coup], as for instance a travelling salesperson. This I did because foreigners do not have access to the society. At the same time the Chilean community accepted me just to a point, for I was a guy who had been successful, I was for them from another class. For this reason I was also a suspect. … Well since it was impossible for me to integrate in the Swedish society, when I couldn't do that, I approached the ghetto [of foreigners].'

In general, the informants' accounts in this sense are consistent with a typical diasporic discourse of social exclusion in the host country, due to unemployment or a feeling of not following one's roots. Chile is seen as the authentic origin of the family and as migrants they do not therefore belong to the Swedish society (Tollefsen Altamirano, 2000). Most of my informants, though, did not immediately mention displacement or discrimination in the host country. On the contrary, especially among the senior informants, it was common to represent Sweden in a positive way and express their gratitude towards the Swedish society for all the support they received as refugees. The reason for the older returnees to represent Sweden in such a positive way, I believe, was not only out of courtesy but because most of them had experienced exile in Sweden at a time when Latin American refugees were highly appreciated and received support, particularly from the socialist movement in Sweden.

Life in Chile

When reflecting on their experiences of being back in their country of origin, most returnees were ambiguous about what they encountered. On the one hand, it was common to express satisfaction over having made the decision to return. The closeness of family, the friendly people, the nice climate and the relaxed lifestyle were often mentioned as some of the advantages of being in Chile again. This picture is present in the informants' accounts, for all ages and also for both early as well as the later return individuals. On the other hand, there were strong narratives that depicted the 'homecoming' in less positive terms. Often there were concerns about how they were treated and reflections about the 'mentality' of the Chileans (in Chile) and the negative changes in the society. Juan, aged 61, illustrated some of these points when reflecting upon his return from his second and 15-year-long exile:

> 'I saw a country that had changed much. It had lost the solidarity that I knew from the Unidad Popular epoch and also the years during the dictatorship when I, myself, was living beside the dictatorship. In the centre of the dictatorship were the ones who lived in Chile.'

Another voice on this theme is that of Andres, who decided to stay in Chile after receiving a literary award in 1996:

> 'I came here to receive a prize. I came because this was my aquarium, I'm from here! But I stayed in a no-man's land. I felt as if I was excluded, there is an exclusion of those who return. I didn't get any work. I had thought that I should find a job very soon.'

Andres was around 55 years old at the time of his return. When I interviewed him, he was still living in Chile and thought that he would still be able to continue his intellectual life. Andres told me that until he was awarded the prize, he had rejected the idea of returning. The award became an inspiration for him; thereafter, he decided to acknowledge his roots and try to live there. Sooner or later, it seems, the realities of everyday life reveal themselves. The returnees missed the Chilean society of the old days. They encountered a Chile that had changed for the worse, with less solidarity and more egoism, towards marked class divisions and corruption and with cynic exploitation of labour and indigenous people.

The critique expressed by Juan and Andres was common among returnees and particularly among the older informants, perhaps as a consequence of how they remembered the Chilean society from the revolutionary period. Some of them claimed that they had become severely depressed over these changes. Such statements of disappointment are not surprising reactions. Returnees confronted an everyday life in a country they had not experienced for so many years. Similar observations have been noted by other researchers (Tollefsen Altamirano, 2000; Jansen, 2008) who suggest that this reaction could be an effect of the 'homeland' being viewed through the lens of the past (Schutz, 1964).

A significant topic in many narratives is annoyance with locals' hostility towards foreigners and their patronising attitudes towards *retornados* (returnees). Experiences of being negatively labelled as a retornado are a central point of reference in many of the narratives. The *retornado* represents a particularly interesting social category in Chilean society, carrying, as it does, deep associations with a return from exile and with political and social tensions in Chilean society itself. There have certainly been ambivalent responses on the part of the local population about the dictatorship and forced exile and, as a result of this, returnees have sometimes been accused of having enjoyed a 'golden' exile and even of economic fraud (Tollefsen Altamirano, 2000:200–215; see also Wright and Oñate 1998; Altamirano, 2009). This would explain the suspicious attitude held by locals and the risk associated with being labelled a *retornado*. In addition the narratives outline a situation in which overt discrimination makes it safer to keep a low profile concerning one's exile background (Olsson, 1997).

Listening to the accounts of the everyday life of returnees is like listening to the 'blues' of a melancholic singer, a song of a society in which they often felt alienated, disappointed and disrespected as exiles. And, of course, the first exiles were also much older when they returned, and less prepared for what they would encounter compared to those whose exile had been briefer. In this sense, the negative experiences of contemporary Chilean society afflicted the older returnees more.

My interpretation of this alienation is that the returnees, when faced with the realities of everyday life in Chilean society, initially confronted the *image* of Chile as it was constructed in diaspora. When meeting a different 'reality' they reacted with something like shock. And when evaluating their own return-projects, informants talked about the tiredness of being forced to cope with the situation of being the homecoming 'immigrant'. Often, they contrasted the lack of public support they received in the Chilean society with the Swedish welfare state. Despite these concerns, however, the returnees did not explicitly consider themselves as immigrants in Chile; the country was still the place of their 'roots'.

Remaining in contact with the diaspora

Most of the informants managed to visit Sweden at least once or a couple of times after returning. The frequency of the returnees' travels between Chile and Sweden is, of course, varied. Many of them regularly travel to Sweden to visit their kin or for the purpose of taking up temporary employment. Of my informants, several were like *semi-returnees* since they lived in Sweden for periods of several months or longer every year, and in a few cases it was difficult to know if he or she had a permanent living arrangement in Sweden or not.

I have had continuous contact with six informants who had returned to Chile during the first few years following the retreat of Pinochet. Five of them were between 34 and 40 years of age when they first returned, but since it was difficult for them to find employment, they had all gone back to Sweden to earn a living. These return projects seem to be 'open-ended' to some extent since these informants later returned to Chile, and in interviews several years later they declared that they could leave for Sweden once again if it became a convenient solution to their everyday problems. Thus, age did not seem to prevent them from being mobile. Instead, as one of the informants added, in relation to the return project it was an advantage being close to retirement since they "don't need to live with this more than for a couple of years until the pension comes".

The pension is viewed as a solution to one's living, but what happens after retirement is not self-evidently decided. One example is Pedro, a key informant since 1993, who moved to Chile in 1990 for the first time. Twenty-two years later, at the age of 57, he still commutes to Stockholm regularly for periods of six to seven months every year, earning a living on temporary employments within the caring-sector. He lives in Chile during the remaining parts of the year (mainly during the Swedish winter), together with his wife and daughter. Once grown up, the eldest son had lived in Sweden, Spain and Chile, but by 2012 he had lived mainly in Sweden for several years. When asked about the future prospects and where to live, Pedro stated that he could easily continue this life until his retirement. He added that if he were offered employment in Chile, he would probably reject it since it would only complicate their lives. He further added that it was not only a matter of economy either since they have a life in both of the countries.

In general, most informants accounted for a similar open-ended return-project. Only a few declared a complete severing of ties with Sweden. Instead, they gave the impression of having frequent contacts with people in Sweden and up to date information about the society there. Apart from reasons of employment, returnees valued the opportunity to return to Sweden for social reasons; to maintain welfare benefits, such as pension or social security; to visit the medical or dental clinic; to attend to their bank affairs, or to renew their Swedish passports or driving licenses. Accordingly, I noted how the majority of my older informants tried to secure visits to Sweden for a period of at least two or three months every second or third year. As previously mentioned, Swedish citizenship made it easier for returnees to travel and access some welfare benefits, not least the pension.

It is not difficult to understand the many conflicting demands that family members of the returnees have when living in different countries, when common functions such as taking care of grandchildren for occasional evenings is impossible. Strategies to compensate include making almost daily Skype internet calls and encouraging the children and grandchildren to visit Chile and live in their houses, as in the example of Sonia in a previous narrative above. The relationships maintained socially with Sweden link the returnees across the national borders and evoke some kind of 'double' belonging. Nicolas, who at the age of 61 runs a private enterprise with business between Sweden and Chile, expresses this as follows:

> 'The exile is over for me, on my part. Because when I come there, I do not feel like an exile-person but as a Swedish Chilean, so to speak. I am a Chilean with Swedish citizenship, I speak the language, I know the culture. I feel good there! Especially in Uppsala, I know Uppsala very well. I don't feel strange there. … Given the circumstances, I have a good life. I feel good with having two countries, two homes. When I need it or want it, at least when my economy improved, I could come there almost as often as I wanted to.'

Communication by means of telephone and (after it became accessible) internet with their friends and relatives in Sweden was a particularly significant part in the social lives of the informants. In fact, the returnees typically make the effort to keep the network and affiliation with the Swedish society and their diaspora intact. This involves a communication that builds on cheap airline tickets and the possibilities to make cheap phone calls as well as access to computer communication. In this sense, there is not a big difference in being a returnee and a 'semi-returnee' with a permanent residence in the diaspora.

The semi-returnees frequently spend some time, from a few months to a year in Chile with the purpose of enjoying their time, meeting kin and friends and in some cases in attempts to find a basis for permanent residence. This, of course, presupposes economic resources but seems to be quite a common pattern among people who are also of retirement age. After receiving a Swedish pension they usually had enough for a comfortable life in Chile – at least as long as they did not need a large amount for health treatment – where the majority of people survive on a monthly salary significantly lower than the pension many of the returnees receive from the Swedish state. Having modest savings in Sweden could also be invested, for instance, in housing in Chile and allow for a comfortable life during periods of extended visits.

Conclusion

The main conclusion of this study is that the returning Chileans conceive of their return-project and encounter the society from the position of diaspora, even a long time after implementing their return-project. Narrative accounts show a conflating of how return is represented in the typical discourses of the diaspora in Sweden. Here, the dominating ideas framed the return to Chile to a great extent as a political act during exile – a representation clearly found in the narratives of those who returned soon after the demise of dictatorship.

In the narratives of the returnees arriving from the late 1990s, the political commitment is less accentuated and the project is instead filled with motives referring to family, life-style issues and 'root' metaphors. This is a consistent change since it has a parallel to the changes experienced by the Chilean diaspora from the late 1980s, when the political exile 'faded out' and was replaced by a more diverse post-exile diaspora. For the migrants who stayed and entered later life during this transition, Chile was still a 'homeland' but quite often became the location for a reunion with families and for the life of their 'real' home instead of being a site for a political mission.

To return to their country of origin is to embark on a journey that may involve material hardships and social alienation. A way of coping with this is to re-connect with the diaspora, as the informants in this study have accounted. Many returnees continue to engage with people in their diasporic social networks using various forms of communication and practices. The link to diaspora is reinforced by the returnees' open-ended return-projects, meaning that they seldom 'close' the door on another residency in Sweden. In this sense they are functioning as 'transmigrants' (Glick Schiller et al, 1995); indeed, many employed moving 'strategies' that encompassed both countries and in other ways conceived of the diaspora as a 'resource' in their return-project. But even those returnees that are older and retired seem to adapt to a transnational life. One of the reasons for this non-decisive return might be that the social ties to diaspora are important for them.

The informants in this study did not completely cut the ties to Sweden where they spent a considerable part of their lives. Often, they had social and emotional ties to Sweden after moving to Chile because their families and kin remained there and they maintained contacts by travelling, if they could afford it, and they continued to correspond with them using other means. And, as we have seen, there were materially pragmatic reasons to spend time in Sweden, particularly for older returnees with limited means and, perhaps, health problems, who could not expect the same public welfare services in Chile; older returnees who were not yet retired and found work could manage to live a quite decent life without such reliance on the Swedish state.

The issue of social engagement following return is a central theme in diasporic contexts (Safran, 1991; Cohen, 1997; King and Christou, 2010), expressing the tension between the 'living here' and the 'desiring of another place' (Clifford, 1994:311). This chapter has demonstrated how the returning migrants developed their return-projects and experienced the Chilean society through the lens of such a diasporic discourse, where the homeland and return from exile and diaspora had significant meanings. It has also demonstrated how the returnees were engaged in border-crossing social ties after returning. The narratives of the returnees accounted for here were, in this sense, a way for the informants to *position* themselves as part of a diasporic transnational social space (Faist, 2000), and speak from a diasporic position, first and foremost, rather than membership of the Chilean society.

The Chilean diaspora in Sweden as well as the Swedish society is not such a distant social reality in the minds of the returning migrants discussed in this chapter. For the older returning migrants with a comparatively independent situation in economic and social terms, the transnational life-strategy provides a more secure and social life. In this sense, the lives of these older migrants indicate that we need to consider the restructuring of the relationship between 'home-' and 'host-societies' (Al-Ali and Koser, 2002:3), as attested by scholars currently investigating transnational approaches to migration and return migration.

Acknowledgements

This chapter draws on empirical research within several projects, among others 'Between Host-country and Homeland' (*Mellan hemland och värdland*) and within the research programme 'Forms of Care in Later Life', both funded by the Swedish Research Council on Social Science and Working Life (*FAS*), and 'Urban Life forms in Larger Cities of the Baltic Sea Region – The Swans' (*Urbana livsformer i större östersjöstäder – Svanarna*) funded by the Baltic Sea Foundation (*Östersjöstiftelsen*). Meanwhile, I have been employed as a researcher at three universities: Linköping University, Södertörn University College and Stockholm University. I am grateful to friends and colleagues at these universities for their helpful comments and criticism on earlier drafts of this chapter.

References

Al-Ali, N. and Koser, K. (2002) 'Transnationalism, international migration and home', in N. Al-Ali and K. Koser (eds) *New Approaches to Migration? Transnational Communities and the Transformation of Home*, London: Routledge, pp 1–14.

Altamirano, D.R. (2009) 'Repatriating women: navigating the way home in neoliberal Chile', in W.L. Alexander (ed) *Lost in the Long Transition. Struggles for Social Justice in Neoliberal Chile*, New York: Lexington Books, pp 185–188.

Anthias, F. (2002) '"Where do I belong?" Narrating collective identity and translocational positionality', *Ethnicities*, 2(4):491–515.

Bauböck, R. and Faist, T. (2010) *Diaspora and Transnationalism: Concepts, Theories and Methods*, Amsterdam: Amsterdam University Press (IMISCOE Research).

Cassarino, J.-P. (2004) 'Theorising return migration. The conceptual approach to return migrants revisited', *Journal on Multicultural Societies*, 6(2):253–279.

Clifford, J. (1994) 'Diasporas', *Cultural Anthropology*, 9(3):302–338.

Cohen, R. (1997) *Global Diasporas. An introduction*, London: UCL Press.

Cornejo, M. (2008) 'Political exile and the construction of identity: a life stories approach', *Journal of Community & Applied Social Psychology*, 18:333–348.

Denzin, N.K. (2004) 'Foreword. Narrative's moment', in M. Andrews, S. Day Sclater, C. Squire and A. Treacher (eds) *The Uses of Narrative. Explorations in sociology, psychology and cultural studies*, New Brunswick, NJ: Transaction Publishers.

Faist, T. (2000) 'Transnationalization in international migration: implications for the study of citizenship and culture', *Ethnic and Racial Studies*, 23(2):189–222.

Glick Schiller, N., Basch, L. and Blanc-Szanton, C. (eds) (1992) *Towards a Transnational Perspective on Migration. Race, Class, Ethnicity, and Nationalism Reconsidered*, New York: Annals of the New York Academy of Sciences.

Glick Schiller, N., Basch, L. and Blanc-Szanton, C. (1995) 'From immigrant to transmigrants: theorizing transnational migration', *Anthropological Quarterly*, 68(1):48–63.

Hassanen, S. (2007) *Repatriation, Integration or Resettlement. The Dilemmas of Migration among Eritrean Refugees in Eastern Sudan*, Trenton and Asmara: Red Sea Press Inc.

Hite, K. (2000) *When the Romance Ended. Leaders of the Chilean Left, 1968–1998*, New York: Colombia University Press.

Jansen, S. and Löfving, S. (2008) 'Introduction: towards an anthropology of violence, hope, and the movement of people', in S. Jansen and S. Löfving (eds) *Struggles for Home. Violence, Hope and the Movement of People*, New York and Oxford: Berghahn Books, pp 1– 24.

Jansen, S. (2008) 'Troubled locations: return, the life-course and transformations of home in Bosnia-Herzegovina', in S. Jansen and S. Löfving (eds) *Struggles for Home. Violence, Hope and the Movement of People*, New York and Oxford: Berghahn Books, pp 43–64.

Kaminsky, A.K. (1999) *After Exile. Writing the Latin American Diaspora*, Minneapolis, MN: University of Minnesota Press.

King, R. (2000) 'Generalizations from the history of return migration', in B. Ghosh (ed) *Return Migration: Journey of Hope or Despair?* Geneva: IOM and UN, pp 7–55.

King, R., Stratchan, A. and Mortimer, J. (1985) 'The urban dimension of European return migration: the case of Bari, Southern Italy', *Urban Studies*, 22:219–235.

King, R. and Christou, A. (2010) 'Diaspora, migration and transnationalism: insights from the study of second-generation returnees', in R. Bauböck and T. Faist (eds) *Diaspora and Transnationalism: Concepts, Theories and Methods*, Amsterdam: Amsterdam University Press, IMISCOE Research, pp 167–184.

Klinthäll, M. (2003) *Return Migration from Sweden 1968–1996. A longitudinal Analysis*, Lund: Lund Studies in Economic History 21, Lund University.

Klinthäll, M. (2007) 'Refugee return migration: return migration from Sweden to Chile, Iran and Poland 1973–1996', *Journal of Refugee Studies*, 20(4): 573–598.

Leiva, M.L. (1997) *Latinoamericanos en Suecia. Una historia narrada por artistas y escritores*, Uppsala, Sweden: Uppsala Multiethnic Papers.

Lundberg, S. (1989) *Flyktingskap: Latinamerikaner i exil i Sverige och Västeuropa* [Refugeeships: Latin Americans in Exile in Sweden and Western Europe] Lund, Sweden: Arkiv förlag.

Olsson, E. (1995) *Delad gemenskap: identitet och institutionellt tänkande i ett multietniskt servicehus* [Dividing Community: Identity and Institutional Thinking in a Multi Ethnic Home for the Elderly], Linköping, Sweden: Linköpings universitet (LSAS).

Olsson, E. (1997) 'Att leva nära en flygplats. Chilenska migranter mellan hemland och värdland' [Living Next to an Airport. Chilean Migrants between home and host country], *Socialvetenskaplig tidskrift*, 4(1):43–63.

Olsson, E. (2004) 'Event or process? Open-ended migration as repatriation practice', in M. Povrzanović Frykman (ed) *Transnational Spaces: Disciplinary Perspectives*, Malmö, Sweden: Malmö University, pp 151–168.

Olsson, E. (2007) 'Familjens plats: återvandring bland sverigechilenska familjer' [The place of the family: return migration among Swedish Chilean families], in M. Eastmond and L. Åkesson (eds) *Globala familjer: Transnationell migration och släktskap*, Hedemora, Sweden: Gidlunds, pp 231–258.

Olsson, E. (2009) 'From exile to post exile: the diasporisation of Swedish Chileans in historical contexts', *Social Identities*, 15(5): 659–676.

Olsson, E. (2013, forthcoming) 'Living next to an airport: diaspora narratives on the return to Chile', in C. Westin and S. Hassanen (eds) *On the Move. Experiences of handling forced migration with examples from Africa, Australia and Europe*, Trenton, NJ: The Red Sea Press (in press).

Safran, W.I. (1991) 'Diasporas in modern societies: myths of homeland and return', *Diaspora*, 1(1):83–99.

Schutz, A. (1964) 'The homecomer', in A. Brodersen (ed) *Alfred Schutz: Collected Papers II: Studies in Social Theory,* Hague: Martinus Nijhoff, pp 106–119.

Somers, M.R. (1994) 'The narrative constitution of identity: a relational and network approach', *Theory and Society*, 23(5):605–649.

Tollefsen Altamirano, A. (2000) *Seasons of Migration. A study of Biographies and Narrative Identities in US-Mexican and Swedish-Chilean Return Movements*, Umeå: Gerum.

Wright, T. and Oñate, R. (1998) *Flight from Chile. Voices of Exile*, Albuquerque, NM: University of New Mexico Press.

Vertovec, S. and Cohen, R. (1999) 'Introduction', in S. Vertovec and R. Cohen (eds) *Migration, Diasporas and Transnationalism*, Cheltenham: Edward Elgar Publishing, pp xiii–xxviii.

Wimmer, A. and Glick Schiller, N. (2002) 'Methodological nationalism and beyond: nation-state building, migration and the social science', *Global Networks*, 2(4):301–334.

Official sources, webpages:

SCB (1991) Sveriges officiella statistik. Befolkning: del 1–2, www.scb.se/Pages/List____283992.aspx

SCB (2013) Sveriges officiella statistik. Befolkning: del 1–2, www.scb.se/Pages/SSD/SSD_SelectVariables.aspx?id=340507&px_tableid=ssd_extern%3aImmiEmiFlytt&rxid=20eda888-9738-4979-ab77-29f9f968a77a

Pensionsmyndigheten (2012) www.pensionsmyndigheten.se

TWELVE

Concluding reflections

John Percival

The collection of chapters in this book provides a substantial contribution to our knowledge of return migration in later life. In particular, this book has provided material and analysis that shows how return migration in later life often involves a complex calculation in which certain factors may all claim attention, and be weighed in the balance, when contemplating, deciding on, or enacting, return. At stake are critical issues, including: family ties, obligations and their emotive strengths; comparative quality, and cost, of health and welfare provision in host and home countries; and older age transitions and cultural affinity with homeland.

Such issues are rightly receiving an increasing amount of research attention, although research findings tend to be as scattered, in terms of their reporting, as the countries being studied. This book provides a much needed synthesis of wide ranging, highly relevant studies and also, importantly, brings together key contributions whose fusion promotes a keen appreciation of these issues in respect of their policy and research implications. This concluding chapter summarises important themes, insights and messages drawn from the book as a whole.

Older migrants' family relationships and responsibilities constitute a highly significant theme in the context of return migration in later life. This is to be expected, perhaps, given Bengtson and Allens' conceptualisation of the family as a 'collection of individuals with shared history who intersect within ever changing social contexts across ever increasing time and space' (1993:470).

Family connections in both home and host country are certainly important to ageing migrants later in life, and location of children in particular can affect decisions, motivations and outcomes as regards return strategies: Ruting's returnees to Estonia (Chapter Eight) visit mainly to rebuild kinship with relatives whose ability to communicate with relatives abroad had been denied by the Soviet authorities; Olsson's political refugees from Chile (Chapter Eleven) similarly prioritise kinship reconnections when considering return from Sweden, despite pragmatic reasons to stay well connected with the diaspora in the host country; Conway and colleagues (Chapter Five) found that lifecourse events may trigger an ability or interest to rejoin family who remained in the home country, providing opportunities for mutual support; and Percival's study (Chapter Six) indicates how family reconnections in the home country, especially with similar age siblings, offer the hope of close and shared bonding that helps replace the loss of spouse, friends or career, bereavements perhaps more keenly felt by the ageing migrant.

Reconnection with extended family members in the home country can also provide 'peer' support that helps reinforce older migrants' cultural identification and may also explain why some returnees are attracted to particular locations in the home country and the sense of familiarity there, as suggested in the respective chapters of Blunt and colleagues (Chapter Seven) and Christou (Chapter Nine).

However, we have also heard throughout the book of competing family expectations and caring priorities: anxieties when family loyalties are put at risk, or divided; tensions that arise when spouses do not share a desire to return to country of origin but find negotiation, or even open dialogue, difficult; pressures when children and grandchildren require emotional or practical support that would be severely limited by the older family member's relocation thousands of miles away, which all affect return migration decision-making and sometimes place the would-be returnee in a state of limbo, what Leavey and Eliacin (Chapter Ten) have referred to as 'being left midstream'. For such reasons, personal aspirations and family obligations may be irreconcilable, not only affecting timing of any possible return but also contributing to possible emotional malaise and social withdrawal, as Percival found (Chapter Six).

One possible compromise, if and when practicable, is to have two bases and spend time in both host and home country. This kind of transnationalism may well facilitate continued social and family relationships across nations, although the resulting dual attachments and characteristics of hybrid identity have received limited attention in the literature; this book raises the positive and negative outcomes that may follow, as ageing migrants celebrate the comfort of having two places called home, or regret the feeling that they do not truly belong to either one. Moving back and forth between places is clearly not just an amenity driven lifestyle choice, as return also takes place to home countries that are economically poorer or politically less stable than host countries. Such returnees, where the option is available, keep a foothold in the host country if they are likely to benefit from better health care and continuing pension provision.

Living costs and economic factors, together with health care and welfare provision, appear as closely connected and prominent themes throughout the book. As we have seen, the incidence of return migration increases after retirement, when the link between income and place of residence weakens. Newbold (Chapter Three) has noted that the geography of ageing is in various ways 'linked' to economic factors, and personal finance is certainly a key factor influencing whether, and how, migrants follow through their desire to return to their homeland. Klinthäll (Chapter Two) has demonstrated that while the numbers of people who return migrate can sharply rise on reaching retirement age, so too does the number of people prompted to return when faced with early retirement due to sickness or redundancy.

The standard of living in the home country, and perhaps ownership of a property there, may also be influential factors, and certainly occupied the minds of Christou's Greek migrants in Denmark (Chapter Nine), Ruting's Estonian migrants in Australia (Chapter Eight), and Olsson's Chilean migrants in Sweden (Chapter Eleven), but are not necessarily decisive factors in planning permanent return migration, as indicated by Bolzman's Spanish returnees from Switzerland (Chapter Four), or Leavey and colleagues' Irish returnees from the UK (Chapter Ten).

Health care concerns and perspectives also occupy the minds of older migrants considering return. Newbold (Chapter Three) reflects that many migrations by older people within Canada may be determined by health related priorities, and similar concerns are prominent in the return deliberations of older migrants interviewed by Christou (Chapter Nine), Bolzman (Chapter Four), Ruting (Chapter Eight) and Olsson (Chapter Eleven), all of who faced the prospect of comparatively poorer quality health care in their respective homelands. Perceptions or experience of home country health and welfare services also appears to affect ability or willingness to integrate fully and identify with the home country, and lead some older migrants to consider the benefits of dual residence, through transnational living arrangements.

Despite these income and health related concerns, emotional and psychological attachments also exert influence on return migration decision-making, especially in connection with the subjective need to reconnect with personal and cultural roots. Older people, particularly those in good health and with reasonable financial support, can look forward to a significant period of time in which to live out dreams and aspirations: a new chapter in their life story, in which return migration can be placed centre stage. As Blunt and colleagues have shown (Chapter Seven), return to specific areas that are personally meaningful may also involve reconnection with local communities, and the opportunity to experience their continuity and change, as well as provide an opportunity to visit heritage and tourist sites that enshrine cultural roots and identity.

Other contributors to this book have also emphasised how cultural 'roots' are engaged with through exposure to broadcast and social media that provides information about, and interaction with, cultural and family life in the home country. Connections can be further strengthened or sustained by access to virtual communication technologies, such as Skype, beneficial tools for those older people less inclined or able to permanently return to their country of origin.

Cultural identification through reconnection with 'roots' communities may assume greater importance in later life, providing an opportunity to construct meaningful personal narrative in the face of bodily and lifecourse changes, an important life review task in later life (Biggs, 2005; Coleman, 2005) and, as such, one that may be expected to assist older people maintain a feeling of order and control. Indeed, thoughts of return do not simply reflect wishes for a golden past but tell us something of our current priorities in life, and older returnees who successfully return to valued places and homelands can be satisfied that a major transition has been accomplished while there is still time.

However, psychological adjustment is also a necessary component of cultural affiliation, as discussed by Leavey and colleagues (Chapter Ten), who, like Christou (Chapter Nine), emphasise returnees' exposure to a complex matrix of changes that can adversely affect mental health and wellbeing. Adjustment to a homeland that has changed and to people who have not shared the returnees' migrant experiences can be very difficult, even traumatic, and can cause some to welcome a continuing link with the host country, the experience of a number of Olsson's Chilean exiles in Sweden (Chapter Eleven), particularly those whose return was met with negative responses or was driven more by political duty to comrades left behind than personal preference. We can usefully reflect on how such personal and cultural disjunctures may possibly accentuate estrangement or outsider status, for example when returning as an unattached or widowed migrant, or exacerbate existential uncertainties about status as an older person and the threat to ontological security (Giddens, 1991).

We appreciate, then, how thoughts and actions in regard to return migration are prompted and influenced by a range of social, pragmatic and psychological factors, whose convergence in later life may be experienced as inspiring or challenging, or both. Moreover, this complex combination of issues has implications for receiving countries. As was noted in Chapter One, there are examples of countries that welcome older returnees, especially those who are able and motivated to contribute valued experience and skills. This book adds weight to the argument, especially in times of economic downturn, for receiving countries seriously to consider the benefits, as well as costs, of the return of older returnees. Many older returnees are well educated and highly skilled, and interested in contributing to their home communities, for example through voluntary work, as noted in the studies reported by Conway and colleagues (Chapter Five) and Percival (Chapter Six). Indeed, Rutter and Andrew (2009) suggest that volunteering is an activity that can assist reintegration and should therefore be better promoted by relevant agencies.

There are other policy-related consequences of return migration that have to be considered. Older returnees may bring their pension rights with them but not have any significant reserves of disposable income or savings and may, as a consequence, put a new and unexpected pressure on the health and welfare sectors in their home countries, a particular challenge for relatively weak economies, perhaps already struggling to adequately support a growing elderly population. Additionally, the provision of informal support by siblings and other family members in the home country, which, as we have seen, can be an important motivation for older migrants' return, may well diminish over time, causing returnees to look for sources of more formal care.

For those returnees with access to alternative informal and/or formal support services in the host country, and the means to travel between countries when required, such a resource may offset any such loss or absence of provision in the home country. However, the increasing focus on transnational movements should not deflect us from the homecomings of permanent returnees, a more sizeable population in the foreseeable future (Stefansson, 2004).

Furthermore, transnational models of migration and return migration in later life raise questions of home and host country obligations and responsibility in regards to public service provision and may be expected to arise more prominently in the future; any policies that ensue would benefit from careful consideration of the temporal and spatial extent of family support.

Clearly, there are important social policy messages arising in this book, and these could profitably be reflected on by relevant organisations: public service providers, government departments, agencies working with and for older people, policy developers, research bodies, and also, perhaps, commercial organisations with interest and experience in travel and tourism. Public services will increasingly have to adjust future projections of need to take account of growing numbers of mobile citizens, not least return migrants in later life. In doing so, relevant organisations may wish to consider strategies for early recognition of needs and difficulties; appropriate health and welfare service partnerships; and collaboration on pensions and social security benefits. Respondents' narratives have also alerted us to a significant need for useful and realistic strategies that help test out the reality of return while minimising financial risk, psychological stress or family disharmony, and to access helpful information and advice.

A potentially beneficial way of allocating resources to deal with such requirements may be through provision of relocation-type services, building on existing models that facilitate the intra- or inter-country travel arrangements and resettlement of younger business people and their families. In this respect, relevant organisations could collaborate to provide a comprehensive information resource, to assist older returnees to become familiar with sources of advice and support in regard to: housing, pensions and social security provision; access to local health and social care systems; and matters related to utilities, banking and insurance.

There may also be a role for these organisations to engage with the tourist industry, to explore how visits to the homeland, whether to see family, enjoy a heritage holiday, or gain insight into daily life through short-term work, could also be packaged as opportunities for familiarisation with the realities of relocation, perhaps incorporating advice and information seminars in popular destinations. There are also travel and tourism implications in respect of older migrants' increasing interest in transnational living arrangements in later life, whether for lifestyle, family, economic or health related reasons.

Adapted models of this kind could be considered in regard to actual or prospective older relocatees to assist in their reorientation and resettlement in their home countries. There is also an argument, based on evidence presented in this book, for host countries to look at ways in which older immigrants considering return migration can access advice and information that helps them share their thoughts and feelings, sometimes difficult to do with close family, and also to discuss pension issues and other practicalities involved with relocation to country of origin.

However, further research in regard to return migration in later life is required, in order to fully understand the optimum ways that relevant organisations can work in partnership to deliver appropriate services to older return migrants. There is a limited body of empirical evidence on older people's return migration, particularly their impact on economic, health and public sector services in host and home regions and countries, and the evidence base from which public policy can be further developed is relatively small, particularly in respect of more micro level issues, such as those affecting emotional wellbeing and marital and kinship relationships.

To this end research could usefully be developed to: obtain new data on marriage patterns and location of children, in order to explore more fully the impact on return migration of family relationships across time and space; examine the circumstances and aspirations of migrants who were exiled from their homeland as children; raise greater awareness of older returnees' health needs and how they are met; contribute a more rounded /complete understanding of the interplay between factors that affect older returnees' personal motivation, psychological wellbeing and physical health.

Such a range of research topics suggests a need to be sensitive to the complex and sometimes competing demands and priorities faced by older migrants considering or realising return to their country of origin, and studies will therefore benefit from employing a range of methodologies. This book has made a significant contribution through its collection of studies that intersect social gerontology, migration, tourism and heritage, and social geography fields of enquiry, and a good case has been made for more inter-disciplinary, mixed methods, research along these lines.

This volume has also presented an analytic and thematic confluence that has enabled us to see more clearly the ways in which factors affecting propensity and motivation for return migration actually play out in the lives of ageing migrants, and are engaged with on individual, kinship and cultural levels. Many of these issues often overlap across chapters, which emphasises their importance and prevalence among different older populations, in diverse geographical locations and in respect of varied migration flows. With any collection of chapters exploiting a variety of methods and relevant fields of enquiry, there are editorial challenges in ensuring a coherent dynamic. Our collective hope is that this volume is appreciated as a significant and consolidated effort to achieve such a goal, not least in order to do justice to the important themes and issues it raises.

References

Bengston, V.L. and Allen, K.R. (1993) 'The lifecourse perspective applied to families over time', in P.G. Boss, W.J. Doherty, R. LaRossa, W.R. Scham and S.K. Steinmetz (eds) *Sourcebook of Families, Theories and Methods: A contextual approach*, New York: Plenum, pp 469–499.

Biggs, S. (2005) 'Psychodynamic approaches to the lifecourse and ageing', in M. Johnson (ed) *The Cambridge Handbook of Age and Ageing*, Cambridge: Cambridge University Press.

Coleman, P. (2005) 'Reminiscence: development, social and clinical perspectives', in M. Johnson (ed) *The Cambridge Handbook of Age and Ageing*, Cambridge: Cambridge University Press.

Giddens, A. (1991) *Modernity and Self Identity: self and society in the late modern age*, Cambridge: Polity Press.

Rutter, J. and Andrew, H. (2009) *Home Sweet Home? The nature and scale of the immigration of older UK nationals back to the UK*, London: Age Concern and Help the Aged.

Stefansson, A.H. (2004) 'Homecomings to the future: From diasporic mythographies to social projects of return', in F. Markowitz and A.H. Stefansson (eds) *Homecomings. Unsettling Paths of Return*, Lanham, MD: Lexington Books.

ENDNOTES

Chapter Three

[1] For the purposes of comparison, older people are compared to the broad labour-force-aged population in the multivariate analysis. This group is not considered in the descriptive analysis portions of this chapter.

Chapter Four

[1] This perspective has been more related to empirical observations in countries such as Germany, France or Switzerland, than in countries such as the United Kingdom or The Netherlands, which developed earlier integration policies and have considered immigrants as part of the national 'ethnic minorities' population (Bolzman et al, 2004).

[2] The situation can change with the economic crises taking place nowadays in both countries, with high levels of unemployment. Emigration will probably increase in the coming years if the economic situation does not improve.

[3] I would like to thank here my colleagues Rosita Fibbi and Marie Vial who have participated in the analysis of the empirical data I am presenting here. The use of the term 'we' indicates that they have also contributed to some of the ideas developed in this chapter.

[4] We are conducting a new survey on these populations, extended to include older Portuguese people; fieldwork is not yet completed.

[5] Question asked: 'Among these assertions, which are the three most important in life?' Possible answers (in decreasing order of frequency): to live in a harmonious family (83%); to be in good health (72%); to have an interesting work (32%); not to be in need materially (30%); to be respected (24%); to live in own country (22%); to have many friends (20%).

[6] We have not observed among Italians living in Geneva or Basle intentions of mobility towards Ticino, the Italian speaking canton. When they want to go back and forth, it is mainly to their region of origin or to a more urban place in Italy. Thus, they have not found a region of substitution within Switzerland.

Chapter Five

[1] Focusing upon US-based research and the resultant literature on retirement migration in that geographically large country and drawing upon it as a comparative source of helpful generalisations does not imply, nor indicate, that there are not equally useful literatures on retirement migration in Europe, Oceania or the wider world that would also have been helpful. Selecting US-based research as a comparative framework for analogous conceptual generalisations about Caribbean return migration in later life, proved to be both sufficient and satisfactory.

[2] All principal investigators (authors of this chapter) conducted some of the person-to-person semi-structured interviews that serve as the empirical 'narratives' of this research. The majority, however, were conducted in Trinidad (with two in Tobago) by Dr St Bernard and a Trinidadian research assistant during the somewhat lengthy time frame indicated as the period from November 2004 to May 2005 (or 2004/2005).

[3] In this project, forty in-depth, qualitative semi-structured interviews were conducted with foreign-born and relatively youthful return migrants residing in Trinidad and Tobago (in 2004/2005 – the time of our interviews). A number of contacts had been made during a preliminary site visit by one of the authors and these were helpful in enabling us to contact the first wave of potential informants. We used length of residence 'away from home' as an important selective criterion for identifying and selecting our relatively youthful respondents, in order to be able to interview returnees who had spent an influential period of time abroad – more than twelve years – yet, who had returned. Snowball sampling was employed thereafter (Atkinson and Flint, 2001) to find, and interview, this 'hard-to-find sub-population' of transnational migrants who had recently returned home; the majority from Canada, the US and the UK.

Chapter Seven

[1] This chapter is part of a broader project funded by the Leverhulme Trust on 'Diaspora Cities: Imagining Calcutta in London, Toronto and Jerusalem.' This project studies the Anglo-Indian, Brahmo, Chinese and Jewish communities in Calcutta, their migration to London, Toronto and Israel since 1947, and the effects of migration for those who have remained in Calcutta.

[2] The Calcutta reunion included a boat cruise to Diamond Harbour to the south of the city, a dance and a quiz focusing on particular Anglo-Indian words, such as the meanings of Calcutta's Ronson Lighter (a lit coir that hangs at

paanshops to light cigarettes) and a Paratha Aloo (someone who attended Pratt Memorial School). Other events in the city have also attracted a large number of visiting Anglo-Indians as well as those who still live in the city, including a concert called 'Down Memory Lane' held in St Joseph's School in December 2007. Such events focus on the past and the nostalgic connection between the community and the city and increasingly form an important part of return visits. The Bangalore reunion in 1998 was the first Anglo-Indian international reunion to be held in India, and was timed to fall in the fiftieth anniversary year of Independence and described as a 'homecoming.' But, 'despite its celebration of return and its theme of "unity and integration", demonstrations were held outside a five-star hotel by some Anglo-Indians resident in Bangalore who could not afford the registration fee. These demonstrations raised questions about who could celebrate a community identity, memory and homecoming, and posed a stark contrast between the poverty of many Anglo-Indians in India and the relative affluence of those who had migrated' (Blunt, 2003:281-2).

Chapter Nine
[1] For a full presentation of the research project and a brief historical overview of Greek migration to Denmark, refer to Christou, 2008, 2009a.

[2] For a detailed discussion on narrative methodologies in (return) migration research refer to Christou, 2009b, 2011.

[3] For a detailed discussion reviewing the concept of 'hybridity' and relevant theories analysing the use of the term in recent social and cultural theory, refer to John Hutnyk, 2005.

Chapter Ten
[1] The authors conducted literature searches for publications on return migration and mental health. They used several search engines and social science databases that include Worldcat, JSTOR, and Academic Search Premier. In our search, we focused primarily on the experiences of adults who returned to their home country after a long sojourn abroad. We excluded studies that focus on other forms of migration such as refugees, expatriates, students studying abroad and second-generation returnees. However, research studies from these fields have informed our analysis, given many similarities in the migratory experience. The authors also drew from their own research focus on Irish and African-Caribbean immigrants in the UK.

[2] Similarly, the target income theory posits that immigrants relocate abroad not with the intention of developing permanent residence in the host country, but with the sole purpose of accumulating enough savings to reach a particular income to improve their life conditions at home. As soon as they reach their target income, they return home; Lindstrom, D.P. (1996) Economic opportunity in Mexico and return migration from the United States. *Demography*, 33: 357–374; Hill, J.K. (1987) Immigrant decisions concerning duration of stay and migratory frequency. *Journal of Development Economics*, 25:221–234.

[3] Unaccountably, Pakistani women do not feature in this discourse.

Index